Making Life More Livable

A Practical Guide to Over 1,000 Products and Resources for Living Well in the Mature Years

Ellen Lederman

A FIRESIDE BOOK
Published by Simon & Schuster
NEW YORK   LONDON   TORONTO   SYDNEY   TOKYO   SINGAPORE

FIRESIDE
Rockefeller Center
1230 Avenue of the Americas
New York, New York 10020

Copyright © 1994 by Ellen Lederman

FIRESIDE and colophon are registered trademarks of Simon & Schuster Inc.

Manufactured in the United States of America

10   9   8   7   6   5   4   3   2   1

Library of Congress Cataloging-in-Publication Data
Lederman, Ellen F.
Making life more livable : a practical guide to over 1,000
products and resources for living well in the mature years / Ellen
Lederman.
p.   cm.
"A Fireside book."
Includes index.
1. Aged—United States—Life skills guides.   2. Aged—Services
for—United States—Directories.   I. Title.
HQ1064.U5L43   1994
646.7′9—dc20   94-21357
CIP

ISBN: 0-671-87531-0

Contents

6   Contents

8   Contents

Using This Book

WHILE LIVING life well is a challenge at any age, it requires even more thought and effort after 50. An enjoyable and fulfilling life doesn't just happen on its own; instead, each of us must resolve to take whatever action is needed to make our lives as livable as possible.

With maturity we become well positioned to take charge of our lives. While aging is typically associated with some physical and financial changes, most of us have developed sufficient wisdom, creativity, and coping skills to continue to maintain a rewarding lifestyle. In fact, many persons find the second half of life to be far superior to the first fifty years!

This book can help you acquire the information, affiliate with the organizations, and obtain the products and services that can make life:

- more independent

- safer

- healthier

- more comfortable

- happier.

There are plenty of ideas that can be implemented immediately, and there are others that may be of value in the future. Browse through the book every few months to see what you may have missed the first time or to find something that didn't interest you previously but now does. Keep in mind that this book is not intended for passive reading. It's up to you to decide what you need and want . . . and then take the steps to get it. Write to manufacturers and suppliers, join clubs and organizations, and investigate services that appear to have some potential for enhancing your life.

The names of individuals and companies offering the products and services described appear in bold print throughout the text. Their addresses and phone numbers are listed in the resources section at the end of the book. Inclusion of a company in the text is not an endorsement of the product or service; you will need to make your own determination of what's right for you. Information in the parentheses is item/product/code numbers used by the company or organization. Prices are provided in approximate ranges and may change at any time. When ordering a product, call or write first to ensure that the price and product number are still the same. Although every attempt has been made to provide accurate and current information, some of the products and services may no longer be available when you read this. If you find an item has been discontinued, write to the president or customer service manager of the company and express your disappointment. If enough interest is expressed, companies will often bring back discontinued items.

While this book is intended primarily for persons over fifty, it can also be used by disabled persons of any age who wish to make their lives more livable. Younger people who care for or about older persons will find the information helpful as well. Many of the products, services, and organizations may also be relevant to persons under fifty who wish to enhance the independence, safety, health, comfort, and happiness of their own lives.

"It is not the years in your life but the life in your years that counts."

—ADLAI STEVENSON

1

A More Independent Life

SELF-SUFFICIENCY is a universal human desire. People dislike having to depend on others for fulfilling their personal needs; we all prefer to be independent so we can be in control of our own lives. Whether it's a basic self-care activity (such as eating, dressing, or bathing) or a more complex task (like cleaning, cooking, or money management), we want to be able to do it ourselves without relying on someone else.

The aging process can challenge our ability to remain as independent as we'd like. Changes in vision, hearing, strength, mobility, and memory may make it difficult to perform activities that didn't present any problems in earlier years. This forces some older persons to rely on a friend, relative, or paid caretaker for assistance (which is inconvenient and demoralizing) or to forgo an activity altogether (which reduces the quality of life).

But there *are* alternatives to depending on others or struggling on your own. A large number of resources are available that can make life easier and more independent. No matter what your age or physical abilities, you'll find something of interest in this chapter. Help yourself to the ease and independence that can be yours at any age.

Accessibility

Private homes and public buildings should be accessible to everyone. Unfortunately, many are not. Steps and other architectural barriers and elements of design can impede mobility and restrict independence in daily activities. Nobody should be a prisoner in his or her own home or denied the right to use a facility or travel anywhere that a more able-bodied person would have the opportunity to enjoy.

❦ Building or remodeling a home

Consultants are available to work with architects and/or clients in reviewing plans, providing designs for new homes or remodeling of existing ones, performing the remodeling, or overseeing the project. They'll go out to the property or work over the phone and through the mail.

Independence Builders, Inc.   *$75 to $125 an hour*

❦ Buying an accessible home

The average real estate agent isn't much help in finding barrier-free, livable homes for persons with physical limitations. But now there are two nationwide networks of professional real estate agents who are knowledgeable about accessible housing. They can search for homes anywhere in the country. The listing service is available at no charge, and completed sales are handled by local brokers at prevailing rates.

Access Real Estate   *Free*
RE/MAX ACTION Specially Challenged Network   *Free*

❦ Renting an accessible apartment: National Accessible Apartment Clearinghouse

A listing of accessible apartments by city, size, zip code, price, and features is available by calling a toll-free number.

National Apartment Association   *Free*

❦ Extendable handrail

People who have difficulty navigating stairs may benefit from this special handrail. When in the wall position, it functions as a standard railing. When pulled out from the wall so that it extends to within 22 inches of the fixed rail on the other side, it allows the user to grasp the railing with both hands while moving up and down the stairs (providing a similar effect to having a walker firmly affixed to the staircase). The system requires less than 5 pounds of pressure for easy opening and closing. Accidental closure is prevented by the rail-

ing locking into place. The company will send instructions for measuring and will custom-make railings when a ready-made system
won't fit.

St. Croix Railings   *$350 to $1,000, depending*
                                                  on length of railing

✺ Home elevators

If stairs are too difficult to maneuver, moving to a one-level house or
apartment is an obvious solution. But for the majority of people who
prefer to remain in the home they've enjoyed for years, an elevator can
be the solution. It operates just like an industrial elevator and provides
a smooth ride between levels. The variety of available finishes can
complement any home decor. For a referral to a local dealer/installer,
contact the manufacturer.

Waupaca Elevator Company, Inc.   *$10,000 to $15,000*
                          (includes installation) for basic models
                          and routine installation; may be more,
                          depending on modifications needed in
                          the structure of the house

✺ Bannister stairway elevators

A less expensive means of getting up and down stairs is to ride in a
seated stairway elevator. No special wiring is needed to install this elevator. The track on which the seat runs is no more than a foot wide,
ensuring that minimal damage results to the walls and woodwork.

Bruno   *$2,500 to $5,000*

✺ *Adapting the Home for the Physically Disabled*

This 22-minute video shows how to modify homes for persons using
wheelchairs or walkers. It includes suggestions for every room, as well
as construction techniques for outside ramps to get in and out of the
home.

Access to Recreation (VH07)   *$75 to $125*

Free information about products and designs for home accessibility
and adaptability is available from a number of sources:

· **National Kitchen and Bath Association** provides lists of certified
  accessible fixtures/designers.

· **Center for Accessible Housing** has a product referral service.

· **Paralyzed Veterans of America** offers information on specific accessibility problems/adaptive techniques.

⚐ The Easy Access Housing for Easier Living
This booklet depicts common accessibility problems in housing and provides adaptation tips for easier access into and throughout the home. Suggested modifications are as easy and inexpensive as possible.

National Easter Seal Society   *Free (with a self-addressed stamped envelope)*

Easy Access Hotline   *Free*

⚐ *The Do-Able Renewable Home: Making Your Home Fit Your Needs*
A variety of techniques and products for making homes more livable for their older occupants is profiled in this booklet.

AARP Fulfillment (D12470)   *Free*

⚐ The Perfect Fit: Creative Ideas for a Safe and Livable Home
Techniques for making homes easier to live in are included in this booklet, including ways to make them safer and more comfortable.

AARP Fulfillment (D14823)   *Free*

⚐ *Lifetime Homes* booklet
If you or an older relative needs a fully accessible home and is in a position to have one built, write for this helpful booklet. It contains actual designs and floor plans to accommodate any disability or accessibility problem.

National Easter Seal Society   *under $5*
Century 21 Real Estate Corporation (local number)   *Free*

⚐ "Tickets" for persons illegally parked in handicapped spaces
Any person who legitimately needs to park in handicapped spaces gets frustrated with able-bodied persons who use these spaces. A cartoon

"ticket" under their windshield wipers may serve as a gentle reminder to these violators that designated spaces for the disabled are no joke and may prevent them from doing it again.

Architectural and Transportation Barriers Compliance Board (ATBCB) *Free (50 tickets to a pad)*

❦ *Access Travel: Airports*

This booklet lists design features, facilities, and services for persons who use wheelchairs, or are sight- or hearing-impaired, or are up in years, at 220 airport terminals in 27 countries.

Architectural and Transportation Barriers Compliance Board ATBCB) *Free*

❦ *Access America: The Architectural Barriers Compliance Act and You*

This booklet explains how to file complaints about inaccessible federal buildings.

Architectural and Transportation Barriers Compliance Board (ATBCB) *Free*

❦ *The Real Guide: Able to Travel*

Practical information on access, facilities, and special tours is compiled by persons with disabilities. The book is edited by Alison Walsh and is published by Prentice-Hall. Local bookstores can special order it or it can be obtained through a mail-order company that carries more than 400 books on disabilities.

Twin Peaks Press *$15 to $35*

❦ Cleaning

Most older homeowners and apartment dwellers prefer to live in a place that is clean and tidy. For some, heavy cleaning can be too difficult. Using a professional cleaning service may be the only option. You can find listings of such services under "Maids" in the local Yellow Pages. Examples include Maid Brigade, Mini Maids, Dust Rag Express, Home Buddies. The charge is typically $30 to $60, depending on the size of the home and what needs to be done. Make sure that the service is licensed, bonded, and insured. For minor cleaning, the following may be helpful.

✒ Long-handled dustpan and brush

The handles on these two items are 33 to 36 inches, so they eliminate the need for bending.

$15 to $35

adaptAbility (17400)
Aids for Arthritis (D-18)
Enrichments (3240-01)
Mature Wisdom (753962)
Solutions (A753962)

✒ Lightweight all-surface sweeper

This self-adjusts to carpet, wood, and linoleum floors and eliminates the need for a heavy vacuum. It's lightweight (less than 3 pounds) and long-handled.

$15 to $35

Enrichments (3242)
Mature Wisdom (753954)

✒ Long-reach duster

Extending 80 inches, this duster prevents the need to climb on chairs or stools to dust in high places.

$5 to $15

Aids for Arthritis (B-21)
Enrichments (3265)

✒ Self-wringing mop

This mop cleans floors as well as any other mop but doesn't require stooping to wring. Instead, the mop cover is pushed down the length of the 16-inch handle.

$15 to $35

adaptAbility (17401)
Home Trends (E005)

✒ Wondermop

An absorbent sponge is attached to a 4-foot curved wand to allow for cleaning tubs, showers, and other areas without straining.

$15 to $35

Comfortably Yours (5229)
Enrichments (3264)

❦ Easy-rise kneeler

Getting into a kneeling position isn't too difficult for most persons, but getting up can be tricky for older individuals. This kneeler makes it easier to stand up, thanks to upright arms that provide support and leverage when rising. The foam-padded platform provides comfortable support while cleaning the floor. Because the device weighs only 7 pounds and has removable arms, it can easily be transported from one location to another. (The kneeler can also be used while gardening, although it's primarily designed for indoor use.)

Comfortably Yours (4904)   *$35 to $75*

❦ Magic sliders

Even young people can't move furniture and appliances very easily. When cleaning, most people find it too difficult to move heavy objects and instead just clean around them. These thin rubber discs enable desks, dressers, beds, sofas, refrigerators, washers, dryers, entertainment centers, and other objects of up to 3,000 pounds to be readily moved for thorough cleaning. When stuck under the feet or base of any appliance or piece of furniture, the sliders allow the object to glide over the floor as if it were on wheels.

$5 to $15 per package of 4

Bruce Medical Supply (BMS1385)
Solutions (6439)

❦ Instant lifter

Heavy furniture and appliances can be lifted up to 3 inches from the floor without any strain when this device is used. Once its lip is placed under the item, stepping on the lever will lift any item weighing up to 440 pounds.

The Safety Zone (182216)   *$15 to $35*

❦ Long-reach window washer

Even second-floor windows can be washed easily and safely with this washer, which extends to 15 feet. It attaches to a garden hose so that the brush pulses water and added soap. In addition to the handle and pulsating power brush, it also includes a scrubbing brush, high-pressure spray tip, and window squeegee.

The Safety Zone (182138)   *$35 to $75*

❦ Cleaning cart on wheels

Extra trips to get and put away cleaning tools and supplies can be eliminated when they're all stored on a single portable cart that can be rolled anywhere in the home. It can stay in a corner or closet when it's not being used.

Home Trends (D904)   *$35 to $75*

❦ E-Z Hose

Vacuum cleaners don't have to be dragged up and down the stairs when this 12-foot-long hose extends the regular hose of the cleaner. It fits all standard vacuum cleaners.

Home Trends (E023)   *$15 to $35*

❦ Under-Vac

With the Under-Vac, hidden dirt beneath appliances like washers/dryers and furniture can easily be reached without bending or stooping or moving appliances and sofas. It's a 3-foot-long hose extension and flat head that fits any standard vacuum hose.

Home Trends (E021)   *$5 to $15*

❦ *Communication*

It's been said that no man is an island, but older persons may well feel that they're living on one if they're cut off from the types of communication younger people take for granted. Impaired hearing may prevent conversation from being understood or television shows from being enjoyed. Visual problems may limit reading ability. Eyesight and dexterity impairments may make writing difficult. Obstacles can even be encountered in using the telephone. There are many steps you can take to ensure that the lines of communication remain as open as possible so you don't lose touch with the world around you.

LISTENING

(See also the Hearing section in Chapter 2.)

The ability to listen is one of the most important aspects of communication. If you have trouble hearing, you won't be able to fully participate in conversation or to enjoy television and radio programs. There can also be problems hearing household sounds such as the doorbell.

This first section covers how to cope with impaired hearing. For specifics on adapting telephones, televisions, alarm clocks, or household objects such as doorbells for the hard-of-hearing, refer to the index to find the pages on which these items are described.

> You may be aware that hearing aids have been improved dramatically within the past few years. Their performance has been improved and the size has been reduced. The majority are custom-made to fit inside the ear. An ear, nose, and throat physician can recommend a qualified audiologist.

✍ Listenaider
This sound amplifier looks like a pocket radio with headphones, but it has a built-in sound reflector and microphone that picks up and magnifies all surrounding sounds up to 25 feet in any direction. It's great for use in church, bingo halls, or small lecture or meeting rooms. A 9-volt battery is required.

$15 to $35

Bruce Medical Supply (NS113)
Enrichments (4088)
Independent Living Aids (437250)
Maxi Aids (20025)

✍ AudioLink
People who have impaired hearing may not be able to enjoy events at public facilities, such as theaters, cinemas, churches, and synagogues. AudioLink uses wireless audio technology in a compact headset that can be customized by a health care professional to accommodate each user's hearing loss. More than 2,000 theaters currently have transmitters that are part of the system. Many rent the headsets, but most users prefer to use their own. The AudioLink can also be used at home for watching television. Send for a free list of facilities that use the AudioLink system or for a referral to a local vendor.

National Captioning Institute   *$125 to $200*
(headset only, for public entertainment use) $200 to $350 (in-home unit for television watching—includes headset, transmitter, and battery charger)

READING

Reading is one of the greatest joys of many older persons' lives. But many have difficulty reading newspapers, magazines, books, and correspondence (as well as labels on food packages or drugs). Obviously, an optometrist or ophthalmologist is the best person to help with visual problems. But there are some things that *you* can do to help you better cope with written material.

❧ Magnifying glass

Many magnifying glasses are available. Some magnify a whole page at once, while others just magnify a few lines or small areas at a time. There are also some that don't need to be held and can hang around the neck and be braced against the chest. Some models feature a built-in light as well.

$5 to $35

Ann Morris Enterprises
Bruce Medical Supply
Independent Living Aids

❧ Proper lighting

When vision is impaired, proper lighting is essential. Check with your eye doctor for recommendations about the best possible lighting and see if you can find appropriate floor and desk lamps at a local lighting store. There are also excellent light fixtures that can be ordered through catalogs. An example of this is the Brite Eye lamp that produces as much soft focused light as five bare 100-watt light bulbs.
Independent Living Aids (130467)   *$125 to $200*

Halogen lamps are another possibility because they can generate over ten times the light of an incandescent bulb and last up to seven times longer, using less than half the power. They're available from any retailer who sells lighting fixtures.

Full-spectrum bulbs are considered to be very close to natural sunlight. Their pure white light helps to increase black and white contrast and shows other colors in their true hues. Persons with eye disorders such as glaucoma and retinitis have been found to see better under full-spectrum light. The 60- or 100-watt bulbs do cost more than incandescent bulbs but last five times longer.

$5 to $15

Lighthouse Low Vision Products (Y3221, 60 watt; Y3222, 100 watt)
Westgate Enterprises

❧ Large-print newspapers
Keeping up with the news is easier with large-type newspapers. There are two weekly papers. One is the *New York Times Large-Type Weekly,* which offers a comprehensive sampling of articles from the week as well as their famous crossword puzzle.

New York Times Large-Type Weekly *$35 to $75 a year*
The other possibility is the *World At Large* weekly tabloid, which presents stories (news, politics, health, arts, and sports) from such sources as *Time* and *U.S. News and World Report.*

World At Large (The) *$35 to $75 a year*

❧ Large-print magazine editions
Reader's Digest contains a variety of human interest, current events, and health articles every month.

Reader's Digest Large-Type *$5 to $15 a year*
Guideposts is an interfaith inspirational monthly designed to develop courage, strength, and positive attitudes.

Guideposts Associates, Inc. *$5 to $15 a year*

❧ Large-print books
Reader's Digest offers their condensed books in large print on non-glare paper. Five volumes of approximately 400 pages are published each year.

Reader's Digest *$5 to $15 for 5 books*
Other large-print books are available from Independent Living Aids.

dictionary (245475)

thesaurus (781160)

world atlas (856300)

bible (King James version) (430722)

cookbooks: *Frugal Gourmet* (341695), *James Beard's Theory and*

Practice of Good Cooking (395626), *Fannie Farmer* (310928), *Love Your Heart* (low-cholesterol cooking) (449268)
Independent Living Aids   *$15 to $35*

⚘ Audio magazines and books

Newsweek on the Air is not specifically designed for older persons or visually impaired individuals, but it's a great alternative for those who have problems with the small print in magazines.

A weekly audiocassette of articles from *Newsweek* is mailed each week, so the listener is assured of keeping up with the latest news about politics, health, science, entertainment, finance, and international affairs.

The interview format features authors, journalists, celebrities, and important newsmakers.

MARK56   *$15 to $35 (10-week subscription)*
If you have lost 70 percent of your vision or you can't hold a book due to severe arthritis, the Library of Congress Division of the Blind and Physically Handicapped/National Library Service for the Blind and Physically Handicapped (NLS) can help. They can provide special cassette players and disc players, discs, and tapes (as well as books in braille). A national network of cooperating local libraries distributes the materials. A wide variety of books and magazines has been recorded on records or tapes, serving every possible taste. Representative titles of magazines include *American Heritage, Analog Science Fiction and Fact, The Atlantic, Consumer Reports, Ebony, Ellery Queen's Mystery Magazine, Farm Journal, Foreign Affairs, Good Housekeeping, Harper's, Historic Preservation, Kiplinger's Personal Finance Magazine, Money, The Musical Mainstream, The Nation, National Geographic, National Review, Natural History, New Choices for the Best Years, New York Times Large-Type Weekly, Outdoor Life, Prevention, Sports Illustrated, Stereo Review, Travel Holiday, True West, U.S. News & World Report, Washington Post Book World,* and *The Writer.* Current issues are mailed to readers at the same time the print issues appear. Thousands of fiction and nonfiction book titles are available, including classics, biographies, gothic novels, mysteries, and how-to and self-help guides. A free subscription to *Talking Book Topics* is available in large-print, cassette, and flexible disc editions. This bimonthly guide features an annotated list of new titles that have recently been added to the collection. Borrowing the

discs, tapes, and equipment is completely free, as is the mailing both ways. Once you finish a tape or disc, all you have to do is replace it in its container, reverse the mailing label, and mail it back. Ask a local librarian at the public library or contact

Library of Congress

Books on Tape claims to have the world's largest selection of audio books. The company specializes in full-length best-sellers on cassette. Inventory includes mysteries, science fiction, classics, history, adventure, travel, general nonfiction, business, and personal development. Average listening time for a book is 8 to 15 hours. Rental prices for a 30-day loan are about the same price as a hardcover book. The books are delivered and returned through the mail.

Books on Tape   *$15 to $35*

Another vendor of recorded books offers a special introductory rate for the first rental. All books are unabridged, single-voice performances on book-packaged cassettes. They are read by experienced stage actors and narrators and are produced in the company's own studio. The majority of recordings are fiction classics such as *To Kill a Mockingbird* and *A Tale of Two Cities*, but there's also a small selection of popular fiction such as mysteries and nonfiction.

Recorded Books, Inc.   *$5 to $15*
                            new customer price for a 30-day rental;
                            additional charge for round-trip postage
                            (regular rentals range from $15 to $35)

The Bible can still be enjoyed by persons who can't read conventional print, thanks to this special service. Cassette tapes contain the Bible and are available in 35 languages. There is no cost or obligation; all the organization asks is medical verification of the visual or physical impairment.

Bible Alliance, Inc.   *Free*

ﻬ **Radio reading service**

People with visual impairments and physical disabilities can keep abreast of local newspapers through a special band on FM radio (as well as some cable TV stations). Contact your local cable company to find out what channel the service broadcasts on or contact the local service center for the visually impaired for the radio station in your area. In some areas, the broadcasts are on regular stations; in others, a special reception box will be needed. The Association of Radio Reading Ser-

vices can assist you as well. You may also contact In Touch Networks, Inc., for more information about their national broadcasts in which articles from more than 100 newspapers and current magazines are read over the air. The stations that provide this service usually do so 24 hours a day and will provide a special radio for listening to the broadcasts.
Association of Radio Reading Services
In Touch Networks, Inc.

❧ Book butler
Holding a book can be painful for arthritic hands, but this device allows the user to enjoy hands-free reading. The book is held in place at an adjustable angle. The spring-action page holders make page turning effortless. The book butler enables books to be held open while reading, cooking, or practicing a hobby.

$15 to $35

Aids for Arthritis (D-17)
Enrichments (4058)
Maxi Aids (18145)

❧ Bookmate
The Bookmate eliminates the need to grip paperback books tightly to keep them open. While it's perfect for individuals with arthritis or weakness of one or both hands, it's also ideal for anyone who wants to free up his or her hands while reading (to eat or drink, for example). The paperback is supported in a vinyl folder with a strap to hold down a page. Pages can be turned without undoing the strap.
Aids for Arthritis (C-46)   *$5 to $15*

❧ Book weight
Still another way to keep a book open without gripping it tightly or using both hands, the leather book weight has lead weights stitched into each end.

$5 to $15

Maxi Aids (91400)
The Vermont Country Store (17554)

Telephones

The phone provides an important link between older people and the outside world, but many senior citizens have problems using the phone. If you have a hearing loss, you may be deprived of the social outlet that the phone offers. Using the phone to obtain information or schedule appointments may be close to impossible. In an emergency, when seconds count, it can be stressful and even dangerous if you have difficulty seeing and using the buttons or dial on the phone. But there are ways to improve your ability to use the phone.

Dial-A-Face phone

This phone features nine large, touch-sensitive buttons into which a photo, drawing, or symbol card (such as 911) can be inserted. One touch dials the number that is programmed, enabling you to reach a relative, neighbor, or emergency medical services with just a push of the button. In an emergency, time isn't lost fumbling for phone books or address books or trying to read small print. The phone also features last number redial, tone/pulse selection, and hearing-aid compatibility. It runs on four AA batteries.

$35 to $75

Independent Living Aids (608923)
SelfCare Catalog (1546)

Push-button phone attachment

This fits over a standard desk touch-tone phone and is secured by mounting tape. The buttons are twice the size of those on standard phones and feature large numerals and letters.

$5 to $15

American Foundation for the Blind (L90030)
Enrichments (4115)
Independent Living Aids (799400)
Maxi Aids (99400)

Large-print telephone dial attachment

The numbers on the dial are twice the size of those on regular phone dials. It's easily attached to standard desk and wall rotary phones with its self-adhesive backing.

under $5

American Foundation for the Blind (L90040)
Maxi Aids (30706)

❧ ITT universal phone

Both visually impaired and hearing-impaired persons can use this phone. It features giant buttons with large black numbers, a neon light to alert the hearing-impaired to incoming calls, volume control on the handset, three memory buttons for emergency or other important numbers, and redial.

Ann Morris Enterprises (AUP1)   *$75 to $125*

❧ Talking phone

The numbers on the buttons in the handset are announced as they are pushed, eliminating incorrect numbers being dialed. Other features include a 10-number memory, redialing, tone/pulse, and speech on/off.

$35 to $75

Ann Morris Enterprises (ATP1)
Independent Living Aids (346892)

❧ Electronic telephone dialer

When dialing is difficult, this device can simplify the process by dialing a complete phone number with the touch of only one number, The dialer can be programmed to dial up to 99 phone numbers. It works by simply placing the dialer against the mouthpiece of a touch-tone phone and pressing the button.

Independent Living Aids (289462)   *$15 to $35*

❧ Sound-booster phone

Older persons can hear, see, and dial this phone without strain. This hearing-aid compatible phone amplifies the incoming voice at the touch of a button. The oversized (1½-inch) white buttons make it easy to see and dial the numbers. It has additional features of other phones, such as ringer/volume control, last-number redial, and tone/pulse switch.

Comfortably Yours (1546)   *$35 to $75*

❧ Voice-activated telephone

The phone dials automatically the person you say you wish to call. It stores up to 50 names by voice (and 100 more alphabetically to be speed dialed at the touch of a button). Both AC power and four AA batteries are used. Other features are hearing-aid compatibility, call timer, and alarm clock.

American Foundation for the Blind (L90080)   *$200 to $350*
Another voice-activated phone is ideal for people who have trouble picking up a handset or getting to the phone to answer it. Totally hands-free, the speaker phone is activated by speaking from anywhere in the room to answer incoming calls. Outgoing calls can be placed by dialing and talking without lifting the handset. It automatically disconnects after the other party hangs up.

Temasek Telephone, Inc.   *$75 to $125*

Speakeasy

If picking up a receiver is too difficult, a speaker phone enables calls to be answered without handling the phone. A microphone and speaker enable both parties to hear each other. A built-in AM/FM radio shuts itself off when the phone is used and turns back on when the conversation is finished. Either an AC adaptor or four AA batteries can be used.

Enrichments (4086)   *$35 to $75*

Telephone amplifier

The handset is placed into a 9-volt battery-operated unit that enables the listener to hear more easily what is being said. It is also convenient because the handset doesn't need to be held up to the ear to talk or to listen. The amplifier can be used with wall or desk phones. It plugs into the phone between the handset and base.

$15 to $35

Maxi Aids (08444)
The Safety Zone (334134)
Another type of amplifier attaches to the telephone earpiece with a strap. The volume can be adjusted. It uses one AA battery. Attaching easily to any standard receiver, this volume booster can be carried in a purse or pocket to use on pay phones.

$15 to $35

Comfortably Yours (5310)
Independent Living Aids (763429)
Maxi Aids (43011)

There are also handsets with built-in amplifiers. The volume of incoming sound is increased more than three times the normal level and with no distortion.

$35 to $75

AT&T National Special Needs Center (G-6)

(may also be leased for under $5 a month)

Hear You Are, Inc. (TL0689)
Maxi Aids (43010)

✳ Clarity Phone

What makes this phone so different from others is that it doesn't just amplify; it has a unique built-in equalizer that automatically tunes, tones, and balances sound to give perfect clarity while boosting volume. High-frequency sounds are increased in volume while low-frequency sounds are filtered out. Every word can be heard clearly and without distortion. The phone also features oversized push buttons and a memory bank for 13 numbers.

$125 to $200

Bruce Medical Supply (UN1000)
Promises Kept (3419)
The Safety Zone (344187)

✳ Handset for speech amplification

If your voice is weak and difficult to hear over the phone, it can be amplified with this unit with adjustable voice volume.

$35 to $75

AT&T National Special Needs Center (G-7)
Maxi Aids (17500)

✳ Ringer adjustment

By altering the ring frequency, the ring pattern, and volume of standard ringing, you can more easily hear the phone ring. TeleChime is programmed to play eight different tunes at various volume levels. The user selects the melody and volume. It's powered by two 9-volt batteries.

Hear You Are, Inc. (TS0406)   *$35 to $75*

Another aid converts the electronic sounds from modern phones into an easier-to-hear, more traditional "bell ring."

$35 to $75

AT&T Special Needs Center
Hear You Are, Inc. (TL0654)

Flashing-lamp telephone-ring alerter

If you have trouble hearing the phone ring, you may do better with a visual signal. When the phone rings, this device causes a lamp light to flash with each signal (whether the lamp is on or off). The phone and a nearby lamp are easily plugged into the telephone ring alerter.

$35 to $75

Hear You Are, Inc. (TL0664)
Independent Living Aids (604279)
Maxi Aids (TR55)

Auxiliary mechanical bell ringer

A ringing phone in another room can be heard with this device. The bell ringer can be installed in any room that has a modular phone jack. It's available at home improvement/hardware stores as well as catalogs.

Independent Living Aids (100529)   *$5 to $15*

Phone holder

When holding the telephone receiver is difficult or uncomfortable because of arthritic fingers, using this padded metal holder can make talking on the phone more enjoyable. The holder fits right onto the receiver, anchored by suction cups or Velcro straps.

$5 to $15

Enrichments (4089)
Maxi Aids (40805)

Telecommunications device for the deaf (TDD)

Deaf, hard-of-hearing, or speech-impaired individuals can use a TDD (very much like a telephone-linked typewriter) to type out their conversations to persons who can hear or other hearing/speech-impaired people. When the telephone receiver is placed into the TDD, letters typed on the keyboard emit special signals that in turn appear as letters on the other person's TDD. The party who is being called, whether hearing or nonhearing, also needs a TDD to communicate back with the hearing-impaired individual. Conversations are read on the TDD display (one to two lines, 20 to 80 characters at a time) or on the print-out of specially equipped TDDs.

$200 to $350

Hear You Are, Inc. (TY0951)
HITEC Group International, Inc. (UT-MC4)
TTY of Carolina, Inc.   122 (compact model)
                              111-1 (printed message)
There are also answering machines that record TDD messages. Standard machines hang up and don't record a TDD message when they hear the beeping tone from a TDD. TDD answering machines will not record a voice call. Answerall is a modified answering machine that records both TDD calls and human voices.

TTY of Carolina, Inc.   *$200 to $350*
A special telephone service (usually called a relay center) enables deaf, hard-of-hearing, or speech-impaired persons to communicate with hearing persons who don't have a TDD. Every state has a relay center that operates 7 days a week, 24 hours a day. Hearing- or speech-impaired individuals type on their TDDs the name and number of the hearing person to be called; hearing persons tell the communications assistant the name and number of the hearing/speech-impaired person they want to call. The specially trained communications assistant relays the conversation word for word and in strict confidentiality. Messages from the TDD user are read aloud to the hearing person; the hearing person's spoken words are typed back to the TDD user. There is no charge for local relays; long-distance calls do not cost any more than the standard charges (and some services even discount the calls). Look in the White Pages of the phone book for the local number of the relay center or contact one of the long-distance companies.
AT&T
MCI
Sprint

❧ Telephone solicitations
People who have difficulty getting to or using the phone may be spared from the bother of answering "junk" calls from telemarketers trying to

sell something or asking for contributions when they request that their names be removed from solicitation lists. Send your name, address, apartment number, zip code, and phone number with area code to the Telephone Preference Service. The local phone company can also be requested not to include you in its "reverse" directory.

Telephone Preference Service   *Free*

✍ Directory assistance

Many older persons have trouble using the Yellow or White Pages to look up phone numbers. Inform the phone company of this to obtain an exemption from directory assistance charges.

TELEVISION

Constant television watching is not beneficial for anyone's physical, intellectual, or social well-being. But television in moderation can be an enjoyable outlet for relaxation and stimulation. If you have trouble watching or hearing standard television sets, there are some devices that can help. You can also consult the Listening section of this chapter for other ideas.

✍ TV screen enlarger

This enlarged screen more than doubles the size of the TV screen. It easily mounts by sliding the braces under television set. Color, brightness, and clarity are retained without wash-out or distortion. One size fits 10- to 15-inch TV screens (measured diagonally); the other fits 17- to 26-inch screens.

	$35 to $75
Independent Living Aids (107092/107095)	*$57.95 or $67.95*
LS & S Group (276-CT-20A/276-CT-30A)	*$39.95 or $54.95*

✍ TV headset

If you or a relative is hard-of-hearing and need to turn up the volume full blast when watching television, it can be difficult for anyone else to be in the room. Neighbors in nearby apartments with thin walls also won't appreciate the volume. By wearing this special headset, the hearing-impaired person can hear well without disturbing anyone else. The headset has preselected stations that correspond to local TV channels. It cannot be used for cable stations.

Independent Living Aids (321678)   *$15 to $35*

A deluxe model features lightweight headphones, larger ear pads, and a padded headband for comfort. There are separate built-in volume controls for each ear. It runs on AAA batteries for 75 hours of television or radio listening. It increases the volume (as well as the clarity) of the broadcasts for the user without disturbing others. The transmitter converts the TV's sound into invisible infrared light waves that are received up to 25 feet away by the headphones.

$35 to $75

Bruce Medical Supply (BMS980)
Solutions (816)

❧ Closed captioning

Deaf or hard-of-hearing persons can still understand all of a program's content and not miss a word of dialogue or narration when a closed-caption decoder is used. Closed captions are subtitles of the audio portion of a television program printed as large, easy-to-read letters on the bottom of the TV screen (just like the subtitles in foreign films). Over 400 hours of network and public television are captioned each week. More than 2,500 video titles are captioned and can be rented or purchased at any video store. There's no monthly charge for captioning; the only purchase needed is the TeleCaption Closed Caption Decoder for sets manufactured before 1993. (All TV sets 13 inches or larger are now equipped with built-in decoder circuitry.) This portable device easily connects to any TV and is compatible with VCRs, cable television, and satellite receivers. It has a 225-channel capacity and includes a wireless remote control.

$125 to $200

Bruce Medical Supply (NC4000)
Hear You Are, Inc. (CC1957)
HITEC Group International, Inc. (NC-NC14)
Maxi Aids (94898)

A mail-order service makes it easy for hearing-impaired video watchers to purchase videos. The Critics' Choice Video catalog indicates which videos in its stock are close-captioned. They also have a Telecommunications Device for the Deaf (TDD) service that allows patrons to call a toll-free number, type in their orders, and obtain a confirmation response via TDD computer.

Critics' Choice Video　　　　　　　　　　　　　*$5 to $75*

For more information on closed captioning, contact
National Captioning Institute

❧ Audiodescription

People with impaired vision can still enjoy television if they know what's going on. Descriptive video describes characters' movements, costumes, body language, and scenery during pauses in the dialogue. To access this service, a separate audio program (SAP) channel must be used. A stereo televison set or multichannel television sound (MTS) stereo VCR is needed to receive the SAP channel. (The SAP button may be marked as SAP, DVS, Bilingual, Audio 2, or Audio B on the stereo TV or VCR.) Monaural TV sets may be converted to stereo with a stereo audio televison receiver called an adapter or decoder. The descriptions are heard through earphones. Audiodescription is also available at some cinemas and theaters, as well as museum exhibits and National Park sites.

Descriptive Video Service/WGBH-TV distributes a listing of distributors and manufacturers of decoder equipment, as well as listings of the public televison stations that broadcast in stereo with the SAP channel. The Nostalgia Channel, a cable television network, programs 6 hours of classic movies and television programs with descriptions each week. The **Narrative Television Network (NTN)** service is available to most cable subscribers. If the local cable system does not carry it, request that they begin to do so or contact NTN for assistance.

Audio Optics can be contacted for information about video films that are audiodescribed.

❧ VCR PLUS Instant Programmer

If programming a VCR is a problem, this device can make it a breeze. Local TV listings in the newspaper or *TV Guide* include a VCR Plus 7-digit number. All that needs to be done is to punch in the code and that show will be recorded. The programmer runs on four AAA batteries and is available wherever VCRs are sold as well as through mail-order catalogs.

Home Trends (M900)   *$35 to $75*

TYPING

Some persons with mild visual impairments can see the keys of a typewriter as they type, but then have difficulty reading the finished product.

⚞ The Canon Typestar 220

This typewriter solves the problem with a special option that allows characters to be printed double size (a full ¼ inches high). It operates on four D batteries.

Lighthouse Low Vision Products (Y1630)   *$200 to $350*

WRITING

Arthritis, tremors, or low vision can impair writing ability. Difficulty in writing letters to loved ones or filling out checks can cause a loss of independence as well as a loss in the fulfillment that comes from communication through the written word. Consider the following products to help write more easily and legibly.

⚞ Plastic/metal signature guides

These stencils are placed on the paper in the appropriate spot so that the signature is confined to the open area of the guide.

under $5

American Foundation for the Blind (B90410, plastic; B90310, metal)
Independent Living Aids (692222, plastic; 224850, metal)
Maxi Aids (92222, plastic; 80420, metal)

⚞ Check stencils

These are available for standard checks or can be custom-made for your personal check, allowing you to fill out a check in the appropriate areas without overwriting preprinted areas.

$5 to $15

American Foundation for the Blind (B90720, standard; B97000, custom-made)
Independent Living Aids (163733)
Maxi Aids (25683)

⚞ Envelope-addressing guide

This plastic guide has three cutouts for the return address and three cutouts for the "address to" area. It fits most standard-sized envelopes.

under $5

American Foundation for the Blind (B90810)
Independent Living Aids (291355)
Maxi Aids (91355)

꠸ Writing guide

Much like the signature, envelope, and check guides, these aluminum or plastic writing aids have ½-inch openings to guide the writer to write in a straight line across the page. They cover an entire letter-sized sheet of paper.

$5 to $15

American Foundation for the Blind (B90700)
Independent Living Aids (435288)
Maxi Aids (35288)

꠸ Credit card guide and magnifier

Charge slips can be signed more readily with this guide, which lets the appropriate line be seen and felt through the opening. It also features a magnifier for reading menus and reviewing bills.

Independent Living Aids (198653) *under $5*

꠸ Big-print address book

Unlike the typical address book with limited space for numbers and addresses, this one has writing spaces ½ inch apart for large print. A wide-tipped black pen is included. This is great for persons with limited eyesight or dexterity who can't see or write the small letters and numbers in the standard address book.

$15 to $35

American Foundation for the Blind (L90280)
LS&S Group (164-BP1)

꠸ Large-print check and deposit register

Older persons with impaired eyesight will still be able to manage their checkbooks with this oversized (8½ by 3½ inches), large-print register for recording checks written and deposited.

Independent Living Aids (430629) *under $5*

꠸ Arthwriter

Arthritic fingers can write more easily with this simple device (a lightweight 3-inch plastic ball with a center hole for the pen).

$5 to $15

Independent Living Aids (089010)
Maxi Aids (73514)

❦ Weight pen

This large-diameter pen comes with miniature weights that can be placed inside the pen to alter the weight from 1.75 to 5.25 ounces. Some older persons with hand tremors may find that the shakiness decreases and writing becomes easier when the hand grasps something heavy.

adaptAbility (11340)   *$5 to $15*

❦ Pen and pencil grips

A variety of special grips are available. Some can be individually customized at home (by heating in hot water and molding) to accommodate grasps that are impaired by arthritis or weakness.

$5 to $15 per set of 10

adaptAbility (11325)
Aids for Arthritis (B-78)
Enrichments (4027)

❦ Nitewriter

For direct light when you write, you may want to purchase this ballpoint pen with a built-in spotlight. It runs on two AAA penlight batteries.

$5 to $15

Independent Living Aids (445100)
Maxi Aids (45100)

❦ *Cooking and Related Activities*

Meal preparation is an enjoyable and necessary activity of daily living. Unfortunately, many older people run into problems in the kitchen. Decreased vision, limited strength, and poor finger dexterity can make cooking unsafe and frustrating. If cooking becomes an unsatisfying experience, you may find yourself avoiding it as much as possible and eating unhealthy foods that don't require much preparation. A loss of independence in the kitchen robs you of the pleasure of preparing and eating food to your liking. To ensure that this doesn't happen, incorporate some of the following ideas into your kitchen.

⚶ Overlay for appliance controls

An appliance company offers a big-type overlay conversion kit to make it easier for older people with limited vision to use a refrigerator, range, dishwasher, dryer, and microwave.

Whirlpool Corporation *Free*

⚶ Liquid level indicator

It can be difficult for some older persons to see when a liquid that is being poured is reaching the top of the container. When this electronic device is placed over the lip of a cup, glass, or bowl, it buzzes or plays a melody when the liquid nears the top. One model vibrates in addition to buzzing.

$5 to $15

American Foundation for the Blind (L90350, buzzer) (L90100, buzzer/vibrator)
Ann Morris Enterprises (KLL1, musical)
Independent Living Aids (457432, musical)
(765444, buzzer/vibrator)

⚶ Easy-to-read kitchen scale

The numbers are easy to read on the dial of this scale with a large detachable bowl and pouring lip. It measures up to 11 pounds in 1-ounce increments.

Maxi Aids (58939) *$15 to $35*

⚶ Talking kitchen scale

Measurements of up to 11 pounds in ½-ounce increments are announced as they are poured into the large mixing bowl. Other features include a rubber nonslip base and a tare feature that allows weighing of more than one ingredient without changing or emptying the bowl. It runs on a 9-volt battery.

American Foundation for the Blind (L90170) *$125 to $200*

⚶ Tactually marked scale

Up to 18 ounces of food can be weighed on this scale with raised dot markings at each ounce or gram. (It can also be used to weigh mail.)

Ann Morris Enterprises (HAS1) *$15 to $35*

❧ No-spill ice cube trays

Older hands can be a little shaky and can spill water from a filled ice tray on route to the freezer. But with this ice bottle, spillage is never a problem. Once it's filled with ½ cup of water, the cap is screwed on and the water is completely enclosed. When an ice cube is needed, the bottle is uncapped and 17 rounded "cubes" can be poured out. Another advantage of the tray is that the cubes are enclosed within the plastic container and never pick up freezer odors.

under $5

American Foundation for the Blind (L90390)
Ann Morris Enterprises (KNS1)
Maxi Aids (36952)

❧ Low-vision cutting board

Depending on the food to be cut, either the black side or the white side can be selected for high contrast.
American Foundation for the Blind (L90021)   *$15 to $35*

❧ Cutting board with guides

Potentially dangerous spills can be avoided with this plastic cutting board. One end is tapered and rimmed so that the board can be lifted and carried to a pot, bowl, or sink without any spillage. The cut-up items can then be easily pushed through the open area to remove them from the cutting board.

$5 to $15

American Foundation for the Blind (L90600)
Independent Living Aids (206862)

❧ Paring boards

Special paring boards have two stainless-steel holding pins to secure food in place for cutting or peeling. Corner guards stabilize bread for spreading butter or jam or cutting sandwiches in half. The board (anchored in place by suction cups) is ideal for one-handed users or anyone who can use a little extra help in preventing items from slipping.
Enrichments (3040)   *$15 to $35*

❧ Slicing aid

Any food (bread, meat, tomatoes, onions, potatoes, lemons, etc.) can be held and sliced evenly with this guide. The item to be sliced is gripped in the stainless-steel "jaws" by squeezing the handles at the top. A narrow-bladed knife cuts between the lines of the ribs. The device is helpful for those with visual or motor impairments.

$5 to $15

Aids for Arthritis (D-7)
American Foundation for the Blind (KC401C)
Ann Morris Enterprises (KTS1)

☘ Swedish slicer
Bread and boneless meats can easily be cut in this special device, which incorporates a cutting board and knife. The thickness of the slices can be adjusted by altering the position of the notches on the slicing guide.
Enrichments (3350)   *$35 to $75*

☘ Bagel buddy
Persons with poor coordination or visual impairment can safely and evenly slice bagels and English muffins with this plastic device. The bagel or muffin is held in place by prongs while it's cut.

under $5

Ann Morris Enterprises (KBB1)
Maxi Aids (10800)

☘ Special knives
Cutting can be very difficult for the older person with limited strength and dexterity. Fortunately, there are ergonomically designed knives that transfer the cutting power from the arm directly to the blade (rather than the finger and wrist strength required by most knives).
Enrichments (1017)   *$5 to $15*
Another helpful device is a pizza cutter/roller knife, which can be used to cut meat, vegetables, fruits, and desserts with a gentle rolling action. They're available in the houseware departments of discount and department stores, as well as from catalogs.
Enrichments (1399)   *$5 to $15*
Rocker knives use a simple rocking motion (rather than sawing back and forth) to cut meat and other foods with arthritic fingers or with only one hand.

$5 to $15

adaptAbility (20114)
Enrichments (1405)

A T-shaped knife has a 4-inch wooden handle and a 4-inch single-edged blade. Less dexterity and strength are required than with regular knives, since the pressure is applied directly above the food.
Enrichments (1411)   *$15 to $35*

⚶ Good Grips kitchen tools
These tools (swivel peeler, bottle opener, kitchen scissors, garlic press, corer, melon baller, grater, whisk, spatula, pizza wheel, spaghetti server, and knives) are designed for comfort, safety, and ease of use.

The enlarged handles are made of a rubberlike plastic and help distribute pressure across the entire hand, eliminating the need for harmful and painful squeezing. They're all dishwasher safe.

$5 to $15

Aids for Arthritis	200, swivel peeler
	201, corer
	203, melon baller
	204, grapefruit knife
	205, grater
	206, bottle opener
	301, squeeze-grip scissors
Promises Kept	2183, garlic press
	2182, whisk
	2152, swivel peeler
	2156, bottle opener
	2155, spatula
	2153, pizza wheel
	2151, kitchen scissors
	2158, spaghetti server

⚶ Locking-lid pot
The locked lid on the stainless-steel saucepan, 3-quart pot or 6-quart Dutch oven makes it easy and safe for people with low vision or lack of coordination to strain water from pasta or vegetables. They have a built-in colander with holes for draining without removing the lid.

$15 to $35

American Foundation for the Blind (L90360, 2-quart saucepan)
Ann Morris Enterprises (KCP3, 3-quart; KCP6, 6-quart)
Independent Living Aids (446655, 3-quart)

⚛ Measuring spoons
Ingredients are less likely to be spilled with these square, deep-sided, stainless-steel spoons.
Ann Morris Enterprises (KMS1)   *under $5*

⚛ Locking double spatula
Food can more easily be turned or flipped over with a double spatula. The spatula can also be used as a salad or pasta server.

under $5

American Foundation for the Blind (L90183)
Ann Morris Enterprises (KDS1)
Independent Living Aids (673330)

⚛ Onion chopper
Tears and cut fingers can be avoided when the onion is dropped into the chopper, the top is screwed on, and the plunger is pushed up and down.
Ann Morris Enterprises (KOC1)   *under $5*

⚛ Pot watcher
Cooks who have difficulty seeing when food is boiling can place the flat glass piece in the bottom of a pot. When the pot vibrates, the liquid is boiling.
Ann Morris Enterprises (KPW1)   *under $5*

⚛ Kettle tilter
Using a standard tea kettle can be difficult if you have weak wrists or tremors. The kettle tilter is a special aid that accommodates any water or tea kettle from 6¼ to 8 inches in diameter. The need to lift the kettle while pouring is eliminated; instead, the kettle is placed in a tilted steel platform support that allows for easier pouring.
Cleo, Inc. (87-1045)   *$35 to $75*

⚛ Screw-cap opener
Any 1¼- to 1⁷⁄₁₆-inch screw cap can be opened without difficulty, even by weak hands, with this opener, which fits into the palm of the hand.
Enrichments (3052)   *under $5*

✹ One-handed jar and bottle opener

Persons who have limited use of one arm after a stroke or limited strength and dexterity in their hands from arthritis or neuromuscular conditions usually have difficulty using a conventional opener for jars and bottles. This opener works for any size screw lid, from toothpaste tubes to gallon jars. It even opens press-and-turn "childproof" pill bottles.

$5 to $15

Aids for Arthritis (E-22)
Bruce Medical Supply (DN4200)
Cleo, Inc. (87-1041)

✹ One-hand can opener

This electric can opener is specially designed for one-handed operation.
Cleo, Inc. (87-1042)   *$75 to $125*

✹ Can-Do can opener

This cordless can opener is ideal for weak or impaired hands because it doesn't require pressing of a hand or lever. Once engaged, it opens the can on its own and stops automatically. It features built-in rechargeable batteries. A recharger is included, as well as a wall bracket for mounting if countertop space is limited.

$35 to $75

Access to Recreation (NC28220)
adaptAbility (26493)
Enrichments (3047)

✹ Electric jar openers

Electric can openers are readily available, but jars and bottles usually have to be opened manually. This presents some problems for weak or stiff hands. But this new appliance eliminates the struggle. It works on anything from ½-inch prescription bottle caps to 4-inch-diameter lids. When the jar or bottle is held up to the cone, the sensor switch activates the motor and does the twisting. It operates on four D batteries.
adaptAbility (10084)   *$35 to $75*

❦ Tab grabber

Flip-top cans and twist-off soda caps can easily be opened with this simple device. Its special slot pries open the metal top of the can, and the molded round opening fits over and removes twist-off caps.

under $5

Bruce Medical Supply (DN4202)
Independent Living Aids (755888)
Enrichments (3089)

❦ Plastic sack opener

Plastic, paper, or foil bags containing potato chips, cake mix, ketchup, nuts, and other items can easily be opened with a pinch of this opener. A tiny protected blade slits the bag.

under $5

For Convenience Sake (3308)
Maxi Aids (24216)

❦ Box-top opener

Hard-to-open boxes of laundry detergent, dishwasher soap, cereal, cake mixes, and pasta can readily be opened when this device is used to pierce the box and then lift the top off.

under $5

Aids for Arthritis (C-50)
Enrichments (3091)
Independent Living Aids (126544)

❦ *Mealtime Manual for People with Disabilities and the Aging*

This classic 267-page spiral-bound book by Judith Klinger gives many valuable tips for streamlining kitchen tasks for older persons to save energy and preserve independence. It even includes recipes.
Access to Recreation (NC28305)　　　　　　　　　*$5 to $15*

❦ Large-print cookbooks

Among the number of large-print cookbooks selling for $5 to $15 are the following:
Eleanor's Big Print Cookbook, **Maxi Aids** (30715)

The Frugal Gourmet Large Print Cookbook, **LS&S Group** (142-142734)
Large Print Weight Watchers Healthy Life-Style Cookbook, **LS&S Group** (142-0-8161-5428-9)
Microwave Cookbook, **Ann Morris Enterprises** (MWCH)

One-handed potato peeler

Potatoes can easily be peeled with one hand when this special peeler is used. Instead of holding the potato in one hand and the peeler in the other, the peeler is placed on the countertop via suction cups or a clamp.

adaptAbility (25001)   *$15 to $35*

EZ-Grip vegetable peeler

Persons with weak hands can easily use this potato peeler because it requires minimal pressure to use. The handle is designed so that the entire hand can be inserted into the peeler.

under $5

Ann Morris Enterprises (KPP1)
Maxi Aids (31107)

Dazey one-hand vegetable stripper

Fresh fruits and vegetables can automatically be peeled and julienned with this electric appliance. The item can easily be placed on the machine by someone with limited dexterity or the use of only one hand. The machine does all the work while it protects the hands from getting cut.

Maxi Aids (11755)   *$35 to $75*

Cheese slicer

Even when strength and dexterity are limited, cheese can easily be cut with this slicer with an angled handler. It's adjustable to allow for varying thickness of the slices.

$15 to $35

Cleo, Inc. (87-1023)
Maxi Aids (10062)

✺ Suction grater

Suction feet hold this grater in place for the one-handed user. It also features a convenient bin for the grated food, which eases cleanup.

$5 to $15

Cleo, Inc. (87-1028)
Enrichments (3294)

✺ Carton Mate

Pouring a half-gallon paper container of milk or orange juice can be difficult for many older persons. This device snaps onto the carton to make it an easy-to-pour pitcher. It features a handle, plastic cap for closing, and a stainless-steel spout blade.

Enrichments (3071)   *under $5*

✺ E-Z pour handle

Two-liter soda bottles become easy to pour when this handle is placed over them. It can be used by the visually impaired or those with weak or arthritic fingers,

Maxi Aids (69101)   *under $5*

✺ Toastmaster broiler oven

Persons with limited eyesight can use this 21- by 10- by 12-inch appliance to bake, broil, and brown because the controls and settings are tactually marked. The glass door removes for cleaning, and the oven has a continuous-clean feature. It's available in most stores that sell small appliances or can be ordered through a catalog.

American Foundation for the Blind (KM880C)   *$75 to $125*

✺ Proctor Silex cool-wall extra-wide toaster

Hands can't be burned when removing toast from this toaster. It's available in most stores where small appliances are sold or can be ordered through a mail-order catalog (with tactile markings placed on the control upon request).

Ann Morris Enterprises (KCW1)   *$35 to $75*

✺ Hot Scoop (for ice cream)

If you love ice cream but have difficulty getting it out of the carton when it's frozen solid, you can prevent wrist strain and still enjoy your favorite dessert with this unique aid. After a 15-second warmup in its stand, the Hot Scoop easily scoops up ice cream. It operates on two C batteries.

Comfortably Yours (4858)   *$15 to $35*

⚜ One-handed rolling pin

A must for the baker who can only use one hand, this tool is double-headed, with a larger roller for making pizza and a smaller one for pastry dough.

Enrichments (3079)   *under $5*

⚜ One-handed beater

The bugle-shaped handle is pumped so that eggs, creams, and sauces can be beaten with one hand. As the pressure is released, spring action reverses the blades.

Enrichments (3309)   *$5 to $15*

⚜ Pan holder

The frame of this device prevents the pot handle from moving. It mounts to the stovetop with suction cups and is ideal for the one-handed cook. When the handle of the pot is placed in the vertical slot, the pot is prevented from spinning during cooking.

                                                                $5 to $15

Access to Recreation (NC28221)
Enrichments (3011)
Independent Living Aids (571480)

⚜ Stationary mixing bowls

Mixing bowls won't move around if they have a suction base or special metal frame to enable one-handed mixing. The bowl can be removed from the suction base by turning it counterclockwise.

Enrichments (3310)   *$5 to $15*

⚜ Dycem

This nonslip material prevents dishes and bowls from moving or slipping. It can also be used to open jar lids.

Enrichments (6613)   *$5 to $15*

⚐ Suction disc

Four inches in diameter and with double-sided suction, this disc secures bowls and dishes to the counter or table. Twist action creates a vacuum on both sides. The vacuum is released with a reverse twist.
Enrichments (1261)   *$5 to $15*

⚐ Long-ring timer

If you're hard of hearing, you may not be able to hear a kitchen timer when it rings for just a second or two. This long-ringing timer (8 seconds) could be the answer. It also features bold, easy-to-read numbers.

$5 to $15

Independent Living Aids (44866)
Maxi Aids (23001)

⚐ High-visibility timer

The 8-inch-diameter face is as big as a kitchen clock and can easily be read by most people from yards away. It easily winds up to 60 minutes. Recessed hanger tabs are included for wall mounting.

$5 to $15

Colonial Garden Kitchen (660274)
LS & S Group (45-8402)

⚐ Sunbeam hot beverage maker

Getting a cup of coffee is more convenient when you don't have to go all the way into the kitchen for it. This appliance can be kept on a nightstand and is completely safe to use. It heats 12 ounces of water in about 90 seconds at the touch of a button. It's also convenient if you live in a situation where you don't have access to a kitchen but would like to be able to get a cup of instant coffee or tea on your own. Look for it in catalogs or wherever small appliances are sold.

$15 to $35

American Foundation for the Blind (L90090)
Independent Living Aids (370820)
Maxi Aids (70820)

⚐ Walking chair

Persons who fatigue easily when standing on their feet will appreciate this rolling chair. Thanks to the adjustable height (27 to 34 inches),

---

OVERHEAD KITCHEN CABINETS

If cabinets are difficult to reach, they can be lowered to 15 inches above the counter instead of the standard 18 to 24 inches.

---

users can still stand on their feet at the counter or sink, but have 90 percent of their weight supported by the seat. The casters can easily roll over carpet, linoleum, tile, or hardwood floors.

$75 to $125

adaptAbility (69011)
Enrichments (3250)
Independent Living Aids (847134)

⚘ Tactile marker (Hi-Marks 3D marker)

Settings on appliances and canned goods can easily be identified by a visually impaired person when marked with this material. Easily applied from a tube onto almost any surface (paper, metal, wood, or fabric), it quickly hardens to form personalized tactile markings.

under $5

American Foundation for the Blind (L90250)
Ann Morris Enterprises (GTM1)
Independent Living Aids (785311)
Maxi Aids (85311)

⚘ Tactile meat thermometer

The temperature of meat can be "read" by feeling the raised dots. Anywhere from 120° to 200°F degrees can be measured (in 20° degree intervals). To use, the meat is removed from the oven or microwave, the thermometer is inserted, and the temperature is read after the thermometer stands for a minute.

Ann Morris Enterprises (KMT1)

$5 to $15

⚘ Candy and deep-fry thermometer

Large tactile dots on this thermometer make it possible for the visually impaired to measure the temperature of candy or oil. The range is 150° to 400° F, in 50° increments. It comes with a bracket for hanging inside the pot.

Ann Morris Enterprises (KCT1)

$15 to $35

✿ Nutcracker
Weak hands can break nuts open with this device, which makes squeezing unnecessary. The nut is placed in the bowl, and the T-handle is turned until the nut is crushed.

Ann Morris Enterprises (KNC2)   *$5 to $15*

✿ Scrub-eeze
If holding onto a ball of steel wool or scouring pad is difficult or uncomfortable, this can be used instead. The right glove has a scouring material on the palm and fingers so that pots and pans or the stovetop can be cleaned easily with an open hand.

Aids for Arthritis (K-14)   *under $5 a pair*

✿ Suction bottle brush
This is a bottle and glass washer for the one-handed homemaker. It's stabilized by a suction base.

$15 to $35

Cleo, Inc. (87-1032)
Enrichments (3223)
Maxi Aids (75349)

✿ *Dressing*

The simple act of putting on clothing can become harder as we get older. Fastening buttons or putting on hosiery can be extremely frustrating when finger dexterity or hip mobility is limited. After a stroke, dressing may have to be done with only one arm. Fortunately, there are a number of devices that increase the ease of dressing.

✿ Button hook
Button hooks were popular many years ago but are not used much these days. You probably can't find one in a local store, but you should seriously think about ordering one from a catalog if your fingers aren't as nimble as they used to be. This inexpensive aid features a wire loop inserted in a large vinyl handle. The hook goes through the buttonhole

to grasp the button and is then brought back the opposite way through the hole so that the button is fastened.

$5 to $15

adaptAbility (34617)
Aids for Arthritis (E-29)
Enrichments (2022-02)
Independent Living Aids (138905)

⚘ Zipper pull

Much like a button hook, this pull can grasp the zipper tab and zip garments closed or open.

$5 to $15

Independent Living Aids (868749)
Mature Wisdom (778902)
Maxi Aids (18108)

⚘ Lace lock

Shoelaces can be secured without tying by sliding the plastic button to lock them in place. Unlocking is as simple as sliding the button in the opposite direction.
Enrichments (6091-02)   *under $5 for 2 pairs*

⚘ Elastic shoelaces

If you have difficulty tying your shoes because you can't easily bend over or handle the laces, elastic laces have enough give to enable the shoes to be slipped on with the bow already tied. Most are available in black or brown for dress shoes and white for athletic shoes.

under $5

Access to Recreation (NC28680-1)
adaptAbility (33512)
Maxi Aids (73786)

⚘ Long-handled shoe horn

This is ideal for the older person who has difficulty using a standard shoe horn due to difficulty in bending over. An extended shoe horn

(12, 18, 24, or 30 inches) will decrease the amount of bending needed to insert the shoe horn into the shoes.

$5 to $15

Access to Recreation (NC28601, 12″; NC28602, 18″; NC28603, 24″; NC28604, 30″)
adaptAbility (31230, 18″; 31231, 24″; 31232, 30″)
Aids for Arthritis (C-90, 24″)
Enrichments (2063, 12″; 2061, 18″; 2064, 24″; 2062, 30″)

✎ Stocking, pantyhose, or sock aid

Donning hosiery can be a struggle even for young women. Older women have even more trouble due to limited flexibility in the spine and hips. A special aid will enable you to put on stockings without reaching all the way down to place them on the toes. Once the hose is put on the plastic sheet, the foot is inserted into the curled sheet. The hose is then pulled up by garters and cloth tapes or a stick. The aid is then removed after the foot is in place. It also works well for men's socks. One company sells a special device for pantyhose as well.

$15 to $35

Access to Recreation (NC28600)
adaptAbility (30892)
Aids for Arthritis (E-21, sock aid; B-26, stocking aid; C-32, pantyhose aid)
Enrichments (2086)

✎ Comfort shoes

Not only are these black or brown shoes as comfortable as house slippers, but they're also sturdy enough to wear outside. Best of all, they're extremely easy to slip into. The shoe's velour front lifts open, then closes and fastens with Velcro. The back seam has a zipper for added ease in donning. They're available in men and women's full sizes (7 to 13 for men, 5 to 12 for women) and adjust to widths of B to EE.
adaptAbility (10006 to 10034)   *$75 to $125*

✎ Single shoes

Shoes are always sold as a matching pair. Personnel in shoe stores routinely check to make sure that both sizes are the same. But some persons have feet that differ significantly in size or wear a brace or other orthotic device that needs a larger size for that foot. Getting into a shoe that's too small for one foot or wearing a shoe that's too big for the other can be difficult and uncomfortable. A shoe exchange service can help solve this problem. When two people wearing the exact opposites are found, the service notifies them so they can make their own arrangements to trade shoes or buy new ones. Many shoe stores also send new single and mismatched shoes to the exchange, so this also increases the possibility of finding the right sizes. A full refund is given if a match cannot be made within a year.

National Odd Shoe Exchange   *$35 to $75 to join; $5 to $15 annual fee*

Another service matches persons with their shoe opposites by computer. Their Shoe Bank has more than 30,000 shoes that can be mailed to interested persons. Photographs of available shoes are sent to the shoe partners; once they decide on which shoes or boots they want and how they're going to share expenses, they send a check to cover the small fee for postage and handling. The shoes themselves (donated by manufacturers and retailers) are free.

The One Shoe Crew   *under $5 to process initial application; $5 to 15 when a partner is located; $5 to $15 handling fee for each item; $5 to $15 postage; send a self-addressed stamped envelope when corresponding*

⚐ Dressing stick

This 26-inch wooden stick has a C hook on one end for unlacing shoes and pulling up socks, as well as retrieving items off closet shelves. The other end has a push/pull hook to pull up pants by a belt loop or pull a footstool closer.

$5 to $15

Access to Recreation (NC28575)
adaptAbility (35410)
Aids for Arthritis (C-45)
Enrichments (2109)

⚐ Sock lock

Sight-impaired persons usually struggle with matching up socks. The sock lock keeps socks paired in the wash and in the drawer, preventing

---

FRONT-CLOSING BRA

Fastening a bra in the back is especially tricky for older women whose range of motion is restricted. Front-closing bras are available wherever lingerie is sold.

---

the wearing of one brown and one black sock. They're sold in packages of 24.

under $5

American Foundation for the Blind (L90200)
Independent Living Aids (699533)

✿ Bracelet fastener

Hooking the two ends of a bracelet can be tricky to do. This fastener eliminates fumbling and needing help from someone else. When the wrist is rested on the holder, the clip on the fastener holds one end of the clasp steady so that the other hand can easily hook the two ends together.

$5 to $15

Dr. Leonard's Health Care Catalog (7796)
Taylor Gifts (4372)

✿ Adapted clothing

Send for information about how to buy and adapt clothing for physical disabilities. A list of fashions and manufacturers is available, as well as listings of trained individuals who can produce garments to meet the needs of persons who have various functional limitations but still want to be fashionably dressed. Fashion technology students are also developing original designs and patterns that will be available for purchase.

Center for Clothing/Physical Disabilities   *under $5*

A mail-order company specializes in easy-access fashions for men and women. For example, sweat suits have snaps in back to prevent the difficulty of pulling the top over the head (205-women's/608-men's, S, M, L, XL, 2X, 3X in an assortment of colors, $15 to $35), some skirts wrap around (250, S, M, L, XL, $5 to $15), and a variety of blouses, shirts, housecoats, and pajamas close in front with Velcro ($5 to $35).

Fashion Ease

JCPenney has a special catalog called Easy Dressing Fashions. The clothes for men and women feature Velcro fasteners instead of but-

tons and zippers, elasticized waists and sturdy fabric pull loops to give more leverage when pulling up skirts and pants, roomier armholes in jackets and tops to allow sleeves to easily slip on and off, and no back openings.
JCPenney (ask for catalog TA 953-4900A)

�֍ *Eating*

The act of eating should be a joy, not a burden. But when handling utensils or using a cup is a problem due to arthritis or tremors, mealtimes become a chore. Older persons with these concerns may not want to eat around other people or may eat less and sacrifice nutrition. Independence may be lost if someone else has to cut the food or assist in any other way. Do everything you can to make sure that eating remains as carefree as it should be.

✖ Grips
If standard utensils are difficult to hold, the handles can be enlarged by sliding them into soft rubber grips. There are four sizes (diameters of ¾, 1⅛, 1⅜, and 1⅞ inches).
adaptAbility (10121 to 10124)   *under $5*

✖ Oversized handle utensils
A secure grip is facilitated by using these lightweight utensils with 1-inch handles. They're available by the piece or as a four-piece set.
$5 to $15 per utensil;
$15 to $35 per set

adaptAbility	21252, fork
	21033, teaspoon
	21034, soup spoon
	21352, knife
	21030, set of 4
Enrichments	1603, spoon
	1610, soup spoon
	1617, fork
	1624, knife
	1631, set of 4

𝅭 Roller knife

Much like a pizza cutter, this knife can cut many foods with minimal pressure or with one hand.

Enrichments (1399)   *$5 to $15*

𝅭 Weighted utensils

The 1-inch-diameter handles add 8 ounces to each utensil, minimizing tremors and shakiness. They're available individually or as a set of four.

$5 to $15 per utensil;
$15 to $35 per set

adaptAbility	21252, fork
	21253, teaspoon
	21254, soup spoon
	21251, knife
	21250, set of 4
Enrichments	1082, teaspoon
	1083, soup spoon
	1085, fork
	1084, spork
	1086, serrated knife

𝅭 Rocker knife

A simple rocking motion (rather than sawing back and forth) allows meat and other foods to be cut by arthritic fingers or by using only one hand.

$5 to $15

adaptAbility (20114)
Enrichments (1405)

𝅭 Rocking T-knife

This T-shaped knife has a 4-inch wooden handle and a 4-inch single-edged blade. Less dexterity and strength are required than with regular knives because the pressure is applied directly above the food.

Enrichments (1411)   *$15 to $35*

𝅭 Scoop dish or plate guard

If poor coordination or failing vision makes it difficult to secure food (such as peas) on a utensil, a dish with a wide rim or a food guard that attaches to the plate with spring-action clips makes it easier to guide food onto the fork or spoon. Plate guards are available in stainless steel or a less inconspicuous "invisible" plastic. Many of the scoop dishes have a suction base to keep them firmly anchored on the table.

$5 to $15

Access to Recreation (NC35244, clear guard; NC35214, plastic scoop dish)
adaptAbility (22480, scoop dish; 22414, clear guard)
Enrichments (1546, scoop dish; 1392, scoop plate)

⚐ Dycem mat
A rectangular piece of Dycem, a rubberlike, nonskid material, makes a terrific placemat that prevents dishes from slipping or moving.
adaptAbility (24001)   *$5 to $15*

⚐ T-grip mug
Fingers can easily be slipped under the T-shaped handle of this mug.
Enrichments (1120)   *$5 to $15*

⚐ Thumbs-up cup
Persons with limited dexterity or strength can stabilize and hold this double-handled cup firmly with both hands and thumbs.

$5 to $15

Bruce Medical Supply (DN8800)
Independent Living Aids (787429)

⚐ *Gardening and Lawn Care*

Gardening is a highly rewarding pastime, resulting in a tangible and beautiful end product. It is also quite physically demanding, requiring frequent or extended stooping, reaching, or aerobic activity. This can be difficult when strength, mobility, or endurance is limited. But no one should be forced to give up such an enjoyable hobby. If you've always been an avid gardener, you can continue to garden with some of the following products.

⚐ No-stoop weeder and trash picker tool
This 3-foot-long weeder eliminates the need to stoop, squat, or crawl to weed and helps to minimize contact with thorns, poison ivy, and

insects. The steel fingers are easily activated by squeezing the contoured grip of the levered handle so that weeds and roots can be pulled out of the ground.

Independent Living Aids (540624)   *$15 to $35*

❧ Weed popper

Another long-handled weeder features a foot lever that does all the work of "popping" out even the most stubborn weeds by their roots. It's 40 inches long and weighs just 4 pounds.

Aids for Arthritis (J-3)   *$15 to $35*

❧ Long-handled flower gatherer

The need to bend over or strain to reach overhead is eliminated with this 31-inch tool that gathers blooms and removes old flower heads.

Walt Nicke Company   *$35 to $75*

❧ Ratchet-cut loppers and pruning shear

These are excellent for people with limited arm and hand strength because of the ratchet action. Branches are cut easily and cleanly. When the handles are lightly squeezed, the user can release his or her grip and the toggle moves to the next notch in the ratchet as the blade remains in the branch. Cutting power is magnified every time the toggle moves. The blades are Teflon coated to prevent rusting. The maxi lopper is 27 inches long and cuts branches up to 2 inches thick; the regular lopper is 19 inches long and cuts branches up to 1¼ inches in diameter; the hand pruner cuts branches up to ¾ inch thick.

The Alsto Company   *pruning shear, $15 to $35*
                                                   regular lopper, $35 to $75
                                                  maxi lopper, $125 to $200

❧ Back-saver rake

This long-handled (60 inches) rake has a natural leverage design that makes it easier to use than standard rakes.

The Alsto Company   *$15 to $35*

❧ Stand-up garden tools

Bending and stooping are eliminated when the 30½-inch tubular steel extender is attached to the spring rake, three-prong cultivator, and digging trowel.

Comfortably Yours (4837)   *$15 to $35*

❧ Upper Hand

This lightweight, durable handle fits any tool (such as shovels, rakes, and hoes) it's placed on. It gives more leverage, power, and control while preventing back and upper-extremity strain.

Aids for Arthritis (J-46)   *$5 to $15*

❧ Handform trowel

Unlike traditional trowels, which must be grasped tightly, the Handform trowel is ergonomically designed to rest against the palm, thus eliminating the need for a tight grip to push the trowel into the soil. It's very useful for gardeners with weak or arthritic hands.

Walt Nicke Company   *$5 to $15*

❧ Lever-Aide Garden Tools

The cushioned leverage bar on these tools transfers the required force to the larger, more powerful arm muscles and away from the weaker hand muscles. Senior gardeners get 100 percent more power with minimized strain and discomfort. The handle of each tool is also ergonomically designed to avoid strain. A cultivator, hand hoe, and hoe-knife weed remover are available.

Lever-Aide Products, Inc.   *$35 to $75 for set of 3*

❧ Leaf bagger

The need to bend over to bag leaves after raking is eliminated with this device. The plastic unit acts like a giant dustpan, allowing leaves to be swept inside the plastic bag. It slips easily into any 30- to 39-gallon trash bag.

Aids for Arthritis (J-98)   *$15 to $35*

❧ Garden scoot

This three-wheel scooter with a tractor-style seat enables older people to sit comfortably while gardening. Its wide tires easily roll through loose, well-tilled, or mulched soil.

                                                         $75 to $125

The Alsto Company
Sporty's Preferred Living Catalog (9972L)

A four-wheel cart is also available that allows the user to sit on a pad-ded seat while transporting gardening tools and supplies.

$35 to $75

Aids for Arthritis (J-28)
Promises Kept (1750)

⚘ **Step N' Start**

Walk-behind lawn mowers are easy to start when this device is used. Instead of bending or pulling to get the mower going, all you have to do is step on the lever and the motor revs up automatically. It fits most mowers except Snapper and Toro models.
Taylor Gifts (859)   *$15 to $35*

⚘ **Garden kneeler**

Gardening (as well as household tasks) is much easier with this pad-ded kneeling platform. It can be turned over to be used as a seat.

$35 to $75

The Alsto Company
Promises Kept (1729)
Walt Nicke Company

⚘ **Hedge hydrant**

You'll never again need to crawl through the bushes to connect the hose when the hedge hydrant is attached to an existing faucet. The faucet extender includes 5 feet of heavy-duty hose and a 16-inch stake keeps the extender off the ground to reduce bending and stooping.

$15 to $35

Promises Kept (1738)
Solutions (5683)

⚘ **Cassette hose**

If lifting, winding, and untangling a heavy hose is getting difficult, con-sider this 50-foot cassette hose that unwinds as you walk and then re-winds quickly. The hose not only becomes more manageable but is safer to use because it prevents tripping over excess cord.
Promises Kept (1740)   *$75 to $125*

❧ Outside faucet turner

Outside faucets can be difficult to turn on. This plastic tool gives extra turning leverage through its extended handle.

Aids for Arthritis (E-26)   *$5 to $15*

❧ Long-reach watering can

The heavy-duty plastic watering can holds 1¼ gallons and is 28 inches long for easy reach without straining.

Walt Nicke Company $5 to $15

❧ Indoor watering hose

The hose connects to the kitchen or bathroom faucet to give 50 feet of convenience in any direction. It saves trips to refill a watering can and is also much lighter in weight to carry. It has an on/off valve for starting and stopping, as well as a spray mister.

Taylor Gifts (66716)   *$15 to $35*

❧ Household turntable

Large potted plants, both indoors and out, can be awkward and heavy to move around for watering and pruning. This plastic turntable with sturdy ball bearings can hold up to 220 pounds, yet it can be turned with just the touch of a finger.

The Vermont Country Store (19259)   *$15 to $35*

❧ Hi-lo hanging basket assist

Older persons may find it difficult to reach hanging plants to water and care for them. With this device, any basket up to 25 pounds can be lowered 3 feet. An automatic locking cam holds the basket in place until it's raised again. The device hangs on any standard-sized bracket or can be fastened directly to the ceiling.

$5 to $15

The Alsto Company
Walt Nicke Company

❧ *Container Gardening for the Handicapped*

People with arthritis and other mobility problems have difficulty bending down to tend a garden. But flowers, vegetables, and herbs can successfully be grown in raised containers. This book by Frank Schweller shows how.

Access to Recreation (BK 14)   *$5 to $15*

❦ *The Able Gardener: Overcoming Barriers of Age and Physical Limitations*

Those who want to begin or to continue to garden can do so, regardless of age and physical limitations, with this helpful book. It covers custom-designed gardens, tools, and methods to make gardening easier. General gardening tips are also provided.

Twin Peaks Press *$15 to $35*

❦ *Grooming and Hygiene*

The desire to present one's best possible appearance to the world isn't restricted to young people. Older persons also want to look well groomed and attractive. Tending to personal hygiene and grooming in the later years of life can be tricky because of declining eyesight, arthritis, and other challenges presented by the aging process. If important grooming and hygiene tasks are neglected, self-esteem suffers. People may even become reclusive when they don't feel presentable. The following ideas can help you make the most of your physical self.

❦ Magnifying mirrors

When vision isn't what it used to be, men may miss areas when they shave and women may not apply makeup neatly or attractively. Bathroom mirrors may not be adequately lit or may not provide magnification. Obtain a suitable makeup mirror from a department or discount store or a catalog. Look for features such as triple magnification and glare-free diffused lighting. Some mirrors have different light settings (such as day, office, home, or evening).

$15 to $35

American Foundation for the Blind (L90600)
Independent Living Aids (187040)

❦ Makeup glasses

Applying eye makeup can be difficult for persons with impaired eyesight. These flip-down magnifying glasses allow the user to see clearly to apply makeup or put in contact lenses. The lenses magnify 2.25

times and flip up individually so you can see with one eye what you're applying to the other.

$5 to $15

Bruce Medical Supply (BMS1549)
Mature Wisdom (785626)
Miles Kimball (0780)

⚘ Magnifying tweezers
Tweezing stray hairs or removing splinters is difficult for older persons whose eyesight isn't quite what it used to be. These ingenious tweezers make things much easier because they have an attached lens so everything can be seen up close.
Promises Kept (1497)   *$5 to $15*

⚘ Sure-grip tweezers
This tweezer is easier to hold and use than standard tweezers, thanks to the extra length (3⅝ inches) and width (⅝ inch on the sides).
Comfortably Yours (4222)   *$15 to $35*

⚘ Nail brush
Persons who have difficulty managing a regular nail brush find nail care easier with this device. The brush is anchored to a convenient surface by suction cups, enabling one-handed or arthritic users to successfully clean their nails.
Enrichments (2076)   *$15 to $35*

⚘ Nail scissors
Especially made for the nails, these scissors squeeze close with the palm, and spring open automatically after each cut. They're ideal for persons with arthritis.
Aids for Arthritis (H-2)   *$15 to $35*

⚘ Easy-hold nail clipper
Specially designed grippers provide easy control. The toenail clipper has a straight cutting edge to prevent ingrown toenails. Both the toe-

nail clipper and fingernail clipper have a built-in compartment to store clippings.

$5 to $15

Bruce Medical Supply (WE7000, set)
Maxi Aids (31040, fingernail; 31045, toenail)

⚘ Nail clipper/file
Holding a nail clipper or emery board with one hand to cut or file nails can be difficult for persons with limited dexterity or use of one or both hands. This clipper is much easier to use than the standard type because suction cups firmly anchor it on a platform.

There's no need to hold the clipper as it is pressed down on the nail to be cut. The device also enables one-handed filing, thanks to the vertical and horizontal slots to hold emery boards.

$15 to $35

Access to Recreation (NC28698)
Enrichments (2076)

⚘ Heavy-duty toenail cutter
Thick or tough toenails can more easily be trimmed with this cutter, thanks to the precision action of the heavy spring.
The Vermont Country Store (14735)   *$15 to $35*

⚘ Toenail Soft
Toenails can become thickened with age, making them difficult to cut. This special aloe-based moisturizing cream softens them to ease cutting.
Mature Wisdom (753087)   *$5 to $15 for 2 ounces*

⚘ Suction denture brush
Limited coordination or paralysis/weakness on one side may make it difficult to handle a denture brush with one hand and dentures with the other. A denture brush that stands upright and stationary on the sink, thanks to two suction cups, can simplify the task.

$5 to $15

Access to Recreation (NC28653)
Enrichments (6338)

� Built-up handle toothbrush

A standard toothbrush becomes easier for arthritic fingers to grasp when the handle is enlarged to a 1½-inch diameter.

Enrichments (6052)   *under $5*

✖ Ergonomically designed toothbrush

The curves on this brush allow persons with arthritis and weak fingers to effectively grasp the brush and use it at appropriate brushing angles. Brush heads can be replaced periodically.

$15 to $35

Aids for Arthritis (H-3,handle and 6 brush heads; H-4, 6 replacement brush heads)

✖ Electric toothbrush

Electric brushes clean teeth more thoroughly, easily, and quickly than manual brushes. They're available wherever small appliances are sold. One mail-order catalog features an Oral B brush with inner bristles to polish the tooth surface and longer counter-rotating bristles to clean plaque between the teeth and along the gumline.

SelfCare Catalog (1817)   *$35 to $75*

✖ Flossing

Dental floss can be tricky for older people to handle. Special flossers can hold the floss at the proper angle and tension. They're available in drugstores in the dental section or through mail-order suppliers.

Access to Recreation (NC44786)   *$15 to $35*

Another option is an AquaFloss machine, which uses pulsating water to stimulate the gums and clean those areas where a toothbrush can't reach. The portable, battery-operated (two AA batteries) AquaFloss water jet pulsates 950 cycles per minute to massage gums and flush away bacteria and food.

$35 to $75

Comfortably Yours (5345)
Promises Kept (1486)

✖ Tube squeezer

To avoid waste and eliminate painful or difficult squeezing of tubes of toothpaste or hand cream, use this simple, keylike device. Once the tube is slid into the grooved key, a turn or two is all that's needed to release the paste or cream. (The key is unwound to remove it.)

$5 to $15

Access to Recreation (NC66623)
Enrichments (3347-01)

✎ Built-up handle comb and brush
The comb and brush are easier to hold with the 1½-inch foam handle.
Enrichments (6050, comb; 6293, brush)   *$5 to $15*

✎ Extended comb and brush
Each is inserted into an easy-to-grip handle approximately 17 inches long, making it easier to reach the back of the head.
Enrichments (6367-04, comb; 6367-05, hairbrush)   *$15 to $35*

✎ Hands-free hairdryer
Older arms and hands can fatigue easily, especially when holding a hairdryer. This special blow dryer has a detachable base (so the dryer can be removed from the stand for hand-held use) that holds the dryer upright while the hair is dried. The dryer is powerful (1500 watts for quick drying) and has two speeds and two heat settings.

$35 to $75

Aids for Arthritis (J-61)
Maxi Aids (09823)

✎ Magic soaper
This long-handled sponge, which has a pocket for soap to be inserted, makes it much easier to wash hard-to-reach body parts like the back. It can be obtained through drugstores, discount stores, and catalogs.

$5 to $15

Aids for Arthritis (B-30)
Cleo, Inc. (86-1025)
Enrichments (6301)

☘ Terry wash mitt

If you can only use one hand, you probably find it difficult to use a washcloth and soap. Simplify things by buying a terry cloth mitt that has a palm pocket for holding a bar of soap.

$5 to $15

Access to Recreation (NC22242)
Enrichments (6335)

☘ Shower/bath seat

If standing in the shower is a problem, there are many shower seats available. Some are so portable that they weigh 8 pounds and can even double as a raised toilet seat, with rails that can be placed over the toilet. They're available in convalescent-aid stores and catalogs.

$35 to $75

Bruce Medical Supply (FHS60)
Enrichments (9940)
Sears HealthCare (11475)

☘ Fluid alert

Individuals who have difficulty seeing when the bathtub has filled up can use this unit to alert them so that the water doesn't overflow. A buzzer is sounded when the bath water reaches the unit. It also has a synthetic voice that announces the water temperature.

American Foundation for the Blind (L90380)   *$15 to $35*

☘ Hand-held showers

These units can allow bathing while sitting. They easily attach to most tubs without any hardware. Hoses are typically 5 feet long, allowing the spray to be directed as desired. The handle can be slipped into the wall bracket when not being used.

$15 to $35

Bruce Medical Supply (BMS443)
Sears HealthCare (2019)

There's also a hose that can enable a sink to be used as a shower, alleviating the need to get in and out of the tub for a shampoo. The 6-foot vinyl hose is attached to a brass adapter that fits all standard faucets.

$15 to $35

Comfortably Yours (4619)
Enrichments (6234)

✍ Bath-O-Matic Hydrocushion

Many older persons are scared or physically unable to get in and out of the bathtub independently. This portable bath lift system weighs only 13 pounds, but enables anyone up to 300 pounds to use the tub. It's completely water-powered; no electricity or tools are required. Either the faucet or shower attachment can power the Bath-O-Matic. The hydrocushion is placed in the tub and filled with water. It inflates to form a seat, which the user can sit on from outside the tub and then slide his or her legs over into the tub. The water valve is opened by gently pulling the drawstring. Water is released into the tub as the user is lowered into the tub to enjoy a bath. (Additional water may then be added to the bath.) After bathing, the valve is reclosed, water is turned on, and the cushion refills so that the user can leave the tub. The manufacturer will refund the entire purchase price if you are not satisfied after using it for 30 days or less. Although there are other bath lifts on the market, this one is about half the price of the others and permits full reclining and freedom of movement in the tub.

International Healthcare Products   *$350 to $600*

✍ Walk-in tub

Shower stalls are easy to get into, but many persons prefer tub bathing. The Kohler Precedence Whirlpool Bath enables older persons to use a tub without having to step over the side to get in or out. This special bathtub has an inward swinging door to allow the user to easily walk right into and out of the tub. When the tub begins to fill, the automatic sensor inflates the seal around the door, preventing any leakage. The gasket is deflated when water is let out. Other special features include a built-in seat and whirlpool jets. Contact your local Kohler dealer (look in the Yellow Pages under "Bathtubs/Bathroom Remodeling") or contact the manufacturer directly.

Kohler Company   *$2,500 to $5,000*

✍ Bed baths/shampoos

For older persons who can't use bathtubs, bathing in bed is the only option. However, in-bed sponge baths and body washes are ineffective, messy, and unsatisfying. The EZ-Bathe provides a real bath in the comfort and convenience of bed. This heavy-duty vinyl unit is placed under the individual and inflated around him or her. Inflating up to 80 inches long, 32 inches wide, and 10 inches deep, it comfortably fits individuals up to 6 feet 2 inches. It features a double-tube design to prevent splashing and spilling, and the cushioning is extremely comfortable and supportive, The unit comes with a wet and dry vacuum for inflating and deflating, as well as a 25-foot shower head and hose. A conventional hose can be attached to the drain hose if the bed is far away from the sink and a longer hose is required. A smaller inflatable basin is available for in-bed shampooing in conjunction with the EZ-Shower.

Home Care Products, Inc.   *$350 to $600 EZ-Bathe;*
$15 to $35 EZ-Shampoo plus
$15 to $35 EZ-Shower

✿ Lotion applicator

Applying lotions, creams, ointments, or sunscreens to the back or feet can be beyond the capabilities of persons with limited reach. This 13¾-inch-long applicator gets the lotion to wherever it's needed, without any strain. The lotion is applied on the soft-sponge pad and is then rinsed off afterward. Replacement pads are available; typically they last 4 to 6 weeks.

$5 to $15

adaptAbility (10202)
Comfortably Yours (5634)

✿ Power toilet elevator

Individuals who have limited strength or mobility problems in their hips or knees can benefit from this innovative power-elevating toilet seat. It lifts to a semi-standing height and returns to standard height for normal use. A switch in the handle controls the electric motor. It can be easily installed or removed in minutes by slipping the unit over a standard toilet.

Med/West   *$600 to $1,000*

✿ Seat lifter

Men and women living under the same roof often battle about whether the toilet seat is left up or down. Older persons in particular can find it difficult to lift the seat or put it down when they have back problems or arthritis. This easily installed white plastic device enables the user to lift the seat without exerting any effort or bending over; stepping on the foot pedal is all that's needed to raise the seat.

(The seat is automatically returned down after the user releases the pedal.)

$15 to $35

Comfortably Yours (3496)
Maxi Aids (13625)

⚴ Raised toilet seat

These white enameled seats securely clamp onto standard and elongated toilet bowls and add from 3 to 6 inches of extra height, enabling you to get on and off the toilet more easily. Some have armrests attached to the seat. They're available at convalescent-aid stores and through catalogs.

$35 to $75

Aids for Arthritis (J-16)
Maxi Aids (65250)
Sears HealthCare

⚴ Toilet safety rails

The rails make sitting down or rising from the toilet much safer and easier in the presence of knee or hip problems. They can be quickly installed by unbolting the toilet seat and placing the bracket between the seat and the bowl, giving something to hold onto on either side.

$35 to $75

Aids for Arthritis (B-33)
Enrichments (5269)
Maxi Aids (04570)
Sears HealthCare (1181)

⚴ Toilet tissue aid

When using toilet paper is difficult because of limited reaching, this 13-inch-long aid can be used. The paper is attached to the molded end for easy wiping without struggling to reach.

Access to Recreation (NC28700)   *$15 to $35*

⚴ Talking scale

Digital displays are fairly easy to read, but some persons with low vision may have difficulty seeing these numbers. A talking scale that announces the user's weight in a clear synthetic voice enables the visually impaired to monitor their weight. Running on two 9-volt batteries, the scale has a volume control and automatic shutoff.

$75 to $125

American Foundation for the Blind (L90020)
Independent Living Aids (850050)
Maxi Aids (57780)

❦ Household Operation

An older person's independence can be severely compromised when routine household objects such as light switches or doorknobs can't be managed. Arthritis and other conditions can make even the simplest acts (using a key or turning on a faucet) tricky. Decreased hearing may prevent the doorbell from being heard. Increase your independence by considering the following.

❦ Support/service dogs
Support/service dogs are to the elderly and physically disabled what seeing-eye dogs are to the blind. Specially trained dogs can help a person transfer from a wheelchair, pull a wheelchair, assist a person to rise after falling, open heavy house and store doors, help with transporting and doing laundry, make beds, turn on and off a light switch, open a refrigerator door, retrieve dropped coins and keys, and pick up the phone. Up to 65 commands can be learned by the dogs. The personal assistance provided by these dogs allows people with a disability to remain at home without an attendant or to save money in attendant care. Dogs and humans are carefully matched for needs, abilities, and personalities. Each pair takes an intensive 2- to 4-week course at a regional training center to learn how to work together as a team. The dogs are placed free of charge.
Assistance Dogs International
Canine Companions for Independence
Independence Dogs
Support Dogs for the Handicapped, Inc.

❦ Doorknob helper
This aid fits on round doorknobs to provide an easier-to-grasp lever handle, allowing the user to open a door with the fingers

placed in a comfortable position. Some of the handles even glow in the dark.

$5 to $15

Aids for Arthritis (B-14, rubber; E-24, metal)
Enrichments (6396-02, rubber)
Independent Living Aids (436755, rubber that glows in the dark)

✴ Knob turner
People with limitations in hand dexterity or strength get extra help in turning appliance knobs and faucets. The device is placed over the knob so that the user gets extra leverage from the extended handle.

$15 to $35

Aids for Arthritis (D-10)
Enrichments (6303)
Independent Living Aids (792528)

✴ No-hands door opener
It can be difficult to open the refrigerator while holding food items, especially if only one hand is functional after a stroke or due to arthritis (or if you have to use a cane). This opener installs without drilling in a few minutes, enabling the refrigerator door to be opened by just stepping on a lever.
Enrichments (3249-01)   *$5 to $15*

✴ Patio slider
Sliding open a glass patio door isn't easy for people with arthritis or limited strength. An electric sliding door operator can solve the problem. The slider surface mounts to the interior of the home. The door can be opened with a push button digital pad, key switch, or remote control and will close automatically from 1 to 30 seconds later (as set on the timer). Upon request, the manufacturer will provide the name of a local professional installer.
Adaptations (PS8700)   *$1,000 to $2,500*

✴ Car door opener
This device with a padded handle and adjustable gripper takes the pressure off weak or arthritic fingers when opening a car door. It can

be carried in a purse or pocket and works on push-button or pull-up handles.

$15 to $35

Access to Recreation (NC2844)
Aids for Arthritis (E-23)
Enrichments (6715)

⚘ Light switch extension handle

This handle fits standard toggle wall switches, bringing the switch 17 inches lower for people in wheelchairs or with shoulder pain/limited arm movement.

$5 to $15

Cleo, Inc. (87-1046)
Enrichments (3426)
Maxi Aids (81910)

⚘ Lamp knob

This three-spoke enlarged knob fits over most standard lamp threads, making it easier to turn the lamp on or off.

$5 to $15 for set of 3

Aids for Arthritis (B-55)
Enrichments (6386-03)

⚘ Light touch

When this converter is screwed into a regular lamp socket, regular light bulbs function as if they were three-way bulbs. The lamp can then be turned on or off or adjusted for brightness with just a touch of the metal base or the frame of the shade, eliminating fumbling for the light switch. The device is ideal for persons who have trouble manipulating lamp switches.

$15 to $35

Bruce Medical Supply (DN8110)
Enrichments (3425)
Home Trends (E902)

⚘ Touch & Glo

Touch & Glo can turn fluorescent lights on and off with the touch of a finger. It attaches to kitchen cabinets or closets with the supplied adhesive tape or screws and plugs into a nearby outlet.

Home Trends (J909)   *$5 to $15*

❦ Remote-control sound-activated switch

Lamps, stereos, or televisions can be turned on and off with a snap of the fingers or a clap of the hand. Installation is as simple as plugging the unit into the wall socket and then plugging the lamp, stereo, or TV into the unit. It can safely be used for any appliance rated between 40 and 400 watts.

Independent Living Aids (657456)   *$5 to $15*

❦ Wireless remote-control system

Appliances (air conditioner, fans, television, stereo, microwave, coffeepots) and lamps can be turned on and off from up to 50 feet away with this system. The Magic Button is a hand-held device that controls lights or appliances with a push of the button. No special wiring is needed; the light or appliance is simply plugged into the receiver. Individuals with mobility restrictions will find the unit invaluable because they can remain in their wheelchair or bed and still control their home environment. Persons who fatigue easily will also enjoy saving steps.

Home Automation Laboratories (5507)   *$35 to $75*

❦ Adjustable key holder

Opening doors becomes easier for those with arthritis when they use this aid. The key holder locks in any position so that the user can hold it in the way that provides the best leverage for turning. Up to three keys can fit into the plastic frame.

                                                                $5 to $15

Aids for Arthritis (C-19)
Enrichments (3206)

❦ Key light

Trying to stab a key into a keyhole on a moonless night is tricky. To help you get into the car or house quickly and without fumbling, slide the plastic case with the light over the top of a key. Press the button to illuminate the keyhole as the key is inserted.

Herrington (M882)   *$5 to $15*

❦ Door light

If you have trouble using a key to let yourself into your home when it's dark outside, install this palm-sized light, which provides a bright beam aimed directly over the lock. The light works on two AAA batteries and has adhesive on the back for easy mounting over the key slot. It's activated by a gentle push. Best of all, it turns itself off after the user goes inside (after 15 seconds).

$5 to $15

Brookstone (15407)
Home Trends (M200)

⚶ SmartFaucet
If a standard faucet is difficult to reach or operate, this faucet with an advanced microprocessor brain and ultrasonic sensor may be an ideal solution. It automatically turns water on and off by sensing the movement of hands, glasses, dishes, and so on. Running on a 9-volt battery, it easily attaches to virtually any faucet. The manufacturer estimates that it can save up to 70 percent of water and energy bills by eliminating unnecessary running of water.
Conservation Corporation of America   *$75 to $125*

⚶ Reachers
To access hard-to-reach objects on shelves, walls, or floors, a reacher can extend your reach. They're generally 2 to 3 feet long and feature trigger action for grasping the object securely.

$15 to $35

Access to Recreation (NC28542)
Aids for Arthritis (H-1)
Enrichments (6109-27)
Independent Living Aids (656260)

⚶ Push-button pusher
The special handle makes it easier to depress push buttons on aerosol cans (such as spray disinfectant, air freshener, deodorant, hair spray, and household lubricant).

$5 to $15

Enrichments (6317-02)

⚶ Thermostat operation
If you have trouble seeing the numbers on your thermostat, you can buy a special magnifier that snaps over an existing round thermostat.
Brookstone (12329)   *$5 to $15*

Or you can replace the thermostat with one that features large numbers and raised temperature settings that click every 2 degrees of dial movement.

$35 to $75

American Foundation for the Blind (L90110)
LS & S Group (152-T87F3467)

✁ Big readable thermometer

This 12-inch thermometer with large numbers can easily be read when placed on a window. The dial is white, the numbers black, and the pointer red.
Maxi Aids (29610)   *$5 to $15*

✁ Doorbell or knocker signaler

Once the unit is wired directly to a doorbell button and a lamp is plugged into the unit, the signaler will flash the lamp for several seconds when the button is pushed. This alerts a hard-of-hearing person who may not be able to hear the bell ring.

$35 to $75

Hear You Are, Inc. (VS0928)
HITEC Group International, Inc. (SA-DS70)
There's also a version that flashes a light in response to a knock on the door. The unit easily attaches to the door with Velcro and operates on a 9-volt battery.
TTY of Carolina, Inc.   *$35 to $75*

✁ Wireless chimes

When it's difficult to hear the doorbell from certain areas of the house, garage, porch, or yard, these chimes can alert the user to a visitor at the door. The doorbell installs without any electrical wires; detachable mounting strips are all that's needed. The base is plugged into an AC outlet up to 50 feet away. When visitors press the exterior button, chimes sound. The unit runs on one 9-volt battery.

$35 to $75

Comfortably Yours (4695)
Home Trends (L910)
Another type of wireless chimes can add to or replace an existing doorbell. The push-button receiver is placed near the door with easy-mounting screws. The receiver chimes may be worn on the belt

or placed anywhere in the vicinity. They can even be taken outdoors.

ID Marketing (WDB-1)   *$15 to $35*

ᘑ Safety bulb changer

When it's difficult or unsafe to climb up a ladder or step stool to change an overhead light bulb, the bulb can still be reached with this device. The bulb changer screws onto any broom handle and has a spring action that holds the bulb for turning. It comes in four light bulb styles: standard, flood, mercury, and track-recessed.

$5 to $15

Comfortably Yours (4833/4/5/6)
Home Trends (J113)

PHYSICAL THERAPY EVALUATION

A licensed physical therapist is the most appropriate professional for determining whether you could benefit from a cane, walker, or wheelchair. Contact your local hospital or home health agency to arrange for a physical therapy evaluation to determine your needs.

ᘑ *Mobility*

For the older person, walking even short distances can present problems. It can also be difficult to rise to standing from a sitting position or to get out of bed. When moving around becomes difficult, quality of life is compromised by the inability to do things independently and the resulting confinement to home and bed. To stay involved in the outside world and remain as self-sufficient as possible, consider the following ideas.

ᘑ Folding adjustable cane

Extremely portable (folding to less than 12 inches), this cane will support hundreds of pounds. It adjusts from 33 to 36 inches. It's handy when a cane is needed only occasionally (such as for extended walking).

$15 to $35

Aids for Arthritis (E-15)
Sears HealthCare (1070)

USE OF A CANE

Cane users need to remember that the cane should be carried on the opposite side from an injured hip or knee. This lengthens the "lever arm" and reduces the forces across the hip joint to less than half of what normally would occur. Too many cane users mistakenly feel that they should carry the cane in the same hand as the injured leg or foot and fail to realize that this prevents a normal reciprocal gait (the right arm and left leg advancing together, then the left arm and right leg).

⚕ Folding seat cane
This cane contains a seat that can be unlocked when you need to sit for a while.

$15 to $35

Aids for Arthritis (B-48)
Enrichments (6801)
Sears HealthCare (1075)

⚕ Cane rest attachment
The spring-tension unit clips onto a cane so it can be rested conveniently on a table, desk, or counter. It alleviates fumbling and reaching for a cane placed on the floor.

under $5

For Convenience Sake (1841)
Maxi Aids (94587)

⚕ Folding seat walker
Using a walker can be tiring. When the person using this walker needs to sit for a while, all he or she has to do is flip down the padded seat. Two of the legs are on casters for easier mobility; the other two have rubber nonslip tips. The handles have cushioned grips.

$75 to $125

Mature Wisdom (754226)
Sears HealthCare (1596)

⚕ Basket walker
This is a well-designed, adjustable walker system that comes with two removable wire baskets, giving the impression of a shopping cart

rather than a walker. It can be used indoors or out, support up to 280 pounds, and has a hand brake system for safety. An attached seat allows resting wherever and whenever desired.

$350 to $600

Bruce Medical Supply (WX21034)
Mature Wisdom (754101D)
Promises Kept (1038)

✥ Wire walker basket or fabric pouch
Objects can be carried in the basket or fabric pouch (which easily attaches to the walker), leaving both hands free to use the walker.

$15 to $35

Cleo, Inc. (39-1005, wire)
Maxi Aids (26150, wire; 13116, denim)

✥ Fanny pouch
Wearing this nylon pack around the waist frees up the hands to use a walker or other assistive device. They're available at sporting goods stores as well as through catalogs.
Independent Living Aids (310655)   *$5 to $15*

✥ Electric three-wheelers
A number of older persons who don't drive have increased their independence through these one-hand-operated vehicles. Intended for the outdoors or indoor commercial establishments rather than for the home, they enable users to go where and when they want, independently or with a companion. They can be used to go to stores or the bank, to visit friends, to get to the golf course or through a park. The marine battery and recharger included in the price allow the vehicle to travel for 20 miles; two golf-cart batteries can be charged for longer trips of up to 60 miles. The vehicle is completely equipped with automatic brakes, a five-gear variable-speed drive, and an adjustable-height swivel seat.
Palmer Industries Inc.   *$2,500 to $3,000 for the 30" single
seater or the 35" double seater;
$350 to $600 for golf-cart batteries;
$5 to $15 for a video preview of the vehicles in use*

Sears HealthCare also has a number of three- and four-wheel motorized scooters, ranging from $2,500 to $5,000.

❧ Luggage cart with seat
If you enjoy travel but get tired walking thr[...]
which has a platform that can be used to s[...]
son, is ideal.
Independent Living Aids (444873)

❧ Porta-ramp
There can be problems when a wheelchair user has to deal wi[...]
pected steps or curbs. This ramp is so light (less than 20 pounds) a[...]
portable that it can easily be carried in the car or on the back of the
wheelchair in its own carrying case.

$125 to $200

Access to Recreation (EZ01)
Cleo, Inc. (53-1103)
Homecare Products, Inc.
Mature Wisdom (751024D)

❧ Lifter seat
The pneumatic lifter assists in getting up and out of a favorite chair or
sofa. The cushion adds almost 4 inches to the height of the chair and
does its magic by rising upward when the person leans forward slightly
and takes some weight off the cushion. It accommodates body weights
up to 300 pounds.

$125 to $200

Dr. Leonard's Health Care Catalog (6474)
Easy-Up
Enrichments (6708)
Independent Living Aids (097042)
There are also electric-lift recliners that operate with hand controls.
They recline completely for napping, recline partially at an angle for
reading or watching television, and tilt forward to help the user to a
standing position.

$600 to $1,000

Dr. Leonard's Health Care Products
Sears HealthCare

❧ Orthopedic chairs
Specially designed chairs (such as the EZ-UP Artherapedic) can be
adjusted to several back positions to eliminate forward trunk lean,

de seats so that legs aren't cramped, and feature extended
to assist the user in entering or exiting the chair. The raised seat
ght conserves energy and protects joints when transferring in or
t of the chair. Footrests provide extra support. While some of
these chairs are available with motorized parts to assist the user in
getting up, a nonmotorized one is preferable if you're able to rise
with only a little help.

Alda Industries *$600 to $1,000*

⚘ **Swivel seat cushion**

For use in the car or on a chair, the top cushion swivels to the proper
position while the bottom cushion remains stationary, making it easier
to turn and get out of a seated position.

$15 to $35

Aids for Arthritis (D-22)
Enrichments (6713)
Mature Wisdom (754283)

⚘ **Leg extenders**

Although it can be difficult for older persons to get out of a low chair,
a favorite chair can still be used by raising it with slip-on molded plastic extenders that add 3, 4, or 5 inches to the height of any chair or
bed with straight legs. The furniture is not damaged by using this device.

Enrichments (6430) *$35 to $75 for set of 4*

⚘ **Helping handle**

This special handle adjusts and clamps onto any standard bed with a
mattress and box spring, making it easier to sit up or change position.

$35 to $75

Aids for Arthritis (F-8)
Maxi Aids (19901)
Sears Health Care (1185)

⚘ **Push-up bar**

Sitting down safely and standing up from the bed or sofa are easier and
safer with this push-up bar with foam-cushioned handles. Made of
lightweight aluminum so that it can be readily picked up and placed

wherever needed, it gives support to help the user out of deep, soft sitting spots.

$15 to $35

Mature Wisdom (556779)
Sears HealthCare (72154)

⚘ Sturdygrip
The vertical pole can be used with or without wall support to help the user get up from bed or a chair or sofa. It runs from the floor to the ceiling. No tools are required for installation.
Sears HealthCare (15562)   *$200 to $350*

⚘ *Monitoring Blood Pressure*

If you need to monitor your blood pressure but have difficulty listening through a stethoscope or seeing the numbers, one of the following items can improve the accuracy and ease of checking blood pressure.

⚘ Master digital blood pressure computer
The cuff self-inflates, takes the reading, then automatically deflates and prints out the date, time, heart rate, and systolic/diastolic blood pressures. It can even print out the last seven measurements for comparison. The large LCD numbers are easy to read. To ensure accuracy, the machine flashes a warning if the arm isn't in the proper position for a correct reading. Either four C batteries or a universal electrical adapter can be used.

$125 to $200

Maxi Aids (11095)
SelfCare Catalog (1110)

⚘ Blood pressure unit auto inflation
Similar to the blood pressure computer above, but without the printed readout, this battery-operated machine (running on four AAA batteries, with an AC adapter available) features a jumbo digital display and a symbol key to indicate errors.

$75 to $125

Bruce Medical Supply (DS7060)
Cleo, Inc. (28-1082)
Enrichments (9980)
Maxi Aids (11081)

❧ Blood pressure/pulse monitor

An index finger is inserted into the compact monitor. The battery-operated mini computer inside does all the work and gives the results (systolic, diastolic, and pulse readings) in just a few seconds on a large-print digital display. It uses two AA batteries.

$125 to $200

Bruce Medical Supply (DS815)
Cleo, Inc. (28-1050)
Maxi Aids (10288)
SelfCare Catalog (1715)

❧ Cardio Vox™ talking blood pressure meter

The electronic voice states the systolic/diastolic pressure and pulse rate readings, time and date, and up to seven stored readings. The arm cuff automatically inflates and deflates. Results may be printed out with the time and date of measurement. Either four AA batteries or an AC adapter can be used.

$200 to $350

American Foundation for the Blind (H90990)
Maxi Aids (10297)

❧ Blood pressure watch

In addition to being a full-function timepiece (with time, date, alarm, stopwatch, and display light), this watch also has a built-in blood pressure monitor. Blood pressure can be taken by placing two fingers on the sensor. The LCD screen shows diastolic and systolic pressures, pulse, and EKG. It stores up to 30 readings with date and time. This watch is an easy way to monitor blood pressure at any time, but is especially effective while exercising.

Mature Wisdom (783597)   *$125 to $200*

❧ Recreation

Life shouldn't be all work and no play. Most retired persons are in a position to pursue whatever gives them pleasure. Retired or not, the aging process may present some challenges in continuing with hobbies or beginning new leisure activities, but the following ideas make it possible to enjoy whatever recreational activity you choose.

BINGO

While bingo may not be everyone's game of choice, there are many older persons who do enjoy it. It's simple enough to play, but impaired eyesight and hearing can make it difficult to see and hear the numbers called.

⚘ Large bingo cards
These cards are much easier to read than standard bingo cards because the letters are ⅝ inch high.

under $5

Ann Morris Enterprises (RBB1)
Independent Living Aids (118743)
LS & S Group (348-CC1A)
Maxi Aids (48725)

(See the Listening section for aids to make it easier to hear the numbers as they're being called.)

BOARD GAMES

Games are fun as well as a great way to get some mental exercise. Plotting strategies and making quick decisions keep the mind alert. Board games also provide an opportunity for socializing. But they can be frustrating for the player who has trouble seeing the pieces or board. Special modifications in certain games make playing much more enjoyable.

⚘ Aggravation
This game for up to four players is played like parcheesi. Specially designed for low-vision use, it features high-contrast colors and large pieces.

$15 to $35

Maxi Aids (10664)
LS&S Group (192-BU-H)

⚘ Backgammon set
Look for sets with an oversized playing field, high contrast, and tactually marked pieces and dice. Some are available wherever games are

sold; others can be obtained through organizations that serve the visually impaired.

$15 to $35

American Foundation for the Blind (G90070)
LS&S Group (192-BU-E)
Maxi Aids (10635)

❧ Checker set
Checkers typically have enough of a contrast to be seen by older persons, but there are some that are especially easy. These have alternating 1-inch squares that are raised and recessed, as well as different shapes for the playing pieces (round for the black, square for the red).

$5 to $15

American Foundation for the Blind (G90020)
Maxi Aids (10625)

❧ Connect Four
This vertical checkers game can easily be played by older adults with low vision because of the high-contrast playing board (yellow) and pieces (red and black, with holes in the middle of the black pieces for tactual identification). It's also a great game to play with grandchildren (aged 7 and up). To win, a player must line up four checkers horizontally, vertically, or diagonally,

$15 to $35

American Foundation for the Blind (G90050)
Independent Living Aids (188643)

❧ Cribbage
A specially modified set has tactually marked pegs for easy identification as well as a board with scoring holes marked by raised metal eyelets.

American Foundation for the Blind (G90260)   *$15 to $35*

❧ Monopoly
The person with low vision can be a real estate tycoon (at least in this game, if not in real life) with this large, easy-to-read playing board. Jumbo-sized cards with braille and large print and a molded overlay on

the game board for easily distinguishing between properties ensure that the biggest struggle will be determining what properties to buy and sell rather than trying to see the game.

American Foundation for the Blind (G90010)   *$35 to $75*

⚘ Othello

This unique game of strategy can be learned quickly but takes a long time to truly master. The magnetic playing board has raised ridges so that the tactually marked pieces don't move during play. Catalog companies have modified the playing surface to give it a higher contrast.

$15 to $35

American Foundation for the Blind (G90080)
Independent Living Aids (564875)

⚘ Scrabble

The large black letters on the white tiles are easy to see. This special set also has a built-in turntable and recessed squares so that the tiles cannot slip out of place.

Lighthouse Low Vision Products (Y2607)   *$35 to $75*

⚘ Uno

Uno is a popular family game for ages 7 and up. Two to ten players can play. Large-print cards can be helpful for persons with diminished sight.

American Foundation for the Blind (G90180)   *$5 to $15*

BOWLING

If bending the fingers is limited because of arthritis, it can be hard to get the fingers into the holes of a bowling ball. The unique handle on this special bowling ball permits the bowler to grasp the ball without the usual finger-hold grip. The fingers are placed under the handle, the ball is rolled, and the handle retracts completely into the ball when released. It's available in 6-, 8-, 10-, or 12-pound weights.

Access to Recreation (BB11)   *$125 to $200*

If arm strength is too limited to hold a ball and roll it down the alley, this long-handled pusher can be used to push and guide the ball once it's placed on the floor. It can be used in a standing or sitting position.

Access to Recreation (BB10)   *$125 to $200*

CROSSWORD PUZZLES

Your mind may be sharp enough to work on crossword puzzles, but your eyes may not be able to read the puzzles printed in newspapers or standard crossword puzzle books. Using the dictionary to look up words can be very difficult as well.

✺ Crossword puzzles in large type

$5 to $15

American Foundation for the Blind (G90200)
Independent Living Aids (205545)

✺ Large-print dictionary
The *Merriam-Webster Dictionary* has over 57,000 entries in large print.

$15 to $35

American Foundation for the Blind (B90100)
Independent Living Aids (245475)

✺ Franklin talking dictionary
This portable electronic dictionary has high-quality speech output for providing definitions for 300,000 words. It also has a spelling checker, thesaurus, and ten educational games (such as hangman and jumbles). Words can be spoken or spelled out on the screen, either as complete words or letter by letter. It includes an earphone, AC adapter, and four AA batteries.

$350 to $600

American Foundation for the Blind (L90500)
Ann Morris Enterprises (ATD1)

EMBROIDERY

Embroidering is a very rewarding pastime for many older persons, but someone with the use of only one hand typically can't manage both the embroidery hoop and the needle . . . unless they have a special holder for the hoop.

✍ Embroidery hoop

The hoop clamps to the table so that the functional hand only has to hold the needle. This device can also be used for darning socks or to hold a knitting or crocheting needle.

$75 to $125

Cleo, Inc. (63-1123)
Enrichments (9455)

FISHING

Fishing is a hobby that can usually be enjoyed at any age, but sometimes physical limitations prevent older persons from participating. When hand or arm movements are limited because of arthritis, stroke, or paralysis, special aids can allow this pastime to be resumed.

✍ Van's EZ CAST

Limited use of one arm is all that is necessity to cast and reel independently. This special unit includes the rod, aluminum casting device, holder, and clamps to anchor the unit on either arm of a wheelchair or lawn chair. The rod is pushed forward so that the line holder releases the line automatically at the exact moment for a good cast each time.

$75 to $125

Access to Recreation (VC01)
J. L. Pachner Ltd. (EZ 101)

✍ Fish grabber

Definitely a help for those with arthritis or tremors, this device keeps fish under control for easier and safer hook removal. The rubber holder wraps around the fish to secure it, protecting the hands from actual contact with the slippery fish.

J. L. Pachner Ltd. (FG 101)   *under $5*

✍ Bait threader and knot tier

Because the line can be held by the teeth while the hand does the work, this stainless-steel needle enables someone with the use of only one hand to thread worms, eggs, grubs, crickets, and to tie trilene or clinch knots on hooks, swivels, and sinkers.

J. L. Pachner Ltd. (KT 103)   *under $5*

❦ Electric-retrieve fishing reels

Persons with the use of only one hand or weakness of the arms can benefit from the electric-retrieve fishing systems. By pushing a button after casting and lowering the rod tip, the slack line is retrieved electronically. It's available from stores that sell fishing equipment or by mail order.

$200 to $350

Access to Recreation (ER112)
J. L. Pachner Ltd. (ER 105)

GOLFING

Many older persons enjoy golf but find that their game isn't quite as good as it used to be. The ball doesn't travel as far or as fast as it has in the past.

Fortunately, major manufacturers now design clubs specifically for senior golfers. Most have graphite shafts, which are lighter than steel but just as strong. More weight is transferred to the club head to hit the ball more forcefully and generate more speed. Because they're ½ inch longer than regular clubs, they also increase speed by extending the radius of the swing. Ask your pro shop or sporting goods dealer for models such as Ben Hogan's Senior Edge Woods and Irons, Slotline's Senior Master, and Wilson's Ultra-SR and Ultra-W (for women).

❦ *Challenge Golf*

This 53-minute video detailing golf for persons with visual limitations, arthritis, limited use of one arm or leg, or standing restrictions offers step-by-step instructions and features actual handicapped golfers at play.

Access to Recreation (VH01)   *$35 to $75*

KNITTING/CROCHETING

Since knitting and crocheting require the use of two hands, people with limited use of one hand due to arthritis or a stroke may mistakenly believe that they're unable to participate in these activities. The following aids provide convincing evidence that these activities can still be pursued.

✿ Knitting needle holder

The holder clamps onto a chair arm or table so that the knitting or crocheting needle can be held firm.

Cleo, Inc. (63-1122)   *$15 to $35*

✿ Crochet grip

To reduce hand cramps and improve the grip of arthritic or weak hands, this mold can be applied to a crochet hook, heated, and custom-molded for individual needs in less than a minute.

adaptAbility (11320)   *$5 to $15 (1-foot length)*

PLAYING CARDS

If you enjoy card games but have difficulty seeing the playing cards or holding them, consider the following aids.

✿ Large-print playing cards

under $5

American Foundation for the Blind (G91180)
Ann Morris Enterprises (RGF1)
Enrichments (9419-02)
Independent Living Aids (402800)

✿ Card holders

These slotted wooden devices can hold 30 to 60 cards securely, enabling the older person with arthritis or with the use of only one hand to play cards.

$5 to $15

Aids for Arthritis (H-14)
Enrichments (9346)
Independent Living Aids (614600)

✿ Magnetic playing cards

Tremors or fatigue can make it difficult to hold cards steadily and continuously throughout a game. This magnetic set is the perfect solution. The cards are easy to handle but stay securely where they're placed on the special magnetized board. Card games can even be played in bed or outdoors without any problems.

$15 to $35

Enrichments (9421)
Independent Living Aids (435322)

❦ One-hand card shuffler
One or two decks can be inserted into the machine to be shuffled. It runs on two C batteries.

$15 to $35

adaptAbility (11475)
Aids for Arthritis (H-6)
Enrichments (9424)
Independent Living Aids (151400)

SEWING

Don't let diminished vision cause you to stop sewing your own clothes or enjoying quilting as a hobby. Before you give away your sewing machine or stop sewing by hand, try the following inexpensive devices.

❦ Sewing machine magnifier
A 2-inch by 3-inch magnifying lens attaches to the sewing machine to make needle threading and sewing easier.

$5 to $15

American Foundation for the Blind (L90312)
Independent Living Aids (690705)

❦ Needle threader
To easily thread a needle, the user with low vision or poor eye-hand coordination just drops the needle into the barrel, wraps the thread around, and pushes a button. Large or thin needles are automatically single or double threaded.

under $5

Maxi Aids (49113)
Independent Living Aids (384222)

✕ Measurement tools

Tape measures, rulers, and framing squares can be tactually marked for persons with visual impairments. Raised dots at each increment make it possible for the user to feel rather than see the markings.

$15 to $35

American Foundation for the Blind (T90212, tape measure; T90240, framing square; T90312, ruler)
Ann Morris Enterprises (HTA2, tape measure)

✕ Rolling scissors

Arthritic or weak hands can make standard scissors painful or difficult to use, but these special scissors don't have handles that need to be pulled open or squeezed shut. Instead, they cut with a gliding motion as the hand gently pushes them to cut coupons, gift wrap, or other paper.

$15 to $35

adaptAbility (10043)
Aids for Arthritis (D-14)
Bruce Medical Supply (BMS1001)

✕ Softtouch scissors

Oversized cushion-grip handles make these scissors easy and comfortable to use. The action spring reopens the blades after each cut to reduce the pressure and motion on the joints. Every pair comes with a lifetime warranty.
For Convenience Sake (1534)   *$15 to $35*

✕ Powered scissors

Any material can be cut effortlessly with these battery-powered (two AA) scissors. The handles are pressed together gently; no squeezing is required. The cutting edge is moved along the material, eliminating the opening and closing of the scissors.
Comfortably Yours (4896)   *$15 to $35*

✕ *Taking Medication*

Almost every older person takes at least one medication. Most take several pills a day. These drugs can do wonders for maintaining health and comfort, but only if they're taken as prescribed. The aging process can impede the ability to take medications correctly. When memory loss, failing vision, or limited dexterity are present, you may encounter difficulty being in charge of your pharmaceutical regimen. With the help of the following aids, you can achieve maximum independence in your own health care.

(See also the Diabetic Care section in Chapter 2.)

❧ Pill splitter
When only half a pill is to be taken, the person with arthritis or sight impairments can easily split the pill by placing it in this simple device, which automatically separates it into two equal halves when the lever is pressed down.

under $5

Aids for Arthritis (C-26)
American Foundation for the Blind (H90201)
Cleo, Inc. (87-1499)
Independent Living Aids (609590)
One pill splitter also has cap-opener capabilities. Lids up to 2 inches in diameter can be popped off with this device, which hooks under the rim of the cap and pulls it off. (Caps on other household products can also be removed with the cap opener.)
Enrichments (9959)   *$5 to $15*

❧ Pill crusher
If you're unable to swallow pills, you can easily crush them by inserting the pill into the crusher and twisting the container. The fine powder can then be stirred into any liquid or soft solid.

$5 to $15

Aids for Arthritis (J-23)
Bruce Medical Supply (BMS506)
Independent Living Aids (308261)

❧ EZ Swallow pill splitter/grinder
People who take half-pill dosages or who have difficulty swallowing will appreciate this three-in-one device. The top section has a splitter with a surgical stainless-steel cutting blade for safe, accurate pill splitting; the bottom features a crusher to grind pills into a fine powder; the middle section can store pills or may be used as a cup.
Mature Wisdom (770909)   *$15 to $35*

⚘ Seven-day pill organizer

A week's worth of medication can be organized so that you readily know what has been taken and what still needs to be taken. The organizer contains seven daily cases, each with four separate compartments for morning, noon, evening, and bedtime. All the cases fit securely in a tray to show the week at a glance or can individually snap out to be carried in the pocket or purse for the day.

$5 to $15

Aids for Arthritis (F-10)
Bruce Medical Supply (BMS503)
Independent Living Aids (850318)

⚘ Healthcheck Rx-Minder Pillbox/Pill Meter II

This easy-to-set pillbox, which has a built-in alarm to remind the user when it's time to take medication, can also double as a travel alarm. It can be set to beep 19 times a day, from 6 A.M. to 12 midnight, on the hour or half-hour.

$15 to $35

Aids for Arthritis (K-8)
SelfCare Catalog (2045)

⚘ Electronic pill timer

This quartz electronic pill timer can be set from 1 minute to 24 hours and will automatically repeat at the programmed interval. Capsules and pills can be stored in a slide-open compartment.

Bruce Medical Supply (BMS507)   *$15 to $35*

⚘ Medi-Track Medication Tracking System and Prescript TimeCap

The user of these unique containers for medication won't ever have to worry about whether or not a dose of medication was taken. They both feature a three-way electronic system that tracks dosage schedules.

· The exact time the last dose was taken is displayed digitally. The time and day when the unit was last opened is always shown.

· A beep sounds when it's time to take a scheduled dose.

· The units flash the "last opened" time if a dose is missed.

The Medi-Track and Prescript TimeCap are as easy to set for individualized medication schedules as a digital watch. Once they're set, the dosage schedule is memorized but can readily be reset if a medication schedule changes. The company will even preset the unit prior to shipment if the dosage schedule is provided. There's an 800 number if assistance is needed in resetting. The replaceable batteries usually last about a year.

The Medi-Track unit can hold approximately seventeen aspirin-sized tablets and is easily transported in a purse or pocket. The Prescript TimeCap comes in three sizes and, while less compact than the Medi-Track unit, may be more appropriate for the person who has to deal with a number of medications. Using a separate Prescript Time-Cap bottle for each medication helps avoid mixups and ensures that the right drug is taken at the right time.

Wheaton Medical Technologies   *$15 to $35*

❦ Aqua Pill Timer

Other pillboxes have programmable alarms to serve as a reminder to take the medication, but they don't do much good if there's no water available for swallowing the pills. This handy pillbox holds 2 ounces of water and comes with a built-in straw (and a slide-out drawer for the pills). It runs on a button cell battery.

Zelco Industries   *$15 to $35*

❦ CompuMed Complete Drug Organization System

Pills are automatically dispensed at the appropriate times and dosages with this system. The CompuMed machine is easily programmed to deliver any combination of pills all through the day. An alarm is sounded every time that medication is dispensed and needs to be taken. Although expensive, the system eliminates even more costly medication errors (such as forgetting to take prescribed drugs or taking them at the wrong time or in the wrong dosage).

Maxi Aids (63399)   *$5 to $15*

❦ Eye Ease Eyedrop Guide

Trembling hands or limited eye-hand coordination can make it difficult to apply eye drops. This device easily attaches to any eyedrop bottle and serves as a base to steady the hand. It fits over the eye so that the bottle is positioned in a stationary position and can simply be squeezed to apply medication.

under $5

Dr. Leonard's Health Care Catalog (8843)
Maxi Aids (78678)

Telling Time

Even if you have some visual or hearing limitations, you can still keep track of time by obtaining timers, wall clocks, alarm clocks, and watches with large faces and numerals or with mechanisms that announce the time or vibrate.

Easy-to-see watches and clocks
Purchase these at most department, discount, or jewelry stores, or order them through a catalog.

$15 to $125

American Foundation for the Blind
Ann Morris Enterprises
Comfortably Yours
Independent Living Aids
LS & S Group
Maxi Aids

Vibrating alarm clock
The vibrating clock is placed under the pillow and vibrates at the preselected alarm time. It runs on two AA batteries. These clocks are available at most discount stores, as well as through catalogs.

$15 to $35

Independent Living Aids (691225)
LS & S Group (134-40001)
Maxi Aids (30-H141)
TTY of Carolina

Transportation and Travel

The need to travel around one's community (and beyond) may diminish somewhat as a person grows older, but it never completely disappears. While some older people may not be going off to a job, there are still a multitude of places they *do* need to go to: shops, banks, physician offices, libraries, church or synagogue, recreational facilities, and the homes of friends and family. Driving is most people's preferred mode of transportation because it enables the greatest degree of independence, but some older persons need to give up driving and find alternative means of transportation.

Traveling long distances can present its own set of challenges as well. This section discusses the various transportation options available to older people, including special services that enable the frail elderly to travel by air.

(See also the Accessibility section in this chapter.)

❧ Free or low-cost van service

Many towns and cities have Ambi-Wagons or Senior Transit programs in which people 65 and older can be transported to doctors and dentists. Arrangements generally need to be made a couple of days in advance. Seniors are picked up at their homes. Contact your local area's **Agency on Aging** for more information. Also check with them to see if there are special programs for reduced taxicab rates for older persons. (If you can't find the local number, call the **Eldercare Locator.)**

❧ MedEscort services

If you would have trouble flying alone because of a physical disability or medical problem but need to travel across the country for medical care, to move closer to family, or to attend a special occasion like a family reunion or wedding, consider hiring a specially trained travel partner. MedEscort is a 24-hour, door-to-door service that assists with all pretrip preparations, makes all the necessary arrangements, and

---

HANDICAPPED PARKING STICKER

If you have trouble walking through large parking lots, you may need to use close-by parking spaces reserved for the handicapped. Obtain a handicapped sticker from the local traffic/ motor vehicles division. A physician's certification of the disability (orthopedic, cardiac, respiratory) will be necessary. A decal of a person in a wheelchair is not sufficient for parking in a handicapped space.

accompanies clients from origin to destination point. They'll even help pack! Skilled nursing care can be provided for clients with needs such as traveling with oxygen or adjusting diabetes medications while traveling across several time zones. The total cost includes the patient's ticket, the escort's round-trip ticket, and the company's fee. The fee could range from $100 for helping with a transfer from an international to a domestic flight to $500 for a nurse or respiratory therapist's services.

MedEscort

❧ Travel planning by phone

Trained specialists at a Philadelphia rehabilitation hospital can help persons with disabilities or illnesses plan trips in the United States and abroad.

Travel Information Service   *Cost is nominal, but varies according to the service*

❧ Evergreen Travel Service

Trying to keep up with able-bodied companions on the typical packaged tour can be stressful for persons with physical limitations. For more than three decades, Evergreen has specialized in domestic and international travel for the physically challenged:

Wings on Wheels tours—accommodate persons in wheelchairs

White Cane tours—for blind travelers

Flying Fingers—for the hearing-impaired

Lazy Bones—geared for those who move slowly

A majority of the staff are trained medical personnel (including registered nurses). There's at least one staff member for every three guests. While assistance is available while traveling (such as help in getting on and off the bus), participants must be able to take care of personal needs in their hotel rooms (or bring a companion). Costs vary according to the destination, length, and activities of each trip.

Evergreen Travel Service

❧ Cruising

It's possible for physically challenged persons to take cruises when they select the right ship. Special travel counselors at a cruise-only

travel agency can steer people to cruise lines that can accommodate persons with special needs. They can arrange for specially equipped cabins, dialysis and oxygen facilities, wheelchairs, and special diets. They'll also make air and transfer arrangements. There is no fee for the service; the agency is paid a commission from the cruise lines. Prices vary according to accommodations, destination(s), and ship.
Cruises Unlimited   *Free*

⚘ Accessible vans
Vacation traveling for wheelchair users is made much easier with these rental vans. The Dodge minivans are modified for complete accessibility. They come equipped with hand controls, four-point tie-down system to secure wheelchairs in place, power ramp, and removable driver and/or passenger seats. The doors are extra wide for easy entrance and exit, and the floor is lowered 10 inches to give passengers more head room. Pickup and delivery are available almost anywhere.
Wheelers Accessible Van Rentals   *$75 to $125 (daily)*
Directory of Accessible Van Rentals by Helen Hecker lists van rental companies throughout the United States that rent lift-equipped vans.
Twin Peaks Press   *$5 to $15*

⚘ Travelin' Talk Network
When traveling, persons with physical limitations can encounter such problems as where to get a wheelchair fixed or where to get medical assistance in case of sudden illness. There are many planning issues to consider, such as which facilities are truly accessible. Travelin' Talk enables persons with physical disabilities to exchange information with each other to plan trips and to solve problems while away from home. In addition to a quarterly newsletter detailing resources and travel trips, the company also publishes a directory of tour operators, hotels, parks, organizations, and other disabled persons who are willing to provide assistance over the phone. Members live throughout the United States, Canada, and abroad.
Travelin' Talk   *$5 to $15 membership; $35 to $75 for the directory*

⚘ *Travel for the Disabled* by Helen Hecker
This large-print 192-page book makes it possible to arrange an accessible trip, tour, or cruise anywhere in the world. It offers hints for traveling by air, bus, car, ship, or train as well as for staying in hotels and

motels. Plenty of how-to and where-to-get travel information is provided.

Twin Peaks Press   *$15 to $35*

℣ Adaptive-driving aids

Persons with physical disabilities can still drive if their cars or vans have special equipment, such as adaptive-driving controls (allowing the brake and accelerator to be controlled by hand, for example) or wheelchair lifts. The Physically-Challenged Resource Center operated by the Chrysler Corporation provides resource information about conversion companies and equipment suppliers throughout the country. By calling a toll-free number, you can obtain referrals to local vendors. The Chrysler Corporation will also provide a cash reimbursement up to $500 to help reduce the cost of modifications to a new Chrysler car, truck, or van.

Chrysler Corporation   *Free*

A similar program is operated by Ford. The company will issue a check for up to $750 toward the installation of adaptive driving or passenger equipment. Its information line provides sources of additional funding and lists of adaptive-equipment dealers and installers or authorized centers to provide evaluations and recommendations for adaptive equipment.

Ford Mobility Motoring Program   *Free*

General Motors also offers a special program for the physically challenged. Representatives at the company's toll-free number identify local driver-assessment centers and installers of adaptive-driving devices or vehicle modifications, suggest which GM cars and light-duty trucks are most suitable for persons with various physical limitations, and direct callers to sources that may help fund the adaptation. When a new GM vehicle is purchased, they'll reimburse adaptation costs up to $1,000.

GM Mobility Program for the Physically Challenged   *Free*

℣ *The Handicapped Driver's Mobility Guide*

This 146-page book published by the American Automobile Association offers a wealth of ideas and resources for improving the mobility of drivers and passengers with disabilities. The publication includes sections on driver education, roadside services for motorists, travel information services, vehicle selection and factory options, additional equipment and modifications, hand controls, wheelchair lifts, augmented driving systems to reduce the effort needed for driving, equipment installation and maintenance, handicapped parking, publications, and organizations that provide materials or services for handicapped drivers.

American Automobile Association   *$5 to $15*

✿ Scooters

Persons who are able to walk for short distances but fatigue easily when they need to walk longer distances (such as through a mall or when visiting tourist attractions) may prefer to use a motorized three-wheel scooter. These have padded seats, removable armrests, a full braking/ steering system. They operate on two 12-volt U-1 batteries at speeds up to 5 miles an hour, indoors and outside.

Bruno Independent Living Aids   *$2,500 to $5,000*

✿ Using a Thermometer

We all need to take our temperature from time to time, but the tiny lines and numbers on a standard thermometer may be impossible for aging eyes to read. A digital thermometer with LCD readout will probably be easier to use. If your vision is extremely low, you may want to consider a talking electronic thermometer.

✿ Thermovoice (TM) II Talking Electronic Thermometer

This machine announces body temperature in either Fahrenheit or Celsius. It runs on one 9-volt alkaline battery; an AC adapter is also available. (Although designed to take body temperature, it can also be used to take water or air temperatures.)

$200 to $350

American Foundation for the Blind (H90110)
Maxi Aids (80651)

✿ When Some Help Is Needed

Almost without exception, one of the primary goals of older persons is to maintain as much independence as possible. But this goal isn't always attainable. Some mature adults are unable to live completely independently. Assistance may be needed to enable some older persons to remain at home. In some cases, a change of residence may be necessary. If you or a relative or friend needs more help than what was described in the preceding pages, here's where to turn.

⚘ Eldercare Locator

The National Association of Agencies on Aging runs this toll-free hotline. They can provide information about any type of service for older people (such as legal assistance, home health, transportation, and adult day-care centers) anywhere in the country.

Eldercare Locator   *Free*

⚘ Aging Network Services

Private comprehensive-care management is coordinated through this service. The central office contacts social workers based in the same area as the older adult. The local social worker assesses mental and physical function, identifies and monitors local geriatric services and resources, coordinates medical and other services, counsels and plans for future needs, and serves as a liaison to family members who live in different cities.

Aging Network Services   *Fees based on hourly rate comparable to those of other private social workers in area; health insurance benefits may cover part of social worker's services*

⚘ National Association of Private Geriatric Care Managers

This professional organization publishes a directory that lists its members, all of whom have at least a master's degree and are highly recommended by peers within their profession. Social workers, registered nurses, psychologists, and gerontologists are available throughout the country to coordinate elder care. They can hire and monitor in-home help; find drivers for medical appointments, trips to the barber, or shopping; and visit or call on a weekly basis.

National Association of Private Geriatric Care Managers
$15 to $35 (for directory); initial assessments range from $200 to $600; fees are then $35 to $200 an hour

❧ Referrals sources for home-care services

Referrals to companies that provide home health and homemaking services, equipment, and supplies are available through the **National League for Nursing** (a professional nursing association).

Free

❧ Publications on caregiving

The following publications on caregiving are available from **AARP Fulfillment** free of charge.

· *A Handbook About Care in the Home* (D955)
Home health care and homemaker services are described, along with tips on assessing home care agencies.

· *Care Management: Arranging for Long-Term Care* (D13803)
Long-term care needs and services are profiled.

· *A Path for Caregivers* (D12957)
Individuals who provide care for older people are helped to identify their needs and develop a plan to meet those needs. A resource list for other sources of information on caregiving is included.

· *Miles Away and Still Caring—A Guide for Long-Distance Caregivers* (D12748)
Relatives and friends who must coordinate the care of a loved one from a long distance need to create a network of family, friends, neighbors, and social service workers who can provide some assistance. This booklet shows how.
AARP Fulfillment   *Free*

❧ Your Home, Your Choice

This workbook is designed to help older persons and their families make decisions about living arrangement alternatives. Options range from services at home to nursing care.
AARP Fulfillment (D12143)   *Free*

❧ ECHO Homes

ECHO (Elderly Cottage Housing Opportunity) homes are also known as Granny flats. They're temporary units built on a family member's property. They enable older persons and their families to live in close proximity to each other so that assistance can be readily available while some privacy and independence are maintained because the unit is a separate and self-contained entity. They're generally about 500 square feet, with one bedroom, a bathroom, a living room, and a full kitchen. There are no wheels or undercarriages; they're placed on piling foundations, so there is no concrete to remove. These manufactured homes are removable and reusable. With no stairs and no painting or maintenance required, the homes are easy to live in. They need to be removed when the older person no longer lives in the unit. Three booklets are available that further explain ECHO homes:

Elder Cottage Housing Opportunity: Restrictions on Manufactured Housing (D1186)

A Model Ordinance for ECHO Housing (D13791)

ECHO Housing—Recommended Construction and Installation Standards (D12212)
AARP Fulfillment   *Free*

❧ Nursing homes
Contrary to popular perceptions, most older persons do not live in nursing homes. Only 5 percent of people over 65 live in a nursing home at any one time. But 20 to 30 percent will spend some time in one during the course of their lives. Most people find it difficult to know what to look for when choosing a facility for a short- or long-term stay. A guide on *Selecting a Nursing Home* can help.
National Council of Senior Citizens   *Free*

❧ *Miscellaneous*

The following products and services can't readily be categorized into any of the preceding sections but are worthy of consideration.

❧ Homemaker, housing, and transportation programs for older adults
The National Association of State Units on Aging can refer you to local programs, in addition to sending you free publications such as *Where to Turn for Help for Older Persons* and *Nationwide Network of State and Area Agencies on Aging*.
National Association of State Units on Aging   *Free*

❧ Locator
Designed as a wireless door chime, this device can also be used to locate items around the house for the visually impaired or the forgetful. The receiver is left on the item to be located (such as a doorway, chair, blanket, keys, etc.) and the transmitter is carried around. When it's time to find the item, the button on the transmitter is pushed and the receiver chimes, alerting the user to the location. It runs on AA and 9-volt cells. The device can also be used as a pager.

Ann Morris Enterprises (ALO1)   *$15 to $35*

❧ Grocery grip
Carrying plastic grocery bags can be difficult and painful for arthritic fingers. This device provides a comfortable padded handle attached to a hook that can support and carry several sacks at one time.

Aids for Arthritis (E-25)   *$5 to $15*

❧ Folding carry-all bags with wheels
Carrying heavy packages can lead to back, shoulder, and arm pain. It is far preferable to save energy and conserve joints by pushing the packages on wheels. This bag folds up to look like a small tote bag, opens to a 21-inch-high, 12-inch-wide, 7-inch-deep bag on wheels.

Independent Living Aids (152623)   *$5 to $15*

❧ EZ read calculator
The visually impaired have difficulty reading standard calculators, but this one is easy to see, thanks to its ⅞-inch numbers. It's solar powered.

$15 to $35

American Foundation for the Blind (N90920)
LS & S Group (183-B-80N)
Maxi Aids (56378)

❧ Talking calculators
In addition to enlarged numbers, some calculators even talk! Numbers are announced as they appear on the screen. The calculator runs on two AA batteries.

$15 to $35

American Foundation for the Blind (R91100)
Ann Morris Enterprises (ATC3)
LS&S Group
Maxi Aids

❦ Computer monitor filters

Computer users with low vision can benefit from these tinted mesh filters, which block up to 90 percent of glare and reflection on the computer screen, enhancing color and clarity on color or monochrome monitors. They also keep the screen clean by eliminating dust buildup.

Maxi Aids (22832)   *$15 to $35*

❦ Large-print computer programs

A variety of special programs are available for magnifying the text and graphics on the screen anywhere from 2 to 16 times the regular size. They work with popular programs such as WordPerfect, Lotus 1-2-3, and Microsoft Windows. One program even enables the printer to print large type as well.

MaxiAids   *$75 to $600*

❦ Diskette hooks

Some older fingers may not be nimble enough to easily insert or remove 5¼-inch diskettes from the computer's disk drive. These hooks attach to the diskettes to enable insertion or removal without having to manipulate the paper-thin diskette.

Enrichments (4053)   *$5 to $15*

❦ *The Hartford House*

This 77-page booklet features tips and products that can help older people maintain their independence at home. It includes sections on lighting, reading, mobility, and kitchen/bathroom use.

Hartford Insurance Group   *Free*

❦ *Independent Living* magazine

This magazine for persons with disabilities offers a variety of information and resources to enable more self-sufficient lifestyles.

Independent Living   *Free*

❦ The Disability Bookshop Catalog

Over 450 hard-to-find books, audiocassettes, and videocassettes that typically aren't available in local bookstores are listed in this 29-page guide. Topics include pain, aging, visual/hearing impairment, exercise, arthritis, computers, resource directories, housing accessibility, cooking, clothing, and other self-help aids.

Twin Peaks Press   *under $5*

❧ ABLEDATA

As the largest information source in the nation on disability-related products to promote independence, this database contains more than 17,000 commercially available products from over 2,000 manufacturers. Categories include personal care, home management, mobility, transportation, seating, recreation, communication, and architectural access. The "information specialists" at the toll-free line can inform callers about the equipment options available, once the caller's functional limitations and the desired task (such as bathing or getting out of bed) are described. They can provide advice over the phone or send written information.

Adaptive Equipment Center   *Free*

❧ Project LINK

Project LINK is smaller in scope than ABLEDATA, but it is especially valuable because it is specifically geared for older adults. Once an individual completes a brief questionnaire about his or her functional limitations and needs, the project's database will search for manufacturers/suppliers of products that could help increase independence. The appropriate catalogs are then mailed to the individual so that he or she can order any desired products. The project workers mail the catalogs to ensure that the catalog or manufacturing companies won't contact the recipients to attempt to pressure them into a purchase.

Center for Therapeutic Applications of Technology   *Free*

2

A Healthier Life

POOR HEALTH is not necessarily an inevitable consequence of aging. With good genes and health-promoting practices, people can enjoy an optimal level of health in the later years. You may not feel quite the same as you did when you were 30 years younger, but you can still be actively and happily involved in life.

Some illnesses and medical conditions can't be prevented, even if you take good care of yourself. But there are things that can be done to minimize pain, discomfort, and dysfunction. While professional medical treatment is essential, there are also many self-help measures that you can take to improve your well-being.

Alzheimer's Disease

Alzheimer's disease is the most common form of dementia (a major form of mental impairment) in older people. It affects the parts of the brain that control thought, memory, and language. The disease can be extremely incapacitating in its later stages. Approximately 4 million people in the United States are estimated to have Alzheimer's disease. While the risk of getting the disease increases with age (typically occurring after 65), it is *not* a normal part of aging. Although there is no effective treatment that can stop the progression of the disorder, some drugs can ease symptoms and provide some relief for both patients and caregivers.

The **Alzheimer's Disease Education and Referral Center,** as a service of the National Institute on Aging, can provide information through its publications or toll-free information line.

The **Alzheimer's Association** offers family support groups in more than 200 chapters across the country.

Publications, information, and services from both organizations are free.

⚘ *Arthritis*

It's been estimated that the majority of persons over 65 (anywhere from 55 to 80 percent) have noticeable symptoms of some type of arthritis. Joint pain and loss of mobility can make it difficult to perform even the simplest of activities. While there's no cure, there's much that you can learn and do to control the symptoms and remediate the problems associated with the disease.

(See also the Education section in this chapter.)

⚘ Arthritis Foundation
This organization provides more than 100 free booklets on different types of arthritis, treatments, and tips for coping with daily activities. Among them are the following:

Coping with Fatigue (9336)

Coping with Pain (9333)

Coping with Stress (9326)

Travel Tips (9071)

Exercise and Your Arthritis (9704)

Guide to Laboratory Tests (9060)

Using Your Joints Wisely (9329)

Guide to Medications (9059)

There are also individual booklets on each of the more than 30 types of arthritis and related diseases, as well as some materials for which there is a small charge—for example the *Guide to Independent Living* (4081), which profiles self-help devices, and the *In Control* videotape (9035), which demonstrates effective ways to manage arthritis).

Answers to questions about arthritis can be provided over the phone, as can referrals to physicians and services who specialize in helping people with arthritis. The Arthritis Foundation also offers classes and workshops addressing medication, joint preservation, energy conservation, water exercise, and gentle sitting exercises. Support groups are available. An annual membership includes the bimonthly magazine *Arthritis Today,* which covers arthritis research, new treatments, tips on coping with arthritis, and stories about persons with arthritis.

Arthritis Foundation   *$15 to $35 a year; local chapters individually set prices for materials and services*

✍ *Arthritis Self-Help, Exercise, and Joint Protection* video
Physical and occupational therapists provide instruction on exercise and activities of daily living for people with arthritis. The tape runs for approximately an hour.

Aids for Arthritis (H-9)   *$35 to $75*

✍ *Best Use of the Hands* video
One tape deals with osteoarthritis; the other addresses rheumatoid arthritis. Each 20-minute tape focuses on pain management and adaptations for daily activities.

Enrichments (8246, osteoarthritis; 8247,   *$35 to $75*
rheumatoid arthritis)

✍ *Arthritis Relaxation/Pain Relief* Audiotape
This 20-minute audiocassette tape program shows how to relax, take control of pain, and reduce stress.

Aids for Arthritis (F-6)   *$15 to $35*

❧ *The Arthritis Helpbook* by James Fries and Kate Lorig

In this informative and comprehensive book, a nurse and physician provide information on coping with pain, using drugs, nutrition, exercises, and self-help.

Aids for Arthritis (B-67)   *$5 to $15*

❧ *Winning with Arthritis* by Harris H. McIlwain

Arthritis can be understood and controlled with the help of this book written by a physician. Diet, exercise, and medication regimens are fully detailed. Both traditional and nontraditional treatments are discussed. The book also includes case studies of arthritis sufferers who have triumphed over the disease. Published by John Wiley & Sons, it can be specially ordered through bookstores or obtained from a mail-order cooperative.

United Seniors Health Cooperative   *$5 to $15*

❧ *Staying Active with Arthritis*

An informative pamphlet for the 37 million Americans with more than 100 types of arthritis can be obtained by sending a self-addressed stamped envelope.

Advil   *Free*

❧ *Exercise Can Beat Arthritis* video

Seated and standing routines are performed to original music. Nine gentle routines are specially designed to increase flexibility, strengthen muscles and joints, and decrease pain and stiffness. It runs for 40 minutes.

Mature Wisdom (784264)   *$15 to $35*

❧ *Hocus-Pocus As Applied to Arthritis*

Fraudulent cures for arthritis are discussed along with medically sound treatments in this seven-page Food and Drug Administration booklet.

Consumer Information Center (537X)   *Free*

❧ *Arthritis Advice*

Suggestions for dealing with arthritis are featured in this two-page publication.

National Institute on Aging   *Free*

❧ *Blood Pressure*

One in four Americans have high blood pressure, and there's an even greater chance of developing the condition in the later years. An estimated one of every two persons over the age of 65 are hypertensive. Although the condition is very treatable, it is a silent killer because there usually are very minimal symptoms (if any) until the disease is quite advanced. Left untreated, high blood pressure can lead to heart attacks, congestive heart failure, strokes, and kidney failure.

Physicians will usually want to treat blood pressure that is 140/90 or higher. Diet and lifestyle modifications can go a long way in controlling blood pressure, but medications may be needed as well.

(See also the Heart Disease and Kidney Disease sections in this chapter.)

❧ *High Blood Pressure: A Common But Controllable Disorder*
This two-page publication offers a number of tips for controlling hypertension.
National Institute on Aging   *Free*

❧ *Blood Pressure*
Blood pressure may be controlled, at least partially, through mental attitude. The calming affirmations and imagery on this audiotape can help reduce blood pressure and maintain it at optimal levels.
Effective Learning Systems, Inc.   *$5 to $15*

PROPER TAKING OF BLOOD PRESSURE

After age 50, blood pressure can be high in one arm and normal in the other if there's a blockage or hardening of the arteries on one side. Therefore blood pressure should be measured in both arms to be sure that the readings match. Hypertension can be undertreated or overtreated if a reading isn't accurate.

NATURAL LICORICE

Scientists and physicians have found that natural licorice (usually imported from England, since artificial flavoring is commonly used in the United States) increases potassium loss and may cause dangerous heart rhythms, so persons taking antihypertensive medications to control blood pressure are usually advised to avoid natural licorice products.

❦ *Cancer*

The incidence of cancer rises with age, so most cases affect adults in mid-life or later. While one of every five deaths in the U.S. is from cancer, the chances of long-term survival are increasing, thanks to early detection and treatment. About half of all cancer patients are alive 5 years after diagnosis.

(See also the Female Health Concerns, Male Health Concerns, Respiratory Concerns, and Skin Health sections in this chapter.)

It's important to follow the American Cancer Society's Cancer Detection Guidelines for early detection:

Breast—every year, women age 50 and over

Cervical—Pap test and pelvic exam every year for women, and endometrial biopsy at discretion of physician

Colorectal—flexible sigmoidoscopy for men and women beginning at age 50, then every 3 to 5 years; fecal occult blood test every year for men and women 50 and older; digital rectal exam every year for men and women 40 and older

Oral—oral exam for men and women every year

Prostate—annual digital examination and prostate-specific antigen (PSA) for men 50 and older

Skin—skin exam every year for men and women over 40

❦ Colon/rectal cancer booklets

Facts on Colorectal Cancer (2004.00)
Colorectal Cancer/Go for Early Detection (2051.00)

Don't Miss Out on Your Sunset Years (2666.00)
Check Yourself Quiz (2729.00)
American Cancer Society   *Free*

⚹ Early detection booklets
Say Know to Cancer (2610.00)
Cancer Risk: What Is Known? What Is Suspected? What Is Myth?
(2651.00)
Cancer Related Check Up (2070.00)
Hopeful Side of Cancer (2012.00)
American Cancer Society   *Free*

⚹ Physician Data Query (PDQ) System
This national computer network provides information about cancer
treatments for every type and stage of the disease, including clinical
trials. It will provide a referral for a second opinion from another physician or send a listing of cancer center and programs. The cancer information specialists who run the toll-free-line are not medical
doctors, but they've been trained to answer questions and send information. They can also arrange a Multidisciplinary Second Opinion
Panel. This volunteer panel of cancer experts will suggest the best
treatment protocol after reviewing the patient's file. Some of these
panels are free, while others are not.
Cancer Information Service   *Free*

⚹ AMC Cancer Information and Counseling Line
This free toll-free line allows callers to ask questions, order publications, and obtain advice.

⚹ *Cancer Facts for People Over 50*
This two-page publication provides important information about the
early detection, prevention, and treatment of cancer in older persons.
National Institute on Aging   *Free*

⚹ I Can Cope and CanSurmount
Cancer patients and family members who participate in these support
groups learn about cancer, how to cope with their feelings, and where
to find local resources.
American Cancer Society   *Free*

❧ Support groups

More than 200 local groups offer support and assistance to cancer patients, families, and other persons with life-threatening illness. The emphasis is on a positive approach and improved coping skills. Home visitation programs are available in addition to group meetings.
Make Today Count   *nominal local dues*

❧ Coping with the side effects of cancer treatments

Radiation and chemotherapy can cause hair loss and affect the skin. An innovative program called Look Good—Feel Better helps cancer patients improve their self-image by enhancing their appearance. It's a joint effort of the American Cancer Society, National Cosmetology Association, and the Cosmetic, Toiletry, and Fragrance Association. The toll-free number refers callers to a local volunteer (trained cosmetologist/beautician) who can show participants how to use makeup, wigs, scarves, and other accessories to look and feel better. Brochures, videos, and makeup sessions are available in English and Spanish.
Look Good—Feel Better   *Free*

❧ *Chemical Dependence*

The popular stereotype of a drug abuser is a younger person (teenager or 20-something), but this doesn't mean that there aren't any people over 50 with chemical dependency problems. It's been estimated that more than 2 million older adults are addicted or at risk of addiction to sleeping pills or tranquilizers. The number of older persons who abuse alcohol is not fully known but is suspected to be substantial. Breaking free of addiction isn't easy, but it *can* be done with the right help.

❧ Hopeline

For help with chemical dependence, contact the **National Council on Alcoholism and Drug Dependence** toll-free "Hopeline." They'll send information about substance abuse and refer you to a local number to call for counseling and treatment.

❧ Support/therapy groups

Rational Recovery groups provide therapy-oriented counseling and stress personal responsibility for recovery.

Alcoholics Anonymous is well known for its support groups.

Secular Organizations for Sobriety offer nonreligious support groups (as opposed to the spiritual focus of Alcoholics Anonymous).

All of these groups will provide free information and referrals to local resources if you send a self-addressed stamped envelope.

❧ *Alcohol: Friend or Foe?*

In just four short pages, this pamphlet discusses facts about alcohol, older adults' increased sensitivity to the effects of alcohol, and drug/alcohol interactions.

Elder-Health Program   *Free*

❧ *Alcohol and Aging*

The problems of alcohol abuse in older persons is detailed in this two-page publication, along with treatment options.

National Institute on Aging   *Free*

❧ *Is Drinking Becoming a Problem?*

In a brief pamphlet, problems relating to alcohol use are discussed. Warning signs and places to seek help for recovery are included.

AARP Fulfillment (D14365)   *Free*

❧ *Chronic Pain*

Chronic pain, defined as pain that does not go· away or recurs frequently, affects people of all ages. The most common types of chronic pain are headaches, back pain, and arthritis pain. Other common types include neck pain, fibromyalgia/fibrositis, myofascial pain, TMJ pain, "whiplash" pain, sciatica, carpal tunnel syndrome, pelvic pain, neuropathy and neuralgia pain, and phantom limb pain. In some cases, the pain may result from an illness or condition such as diabetes, osteoporosis, lupus, or scleroderma; in many cases, however, the cause is unknown. Chronic pain impacts every aspect of a person's life: work, play, relationships, self-esteem, and emotional well-being.

If you or a loved one number among the more than 25 million persons affected by this condition, it's important to learn more about coping with pain and seeking support.

⚘ National Chronic Pain Outreach Association

A national organization can refer you to local support groups and pain management programs. A quarterly newsletter, *Lifeline,* is included in the price of membership, as are up to five publications. (Additional publications cost less than under $5 each.) Among the many available publications are the following:

Pain Management Strategies

Flare-Up Coping Tips

Choosing a Pain Clinic or Specialists

Heat, Cold, or Both for Pain Management

Humor for Pain Management

Breathing for Pain Management

Distraction for Pain Management

Touch and Simple Massage for Pain Management

The Aging Spine: Degenerative Disc Disease

Depression and Chronic Pain

Communication: Getting the Most from Your Doctor-Patient Relationship

National Chronic Pain Outreach Association   *$15 to $25 a year*

⚘ Headaches

If you're one of the 45 million Americans who suffer from frequent or debilitating headaches, you can obtain information about causes and treatment by calling a toll-free hotline or subscribing to a quarterly newsletter. A list of physicians who specialize in treating headaches is also available.

National Headache Foundation   *Free phone call; self-addressed stamped envelope for list of physicians; $15 to $35 a year for newsletter*

⚘ Back pain

Say Goodbye to Back Pain is a 96-minute tape that features exercises used at YMCAs throughout the country to reduce or eliminate back pain caused by minor backaches or more serious disorders (such as slipped discs). Self-tests help identify problem areas. Exercises relieve pain while reducing stress. Practical tips help prevent pain while performing normal activities of daily living.

Lifestyle Resource (4570)   *$35 to $75*
Promises Kept (5051)
Relief from Back Pain is a 57-minute video that shows techniques and exercises to reduce and avoid back pain. No special equipment is needed for the safe, simple exercises.
Mature Wisdom (784249)   *$15 to $35*

Anxiety and stress
Three double-sided audiocassette tapes deal with muscular relaxation, controlled breathing, meditation, and positive thinking. They help people learn to minimize insomnia, anxiety, and pain.
Enrichments (8455)   *$35 to $75*

Peaceful Sensations
These two musical audiotapes provide calming background music for stress-management and relaxation techniques. They emphasize the sounds of nature, such as the ocean.
Enrichments (8479)   *$15 to $35*

Pain Relief
While this tape is not a substitute for professional medical diagnosis and treatment, its positive statements and imagery can lead to more effective coping with pain.
Effective Learning Systems, Inc.   *$5 to $15*

Dental Care

Whether you have your own teeth, dentures, or bridges, it is important to take care of your mouth. Oral hygiene and health measures are essential to be able to eat and talk well and also have a great impact on your appearance.

Taking Care of Your Teeth and Mouth
This two-page publication instructs older persons on oral hygiene and health.
National Institute on Aging   *Free*

✿ Geriatric dentistry
For referrals to dentists with a special interest in older persons, contact the **American Society for Geriatric Dentistry.**

✿ Aqua Floss water jet
Bacteria and food are flushed away while gums are massaged. The American Dental Association approves of this battery-operated device.
Promises Kept (91486)   *$35 to $75*

✿ Sonic dental cleaner
Plaque and tartar buildup on dentures can affect the fit and cause bad breath. "Electrosonic" vibration and brushing are very effective in preventing these problems. Dental offices have used this cleaner for years, but it hasn't been available for home use until recently.
VibraSonics   *$35 to $75*

✿ Dental implants
Artificial teeth can be attached directly and permanently to the jawbone, avoiding the discomfort and problems often associated with dentures. Implants are much more expensive than dentures (approximately $1,000 to $2,500 for a single tooth), but many persons feel they are well worth the price. They can last for a decade or even longer. Further details about implants are available free of charge by sending a self-addressed stamped envelope to the professional dental associations that specialize in gum disease or oral surgery.
American Academy of Periodontology
American Association of Oral and Maxillofacial Surgeons

✿ *Denture Facts*
The 11 most common myths about dentures are addressed in this pamphlet.
Dentsply   *Free*

✿ *Periodontal Disease and Diabetes: A Guide for Patients*
The connections between periodontal diseases and diabetes are explained in this pamphlet, which also gives tips for protecting teeth and gums.
National Institute of Dental Research   *Free*

❧ *Diabetic Care*

A late-in-life diagnosis of diabetes is cause for concern but not alarm. In most cases, the condition can be successfully controlled through diet and/or medication. If you have recently been found to be diabetic, you need to do all you can to learn about, monitor, and control the disease. Even if you have been a lifelong diabetic with years of experience in dealing with the condition, you may not be aware of all the available new products.

❧ American Diabetes Association

Membership includes a monthly subscription to *Diabetes Forecast* (containing ideas for healthy living and updates of medical research and practice), discounts on diabetes books, and membership in a local affiliate (including support groups and seminars).

American Diabetes Association   *$15 to $35 a year*

❧ Diascan-SVM glucose monitor/One Touch blood glucose meter

Visually impaired diabetics can accurately monitor their blood glucose levels with this device. A smear of blood on the test strip is all that's needed. The results are announced by the electronic voice. The system is considered to be very user-friendly and easy to learn.

$350 to $600

American Foundation for the Blind (H90610/H90410, monitoring system and voice synthesizer)
Independent Living Aids (235720 Diascan)
Maxi Aids (15500)

❧ Magni Guide

This precision optical system magnifies the entire length of the syringe scale for easier reading and simplifies the mixing of insulins, including helping to locate bubbles in the syringe. It fits both 1-cc and ½-cc insulin syringes.

under $5

American Foundation for the Blind (H90202)
Independent Living Aids (454500)
Maxi Aids (54500)

✻ Insul-eze syringe loading device
Unsteady hands and impaired eyes can make it difficult to self-administer insulin, but this device holds the insulin bottle and syringe firmly together while providing 2.5X magnification for the full length of the syringe.

$5 to $15

Independent Living Aids (387420)
Maxi Aids (94327)

✻ Autojector
This device automatically injects the needle at a prescribed depth and administers the insulin. A push of the button results in a perfect injection. The device accepts most brands of disposable insulin syringes.
Independent Living Aids (097037)   *$35 to $75*

✻ Insulin needle guide
The syringe needle is placed into the funnel-shaped inner contour of the guide to prevent bending and contamination of needles. It can be used only with Eli Lilly insulin bottles.
American Foundation for the Blind (H90203)   *$5 to $15*

✻ Palco Load-Matic
Syringes can be quickly and accurately loaded by touch alone. The needle is aligned with the bottle top while the syringe is loaded in single-unit increments. Dose settings can be checked by feeling the raised dots. The device comes with an audiocassette and written instructions.

$35 to $75

American Foundation for the Blind (N90400)
Bruce Medical Supply (PL700)

✻ Monodose liquid medication guide
Half-teaspoon increments are tactually marked for the visually impaired.
American Foundation for the Blind (H90200)   *under $5*

✻ Sleep sentry
To alert the diabetic to hypoglycemic symptoms (such as perspiration and a drop in skin temperature) while he or she sleeps, this watchlike

device is worn on the wrist. It emits a loud beep when changes in skin temperature or moisture occur. The sleep sentry operates on two hearing-aid-type batteries.

$200 to $350

Independent Living Aids (695294)
Maxi Aids (94512)

❧ *Buyer's Guide to Diabetes Products*

The features of every diabetes product (insulin, syringes, aids for the visually impaired, and blood-glucose monitors) from a variety of manufacturers are compared in this 42-page guide.

American Diabetes Association (#CMISBUY)   *under $5*

❧ *The Diabetic Traveler*

This quarterly newsletter offers a free index to past issues and a free insulin-adjustment guide for jet travel across multiple time zones. Past issues have focused on such topics as spa vacations, cruises, healthful eating on the road, Mexico, Hawaii, Spain, London, and Tokyo. Much of the information provided about health and safety is helpful for diabetics and nondiabetics alike.

The Diabetic Traveler   *Free insulin-adjustment guide; $15 to $35/year subscription*

❧ **Tele-Library**

Recorded messages about diabetes (facts, blood glucose testing, and diabetes research) are available by calling the toll-free number of the Lifescan health care company. Messages about the company's promotions (such as rebates) and customer service programs (such as video and audio cassettes showing how to use its blood glucose–monitoring products) are also included. For questions that remain unanswered after listening to the taped messages, a special toll-free line allows callers to speak to trained technical service representatives.

Lifescan Tele-Library   *Free*

❧ *Dealing with Diabetes*

This two-page publication includes a number of suggestions for coping with diabetes in the later years.

National Institute on Aging   *Free*

⚕ *Type II Diabetes: Your Healthy Living Guide*

Touted as the first all-in-one sourcebook for diabetes management, this 235-page guide discusses diet, exercise, medications, and the prevention of complications of the nerves, eyes, and kidneys.

American Diabetes Association (#CTIIHG)   *$15 to $35*

⚕ *Diabetic Foot Care*

This 12-page booklet provides information about the early detection and treatment of diabetic foot problems.

American Diabetes Association (#PMFOOT)   *under $5*

⚕ *Dental Tips for Diabetics*

This leaflet discusses oral hygiene techniques for diabetics.

National Institute of Dental Research   *Free*

⚕ *Exchange Lists for Meal Planning*

The six Exchange Lists are detailed through charts and easy-to-understand language, so that meals can be properly planned.

American Diabetes Association (#CELMP)   *under $5*

⚕ *Month of Meals Set*

This revolutionary meal-planning device allows users to forget figuring fats, calories, and exchanges. Instead, the unique format of pages split into thirds allows any combination of menus—breakfast, lunch, and dinner. No matter which combinations are chosen, nutrients and exchanges are still correct for the entire day. Easy-to-fix recipes are included. Three interchangeable books include basic menus, ethnic foods, and even fast foods!

American Diabetes Association (#CMPSET3)   *$15 to $35*

⚕ *Family Cookbooks*

A series of cookbooks published by Prentice-Hall Press and coauthored by the American Diabetes Association and the American Dietetic Association feature a large number of healthy recipes, complete with a breakdown of nutrients per serving and exchange values. It can be ordered through bookstores or the American Diabetes Association's order service.

American Diabetic Association   *$15 to $35*

Family Cookbooks I, II, III, IV (#CCBF1, CCBF2, CCBF3, CCBF4)

Holiday Cookbook (#CCBH)

Special Celebrations and Parties Cookbook (#CCBSCP)

❧ Diabetic Retinopathy

To better understand how diabetes can cause visual impairment, what the symptoms of diabetic retinopathy are, and how to correct any vision loss, send for this six-page booklet prepared by the National Institute of Health.

Consumer Information Center (413X)   *under $5*

❧ Digestive Concerns

When the digestive system malfunctions, conditions such as gas, heartburn, and indigestion may occur. These can be annoying but usually are not serious. However, other digestive disorders such as pancreatitis, inflammatory bowel disease, hepatitis, ulcers, and gallstones are cause for concern because they have the potential to be life-threatening.

   Comprehensive information about digestive health and disease is available through the federal government in publications such as the following:

Digestive Health and Disease: A Glossary (DD-01)

Facts and Fallacies About Digestive Disease (DD-02)

Your Digestive System and How It Works (DD-03)

Smoking and Your Digestive System (DD-52)

Harmful Effects of Medicines on the Adult Digestive System (DD-116)

Crohn's Disease and Ulcerative Colitis (DD-103)

Diverticular Disease (DD-104)

Gallstones (DD-105)

Irritable Bowel Syndrome (DD-106)

Ulcers (DD-107)

Gastroesophageal Reflux (DD-108)

Lactose Intolerance (DD-109)

Hepatitis (DD-101)

Gastritis (DD-113)

Hiatal Hernia (DD-115)

Digestive Diseases Organizations for Patients (DD-05)

**National Digestive Diseases Information
Clearinghouse** *Free*
Constipation and *Digestive Do's and Don'ts* both include a wealth of tips for better digestion in older persons.
National Institute on Aging *Free*

❧ Education

No one is ever too old to learn more about his or her body and how to take care of it. Both nonprofit and commercial publishers are recognizing this fact and have begun to offer an ever-increasing number of educational materials. Some are geared specifically for senior citizens, whereas others are intended for a more general population (but are still very relevant for older people). One or more of them could make a big difference in improving your physical and emotional well-being. Also take advantage of helplines that provide prerecorded or individualized information.

❧ *Coming of Age* video
Tips are given for keeping bones strong, heart healthy, preventing cancer, and keeping the mind alert. The tape is an hour long and is hosted by Eddie Albert.
SelfCare Catalog (1012) *$15 to $35*

❧ *DocTalk* tapes
These lively conversational tapes by board-certified physicians feature practical information on prevention, early diagnosis, treatment, and self-help for such conditions as high blood pressure, high cho-

lesterol, and arthritis. Each 40-minute tape includes questions to discuss with your personal physician and reference books for further study.

SelfCare Catalog   (impotence, 2098; breast cancer, 2096; high blood pressure, 2095; cholesterol, 2101; living with arthritis, 2099; cancer prevention, 2097) $15 to $35 each

৺ Healthwise for Life: Medical Self-Care for Healthy Aging

Over 115 of the most common health problems of older adults are profiled in this easy-to-read book. Information was compiled from physicians, nurses, pharmacists, physical therapists, and nutritionists. Symptom identification, home treatments, the need for a medical consultation, and techniques for preventing the problem from getting worse are described.

For Convenience Sake (9960)   *$5 to $15*

৺ Healthy Older People Hotline

Information specialists can provide educational materials and technical assistance regarding a variety of health issues. They can refer callers to the appropriate health-related organization for further help.

National Health Information Center   *Free*

৺ 900-number medical information

Eighty licensed MDs staff this service, which provides information and advice about any medical concern. Obviously, they're unable to make a definitive diagnosis or prescribe treatment over the phone, but they can advise callers as to what the problem might be and whether a visit to the doctor is recommended.

Doctors By Phone   *under $5/minute*

৺ Ask A Nurse

A toll-free call will direct you to a local hospital with the nearest Ask A Nurse program. The registered nurses do not diagnose a problem over the phone but will provide health information on virtually any topic and answer questions.

Ask A Nurse   *Free*

❧ Checking physician credentials

To know whether your doctor is board certified in his or her specialty (by passing proficiency examinations and continuing education), call the board hotline.

American Board of Medical Specialties Certification Hotline   *Free*

❧ Tel-Med

A variety of 3- to 5-minute tape-recorded health messages written by physicians is provided by many hospitals, universities, medical societies, universities, and libraries. This information (on such topics as alcoholism, arthritis, bee stings, cancer, diabetes, drug abuse, flu, mental health, nutrition, and smoking) is available over the phone. Contact your local hospital, college, library, or medical society to see if they offer this service.

❧ *Prevention Magazine*

This monthly magazine is a treasure trove of tips relating to nutrition, exercise, and general health concerns.

Rodale Press   *$15 to $35 a year*

❧ *Johns Hopkins Medical Letter—Health After 50*

This eight-page monthly newsletter by the doctors at Johns Hopkins School of Medicine and its medical institutions addresses all the issues that impact an older person's health. It provides the latest information on new drugs, surgical procedures, and nutritional guidelines, focusing on the subjects that are most relevant to the aging reader (such as cholesterol, osteoporosis, hypertension, cancer, and arthritis). In an easy-to-read format, the newsletter helps sort out research findings from a variety of sources and offers recommendations from the Johns Hopkins doctors.

Johns Hopkins Medical Letter Health After 50   *$15 to $35 a year*

❧ *Healthline*

The contents of this monthly periodical educate readers about ways to help avoid illness and live longer, healthier lives. Articles can range from choosing hearing aids to the need for annual rectal examinations to profiles of essential vitamins and minerals to coping with pet allergies to choosing a sunscreen.

Mosby-Year Book, Inc.   *$35 to $75 a year*

❧ *United Seniors Health Report*

Published five times a year, this newsletter addresses new developments in senior health care issues. Recent editions have focused on proposed changes in Medicare, nutrition, and long-term care insurance.

United Seniors Health Cooperative   *$5 to $15 a year*

❧ Books on disabilities

Virtually any book on disabilities can be obtained through this mail-order firm. Ask for its free catalog.

The Disability Bookshop

❧ *Complete Guide to Symptoms, Illness, and Surgery for People Over 50*

Written by H. Winter Griffith, this 800-page book is filled with information about every type of medical concern. While there are other home medical references, this is one of the few specifically written for persons over 50. Your local bookstore can order it. The publisher is Body Press/Perigee.   *$15 to $35*

❧ *Healthy Questions*

Selecting and using the services of health professionals is a little easier with the help of this guide. Emphasis is on the appropriate questions to ask physicians, dentists, vision care specialists, and pharmacists. These questions ensure that the best health care providers will be chosen and that a mutually beneficial relationship is established.

AARP Fulfillment (D12094)   *Free*

❧ NIA's Age Pages on Medical Care

Each of these two-page publications provides a wealth of information on using the health care system most effectively. Four titles are available:

Considering Surgery?

Finding Good Medical Care for Older Americans

Hospital Hints

Who's Who in Health Care

National Institute on Aging   *Free*

❧ *Exercise*

It's extremely important for older people to engage in some kind of exercise to maintain muscle tone, strength, flexibility, and stamina. Some octogenarians participate in vigorous outdoor activities, while other people in their sixties can only engage in sedate exercises at home. **Check with your physician first to find out what type of exercise is advisable before beginning an exercise program.**

The American College of Sports Medicine recommends 20 to 30 minutes of aerobic exercise 3 to 5 days a week and 20 minutes of strength training twice weekly. This level of exercise has been found to stimulate the production and distribution of human growth hormones, making the exerciser look younger. A Harvard research study revealed that senior citizens who swim have sex lives comparable to persons in their late twenties! Other studies have shown that even the oldest exercisers (85 to 100 years old) doubled the strength of their legs and took 20 percent less time to walk down a hall or up stairs after maintaining a regular exercise routine for several months. Most were able to stop using walkers and canes.

❧ Planning an exercise program

A physical therapist can be invaluable in planning an exercise program for an older person. A consultation can be arranged with a therapist in the outpatient department of the local hospital or in private practice (consult the Yellow Pages under "Physical Therapists").

EXERCISE EQUIPMENT

Be aware that some exercise equipment is not suitable for people over 60, especially those with certain conditions or limitations. Stair machines may be too physically demanding for many older hearts. Rowing machines are contraindicated for back problems and hypertension. Treadmills are inappropriate for people with balance problems. Cross-country ski machines are extremely physically demanding and require excellent coordination. Persons with arthritic knees or balance problems should not use exercise bikes. Read the sections on bicycling and walking for descriptions of appropriate equipment.

❦ Exercise Motivation
This audiotape provides encouragement and helpful hints for beginning an exercise program.
Effective Learning Systems, Inc.   *$5 to $15*

BICYCLING

Whether cycling is done inside on a stationary exercycle or outdoors on a regular bike, there are a number of products that can make it easier and more enjoyable for the older exerciser.

❦ Reading stand for exercise bikes
Stationary bicycles provide excellent cardiopulmonary benefits, but they're not used regularly enough because people often find them boring. Reading while pedaling takes the boredom out of exercising and stimulates the mind as well as the body. You may find you use the bike more often if you have a reading stand for it. The steel rack attaches to the bike handbars without tools to hold books or magazines.
Promises Kept (1018)   *$15 to $35*

❦ Video bike tours
Avid cyclists enjoy touring the country on two wheels. But you don't have to leave home to enjoy breathtaking scenery and an invigorating bike ride. Just pop the video *Stationary Bike Tours of America* or *Videocycle Tours* into the VCR and pedal away on your exercise bike. Twenty minutes on the bike will go by quickly and pleasantly while you watch these special travelogs, which contain narration as well as lively music.

$15 to $35

Relax Video (Stationary Bike Tours)
SelfCare Catalog (Videocycle Tours—1506, San Francisco; 1507, Hawaii; 1508, Vermont Autumn Colors; 1509, Oregon Coast; 1510, British Columbia)

❦ Easyseat
The standard saddle-style bicycle seat for street and exercise bikes can chafe and cause numbness. The Easyseat is much more comfortable because it has two separately adjustable cupped cushions that provide a larger riding support.
The Alsto Company   *$15 to $35*

⚘ Comfort seat pad

The degree of cushioning is controlled by squeezing the pump to increase or decrease the amount of air in the seat. The cover is nylon bonded to rubber foam. The seat pad makes exercise bikes more comfortable and supportive and decreases seat friction and jolts from bumps on regular bikes.

Comfortably Yours (4889, regular bike; 4930, exercise bike)

$35 to $75

⚘ Good Life Bike

You don't have to be over 50 to enjoy this bicycle, but you'll especially appreciate this new design if you've reached the age at which standard bikes leave something to be desired. Its exclusive heads-up riding position keeps the back and head erect, while the "step thru" frame makes it easy to get on and off. The adjustable wide-saddle seat provides both padding and a spring suspension for comfort. A reassuring safety feature is the power-response rim band brake, which gives three times the braking power of ordinary caliper brakes—in one easy-touch lever motion. An indoor fitness stand allows the bike to be used as a stationary exerciser at home.

NordicTrack (6140)   *$200 to $350*
(7000, fitness stand)   *$75 to $125*

⚘ Adult tricycle

Persons who enjoy riding a bicycle but want more stability than two wheels can provide will enjoy a three-wheeler. Some have high-backed molded seats for full back support, an open walk-in frame, and swing-up handlebars for easy access.

Sears HealthCare (47856)   *$200 to $350*

⚘ Pedaler exerciser

You can receive the benefits of bicycling (improved lung capacity, circulation, and flexibility) even if you have difficulty climbing and sitting on an exercise or regular bike. Instead, you can sit in a favorite chair, insert both feet into the foot-strapped pedals, adjust the resistance, and pedal away. By placing the device on the table, the arms can also be exercised.

$35 to $75

adaptAbility (49500)
Aids For Arthritis (E-7)
Comfortably Yours (5316)
Promises Kept (1005)

HAND EXERCISES

Exercises to keep hand muscles strong and finger joints limber can be done while watching television. The following are good hand exercisers.

⚘ Therapeutic putty
The putty can be manipulated in a variety of ways to improve strength and dexterity. It is available in four strengths: extra soft, soft, medium, and firm.
adaptAbility (41311, extra soft; 41331, soft; 41351, medium; 41371, firm)   *under $5*

⚘ Exer-grip
Squeezing the springs on the gripper strengthens the hand, wrist, and forearm.
adaptAbility (43650)   *under $5*

⚘ Exer-ball
This foam ball provides a simple but effective way to exercise.
Cleo, Inc. (11-1077)   *$5 to $15*

⚘ Hand helper exerciser
Rubber bands provide resistance while the user squeezes the plastic frame.
adaptAbility (45511)   *$5 to $15*

SWIMMING/AQUATIC EXERCISE

Water exercise provides a complete workout in a no-impact environment that cushions and protects joints. It improves cardiovascular functioning, increases joint range of motion, and enhances muscular strength. Swimming is, of course, the predominant form of aquatic exercise, but walking in the water is also very beneficial. (Walking at a pace of 3 miles per hour burns twice as many calories as walking the same speed on land because water has greater resistance than air.) For safety purposes, older persons always need to have someone else around when exercising and to keep the water at 84°F or more.

❦ Aqua Jogger
This device is worn around the waist to provide buoyancy, so that the arms and legs are free to move for gentle stretching or calisthenics. It keeps the user upright for jogging in the pool.

$35 to $75

Promises Kept (1009)
Solutions (5771)

❦ Aqua Jogger video
This 45-minute videotape shows the basics of using the Aqua Jogger and demonstrates ways to develop personalized water workouts.
Solutions (877)   *$15 to $35*

❦ Weighted swim mitts
These fingerless gloves contain up to three removable ⅓-pound weights. Wearing them while walking in water or swimming helps tone the upper body muscles and strengthen the heart. They're available in sizes small (7–8), medium (9–10), and large (10½–12).

$35 to $75

Promises Kept (1057)
Solutions (5129)

❦ Kickboard
A kickboard allows the user to keep his or her head above water and concentrate on kicking to strengthen the heart and tone the legs. Kickboards are available at sporting goods departments or from catalogs.
Promises Kept (1056)   *$15 to $35*

❦ Swim goggles
Traditional swim goggles can be uncomfortable if they rub the tender tissue around the eyes. The patented sponge frame of Barracuda swim goggles effectively seals out water while comfortably fitting around

the eye sockets. The goggles are available in two lens colors: smoke for outdoors and clear for indoor swimming.

Solutions (5554)   *$15 to $35*

⚘ Lap counter

To monitor progress, swimmers can use an electronic lap counter to record total swimming time, average lap time, fastest lap, slowest lap, total laps, and calories burned. The counter pad attaches with suction cups to the pool wall and can easily be transported, placed, and removed. The swimmer touches the pad with hands or feet at the end of each lap. Four D batteries operate the system.

Promises Kept (1045)   *$125 to $200*

⚘ Water exercise classes

A variety of classes is offered at health clubs, schools, community centers, and Ys. To find out what water exercise classes are available locally, send a self-addressed stamped envelope to the national association that deals with aquatic exercise.

U.S. Water Fitness Association   *Free*

Two other aquatics brochures detailing water exercise classes are available from another water fitness association.

Aquatic Exercise Association   *under $5 (for both)*

VIDEOS FOR GENERAL FITNESS

It's true that the majority of videotapes feature strenuous workouts for younger persons, but there are a number of tapes specifically designed or suitable for the mature exerciser.

⚘ *Dancin' Grannies*

This is one of the few aerobics videotapes specifically geared toward mature women. It features exercisers over 55 in heart-smart workouts that increase coordination, flexibility, endurance, muscle tone, range of motion, and self-confidence. Two 55-minute tapes are available. Tape 1 has aerobics for beginners. Tape 2 focuses on limbering, stretching, body sculpting, and relaxation.

Dancin' Grannies order service   *$15 to $35*

⚘ *Prime Time Fitness*

On this exercise video featuring mature adults, the workout includes stretching, strength training, and low-impact aerobics. It is led by Bev

Harris, a 50-year-old who runs the Prime Time Fitness studio in Tampa, Florida, specializing in fitness for older adults.

Delo Books   *$15 to $35*

❧ *Senior Fitnessize*

This 30-minute video presents muscle-toning and range-of-motion exercises in a standing or sitting position. There is also educational information about the various exercises in addition to the demonstrations by retirement home participants.

Senior Fitnessize   *$15 to $35*

❧ *Senior Stretch for Women*

This hour-long tape features simple movements to increase flexibility and coordination while minimizing any pain and stiffness.

Mature Wisdom (784280)   *$15 to $35*

❧ *Angela Lansbury's Positive Moves*

In an hour-long video, the popular actress shares her personal plan for fitness and well-being for the mature years.

Critics' Choice Video (DAWKV001016)   *$15 to $35*

❧ *Chair Dancing* **tapes**

A dancer created these sitting routines when she fractured her ankle and had to teach dancing from a chair. The 45-minute tapes provide aerobics, toning, and stretching at three levels.

❧ **Chair Dancing order service**

$5 to $15 audio;
$15 to $35 video

❧ *Any Body Can Sit and Be Fit*

All the exercises in this 20-minute video can be performed while sitting in an armchair. They help to relieve muscle tension, burn calories, and increase circulation.

Cleo, Inc. (12-1254)   *$15 to $35*

❧ *Armchair Fitness*

This 60-minute videocassette provides a graduated set of aerobic exercises with stretching and strengthening. All exercises are performed sitting in a chair to the sounds of original Big Band music.

Access to Recreation (8250-01)   *$35 to $75*

❧ Keep Fit While You Sit

A disabled person and a physical therapist developed this 45-minute video. The aerobic exercises (all done while sitting) work the arm, torso, neck, and shoulders. Both cardiovascular endurance as well as upper body strength are increased.

Twin Peaks Press   *$15 to $35*

❧ Good Housekeeping Fat-Burning Workout

This 45-minute video for beginners features low-impact aerobics with overall stretching and toning.

Good Housekeeping Order Service   *$15 to $35*

WALKING

Walking can be an ideal form of exercise for older people. It doesn't place excessive strain on the joints, it offers excellent aerobic activity if done briskly, and it gives a change of scenery and an opportunity to see other people.

❧ Mall walking

If you would like to walk but your neighborhood isn't safe to walk around or the terrain is too challenging (rocky or hilly), find out whether a local shopping mall has special provisions for mall walking. Many malls have special clubs that attract senior citizens who prefer the safety and controlled climate. Some open early so that walkers can have the mall to themselves. Contact the management office of the mall closest to you. There's even a National Organization of Mall Walkers (NOMW) for recognition of accomplishments. Once an individual purchases a log book from NOMW, he or she receives awards (such as certificates, emblems, hat pins, and medallions) after logging 50 miles, then at 100, 250, 500, and every 250 miles thereafter. Membership in the NOMW entitles you to free and reduced log books, the NOMW Mall Walkers hat, and information about beginning a walking program.

National Organization of Mall Walkers   *$15 to $35 initial membership; $5 to $15 yearly renewal; $5 to $15 logbooks*

❧ Prevention Walking Club

Prevention Magazine sponsors a walking program that encourages participants to develop a healthy walking habit. Membership in the

Prevention Walking Club includes a *WalkPower* booklet with tips on starting the program and a year-long walking log with inspirational quotes. Special certificates and stickers are awarded to chart progress.
Prevention Walking Club   *under $5*

⚘ *Fitness Walking Guide*
This booklet, developed by the Rockport shoe company and the Metropolitan Life Insurance Company, contains a step-by-step program and two pages of daily walking logs.
Rockport Fitness Walking Guide   *Free*

⚘ *Pedometer*
You may want to obtain a pedometer to measure the distance you walk; these are available at all sporting goods stores. To add pleasure to your walks, use a personal radio or tape player with headphones. There is even a combination stereo/pedometer available that features an AM/FM radio; cassette player; electronic digital readouts for correct time, time elapsed, and distance covered; and a metronomic tone to help establish the desired pace. It runs on two AA batteries.
SelfCare Catalog (2020)   *$35 to $75*

⚘ *Walking* magazine
Look for *Walking* magazine at the newsstand for articles on such subjects as customizing a workout for your body type and goals or evaluating 40 kinds of footwear. Published monthly

under $5 per issue

⚘ *Walker's World Newsletter*
Every other month, *Prevention* publishes a *Walker's World Newsletter* in the back of the magazine. Featured are walking vacations; products to make walking easier, safer, healthier, and more fun; and inspirational stories from Walking Club members.
Rodale Press   *$15 to $35*

⚘ *Walking for Exercise and Pleasure*
The 13 pages of this booklet detail how to warm up and how far/fast/often to walk for best results. It was prepared by the President's Council on Physical Fitness and Sports.
Consumer Information Center (108X)   *under $5*

❧ Vitamaster WalkSafe

Most exercise equipment is not designed with the needs of older users in mind. But this treadmill has several unique features that recognize what mature exercisers want and need. Both safety and comfort are considered. The monitor is easier to use than the typical ones on electronic treadmills; the reset button is pushed to start. A quick-stop safety switch ensures that the treadmill can be stopped immediately if need be. For an easier walk, the extra-large handrails have soft hand grips. The speed can be adjusted from 0 to 6 miles per hour. For a softer walk, the thick shock-absorbing cushioning under the treadmill minimizes body stress. The walking surface is extra wide (16 inches) to provide a wider base of support when exercising. The treadmill can be purchased at WalMart or Montgomery Ward, or contact the manufacturer.

Readmaster Corporation   *$600 to $1,000*

❧ *Walking Tapes*

These audiocassette tapes motivate the listener to keep on walking. Each set of three tapes includes classical and popular music. They're available in beginner (104–120 beats per minute, 3 miles an hour), intermediate (120–134 bpm, 4 mph), or advanced (128–148 bpm, 4½ mph) modes.

Signals   *$35 to $75 (set of 3)*

❧ *Fitness Walking* audiotapes

Three cassettes feature popular tunes from the 1940s through the 1980s. The beginner mode is a 20-minute mile; intermediate is an 18-minute mile; advanced is a 16-minute mile.

Comfortably Yours (5427)   *$15 to $35*

❧ *Take a Walk with Me*

This hour-long audiocassette features walking tips and peppy music.

Dancin' Grannies order service   *$5 to $15*

MISCELLANEOUS

Although the following don't specifically fit into any of the other categories, they're definitely worth looking into.

⚜ Volkssporting

Volkssporting (meaning "the sport of the people" in German) originated in Europe in the mid-1960s and began in the United States about a decade later. The philosophy behind volkssporting is that every person, regardless of age or physical ability, can enjoy some type of outdoor sport on a noncompetitive basis. Each participant chooses the sport, distance, and pace. Walking is the most popular volkssporting activity, but there are also swimming, biking, cross-country skiing, snowshoeing, and roller/ice skating events. Trails are carefully laid out and marked at historic or scenic sites. In addition to receiving the benefits of improved health and fitness, participants can also make new friends and enjoy wonderful scenery either near or far from home. There are more than 550 clubs throughout the United States offering over 2,500 events throughout the year.

American Volkssport Association   *$15 to $35 a year*

⚜ *Pep Up Your Life*

This booklet profiles an exercise program designed for adults over the age of 50.

AARP Fulfillment (D549)   *Free*

⚜ *Staying Fit Over 40*

Appropriate for both men and women, this informative booklet details the health risks of inactivity, the benefits of regular exercise, and techniques for exercising safely and effectively.

Advil Forum on Health Education   *Free*

⚜ *Pretend Your Nose is a Crayon (and Other Strategies for Staying Younger Longer)*

Written by Carol Greenberg and published by Houghton Mifflin, this instructive 150-page fitness book presents techniques to improve breathing, heart function, bone density, mobility, and mood. Most bookstores carry (or can order) the book, or it can be obtained through a mail-order cooperative.

United Seniors Health Cooperative   *$5 to $15*

Female Health Concerns

Many women mistakenly feel that they don't need to continue seeing their gynecologist once their reproductive years are over. Nothing could be further from the truth. The risk of both breast and cervical cancer increases with age, so it becomes more important than ever to monitor the health of the breasts and cervix. Medical care should also be sought for dealing with any problems associated with menopause.

(See also the Cancer and Osteoporosis sections of this chapter.)

Mammograms

Annual mammograms are recommended for women over 50 because the incidence of breast cancer significantly increases after this age. Less than 2 percent of women in the United States get breast cancer before age 50, whereas 11 percent do by age 85. It's important to go to a mammography facility that is accredited by the American College of Radiology. This will ensure that the center uses the lowest possible radiation, produces the highest-quality pictures, and has adequately trained personnel, including a radiologist who is board certified or has special mammography training. The **American Cancer Society** can advise whether or not a center meets these standards.

Breast Self-Examination pamphlet

A pamphlet on *Breast Self-Examination: A New Approach* explains how to perform monthly exams at home.

American Cancer Society (2088.00) *Free*

Chances Are You Need a Mammogram

Just because women are past childbearing age doesn't mean that they're exempt from taking care of their health. This booklet presents convincing advice on the importance of preventive and diagnostic monitoring.

AARP Fulfillment (D14502) *Free*

❧ Smart Advice for Women 40 and Over: Have a Mammogram

The National Institutes of Health has published a small but comprehensive pamphlet that details the need for regular mammograms in older women.

Consumer Information Center (524X)   *Free*

❧ Breast self-exam cards for the shower

Waterproof, laminated instructions for breast self-examinations are available through a breast cancer foundation. These cards can be hung up in the shower to serve as a reminder to take a few moments to do this important exam each month.

Susan G. Komen Breast Cancer Foundation   *Free (donation requested)*

❧ Reach to Recovery

This short-term peer-visitor program for women who have or have had breast cancer is sponsored by the American Cancer Society. Physical, emotional, and cosmetic needs are addressed. Support and information are provided by women who have recovered from breast surgery and want to help other women through the trauma.

American Cancer Society   *Free*

❧ Gynecological care

The national association for gynecologists can make referrals to local qualified physicians. They also provide such pamphlets as *Preventing Osteoporosis, The Menopause Years,* and *Estrogen Use.*

American College of Obstetricians and Gynecologists   *Free*

❧ Pap smear

Although cervical cancer is most likely to occur in postmenopausal women, this age group is the least likely to get a Pap smear. This fast and painless test can be performed by any gynecologist and most general/family medicine/internal medicine practitioners. To learn more about Pap smears and uterine cancer, send for *Stay Healthy! Learn About Uterine Cancer.*

American Cancer Society (2062.00)   *Free*

❧ Menopause

This informative 36-page publication profiles the options for treating menopause. Concerns about osteoporosis, breast cancer, and cardiovascular disease are discussed. It also includes a list of organizations to contact for further information and recommended books to read.

National Institute on Aging   *Free*

❧ *Hot Flash*

This quarterly newsletter for older and mid-life women features many informative articles about relevant health concerns (such as osteoporosis, incontinence, menopause, and pain management).

National Action Forum for Midlife and Older Women   *$15 to $35 a year*

❧ Foot Health

It is difficult to walk comfortably and efficiently when you have foot problems. Aging does bring about some changes in the feet, but there are a number of ways to maintain and improve their health.

   (See also the section on Diabetic Care in this chapter and the section on Feet in Chapter 4.)

❧ *Your Podiatrist Talks About Aging*

This informative pamphlet addresses the effects of aging on the feet and offers tips on keeping the feet in shape. (Other pamphlets are available on general foot health, diabetes, arthritis, high blood pressure, foot orthoses, surgery, Medicare coverage, women's feet, walking, and nail problems.) Upon request, the national podiatric medicine organization that publishes the pamphlets will also make referrals to local podiatrists.

American Podiatric Medical Association   *Free*

❧ *Foot Care*

The care of older feet is discussed in this two-page publication. It touches upon the foot problems that more than three-quarters of all adults past middle age experience.

National Institute on Aging   *Free*

❧ Hearing

Although the majority of older adults tend to experience partial hearing loss and at least 40 percent have a significant loss, many are reluctant to admit to the problem and seek help. This is unfortunate because there are many resources available to help deal with hearing problems. Take advantage of them to ensure that you do everything possible to preserve and maintain your hearing ability.

(See also the Communication section in Chapter 1.)

❧ Better Hearing Helpline

A hearing screening can be conducted over the phone. All it takes is a quiet room and 2 minutes. While not a complete test, it can alert the user to the possibility of a hearing loss. The operator at the toll-free number will refer you to a local number to call for the screening.

Better Hearing Helpline   *Free*

❧ *Your Guide to Better Hearing*

This booklet discusses ringing in the ears and medical assistance such as surgery, hearing aids, and hearing conservation. It even contains a self-administered hearing test with eight questions evaluating the ability to hear in different circumstances and helping to determine whether hearing assistance is needed.

Better Hearing Institute   *Free*

❧ *Hearing and Older People*

This two-page publication details problems and solutions relating to hearing loss in older people.

National Institute on Aging   *Free*

MEDICAL HELP

Hearing loss can be corrected or compensated for—*if* you seek professional help. Too many older persons are unwilling to see an otologist or otolaryngologist (physician who diagnoses and treats diseases of the ear) because they think it will inevitably lead to a hearing aid. In many cases, the treatment may be as simple as having plugs of hardened ear wax removed. In other cases, surgery may be indicated. The physician will be able to advise you about whether a hearing aid would help. Ask your family physician to make a referral to an ear-nose-throat specialist.

✒ *Hearing Loss*

Reading lists and summaries of current research are provided in this information packet.

National Institute of Neurological and Communicative Disorders and Stroke (82-157)   *Free*

✒ *Have You Heard?*

Hearing impairments associated with aging are described in this publication. Techniques for coping with hearing loss are also presented, including when and where to go for hearing aids.

AARP Fulfillment (D12219)   *Free*

✒ *Product Report: Hearing Aids*

Specific information about products and services related to hearing loss is provided in this booklet. Tips on selecting an appropriate hearing aid are included.

AARP Fulfillment (D13766)   *Free*

✒ **Hearing Aid Helpline**

Information on hearing loss, hearing aids, and how to locate a qualified hearing aid specialist is available to the public via a toll-free helpline. Consumer complaints about hearing aids are also handled at this number.

International Hearing Society   *Free*

✒ **Self Help for Hard of Hearing People (SHHH)**

As the largest international consumer organization dedicated to the 24 million persons who do not hear well, SHHH educates members, their families and friends, and society about hearing loss. Affiliate chapters across the country meet regularly to learn about hearing loss, offer support, and promote self-help. Membership includes a subscription to a bimonthly magazine (*SHHH Journal*) as well as free or discounted publications. Among the many offerings for under $5 are the following:

Living Alone with a Hearing Loss (201)

Persuading Your Spouse/Relative/Friend to Acknowledge a Hearing Loss and Seek Help (202)

Beyond the Hearing Aid with Assistive Listening Devices (251)

The Hearing Aid Handbook: User's Guide for Adults
Self Help for Hard of Hearing People   *national membership: $15 to $35 a year*

⚶ Tinnitus
Constant ringing or buzzing in the ears or inside the head is found most often in people 55 years of age and older. The national association for this disorder sponsors self-help groups nationwide and offers such publications as *Information About Tinnitus* and *Coping with the Stress of Tinnitus*.
American Tinnitus Association   *Free*

⚶ Communication disorders helpline
A toll-free information service answers questions from the public about communication disorders and offers the names of certified audiologists who diagnose hearing problems and fit hearing aids and also speech/language pathologists. Fact sheets on the diagnosis and treatment of speech, language, and hearing disorders are also available.
American Speech-Language-Hearing Association   *Free*

⚶ Heart Disease

As hearts age, they tend to pump a little less efficiently. This may be unnoticeable when a person tries to stay heart-healthy through exercise, diet, and refraining from smoking. In cases of actual disease, there can be symptoms and consequences that are uncomfortable, limiting, or life-threatening.

(See also the sections on Blood Pressure, Stroke, Respiratory Concerns, Education, and Exercise in this chapter.)

⚶ American Heart Association
This voluntary health organization funds research and sponsors public education programs to reduce disability and death from cardiovascular diseases and stroke. Local heart associations sponsor stroke clubs, in which patients and families exchange practical advice on recovering from a stroke and listen to speakers discuss the latest research and state-of-the-art treatment. The Mended Hearts offer similar local

groups for people with heart disease. They also sponsor smoking cessation groups. A number of free pamphlets are available, including:

After a Heart Attack

How You Can Help Your Doctor Treat Your High Blood Pressure
Coronary Artery Bypass Graft Surgery

Recovering From a Stroke

Cholesterol and Your Heart

Walking for a Healthy Heart

An Older Person's Guide to Cardiovascular Health

American Heart Association   *Free or nominal dues*

❦ Publications on heart disease
A Handbook of Heart Terms, How Doctors Diagnose Heart Disease,
Heart Attacks, and *The Human Heart: A Living Pump* are available
for the asking.

National Heart, Lung, and Blood Institute   *Free*

❦ *Heart to Heart: What Older Women Need to Know About Heart Disease*
This fact sheet profiles prevention techniques for heart disease (the
number-one killer of older women).
AARP Fulfillment (D14260)   *Free*

❦ *So You Have High Blood Cholesterol*
The National Institutes of Health has published a practical 28-page
guide to lowering blood cholesterol through diet, medication, and
exercise.
Consumer Information Center (127X)   *under $5*

❦ Transtelephonic pacemaker testing
Pacemakers can easily be checked in the comfort and privacy of the
home with this nationwide special service. All that's required is a
phone and a portable transmitter provided by the monitoring company. A trained technician calls at the patient's convenience and receives the heart rhythm over the telephone lines. The pacemaker

impulse and heart rate activity are recorded on a computerized graph, similar to an EKG done at a doctor's office. The test results are then forwarded to the referring physician. (A doctor's prescription is needed to enroll in the program.)

Pace Link   *Covered by Medicare and most private insurers; company will bill insurance directly*

❧ Kidney Disease

Kidney disease is not necessarily associated with aging. In fact, most healthy older people still have kidneys that function well. But a small number of persons over 50 do have some kidney problems.

❧ American Association of Kidney Patients

Access to a wide range of pamphlets and brochures on kidney disease and its treatment is available, as well as local support groups. The NA–K (sodium-potassium) Counter, while designed for dialysis patients, is also helpful for family and friends who want to decrease their salt intake and need to know how much salt is in specific foods.

$15 to $35 annual dues

❧ National Kidney Foundation

This national organization provides a number of services, such as publications, support groups, and transportation to dialysis.

Local chapter dues vary

❧ Male Health Concerns

Eighty percent of all men over 55 have experienced symptoms of non-cancerous enlargement of the prostate gland. It's important for older men to learn more about the prostate so that any dysfunction can be diagnosed and treated.

(See also the Cancer section in this chapter.)

❧ Cancer Facts for Men

Facts about diagnosing and treating prostate and testicular cancer are the focus of this booklet.

American Cancer Society (2008.00)   *Free*

⚜ *Prostate Enlargement* booklet

For more information about the condition and ways to monitor and treat it, send for a free booklet.

National Kidney and Urologic Diseases Information Clearinghouse   *Free*

⚜ *What Every Man Should Know About His Prostate*

This booklet explains the role of the prostate in the body and the prostate changes that tend to occur with aging. It also discusses several prostate-related conditions and the steps to take to ensure early diagnosis of prostate disease.

Merck   *Free*

⚜ *Prostate Enlargement: Benign Prostatic Hyperplasia*

This 14-page National Institutes of Health booklet describes the symptoms, causes, treatment, and recovery of an enlarged prostate.

Consumer Information Center (418X)   *under $5*

⚜ Prostate Problems

This two-page publication describes prostate dysfunction in older men.

National Institute on Aging   *Free*

⚜ *Medications*

Prescription drug overdose is a common but often unrecognized problem in older persons. Government studies have revealed that 2 million older Americans overdose on medications or risk a potential addiction to tranquilizers and sleeping pills. It has been estimated that more than 200,000 hospitalizations each year are caused by drug misuse. Other problems include side effects such as dizziness, drowsiness, or confusion.

It's not that most seniors intentionally abuse drugs; rather, they misuse them. They may double their dose to get more relief from symptoms or use alcohol or over-the-counter drugs that adversely interact with their prescription medication.

Physicians are also to blame. Too many doctors neglect to decrease the standard dosage for older adults and as a result prescribe a dose that's too strong for frailer bodies with slower systems. Or if a patient sees more than one physician, each doctor may prescribe medications that would be fine on their own but interact dangerously when taken in combination.

To combat these problems, knowledgeable physicians are prescribing medications tailored to the needs of older persons. New low-dose versions of standard drugs can help. Slow-release formulas taken once or twice a day prevent the likelihood of overmedication from a faster-acting dose.

Older persons also need to take responsibility for ensuring that optimal benefits are received from medications (and side effects minimized). By alerting their physicians to all other drugs they are taking and using only one pharmacy so that a complete record can be maintained, they enable their doctors and pharmacists to foresee potential complications from the combination of medications. Because many medications can't be taken with alcohol, each patient needs to be aware of which drugs fall within this category and curtail drinking when advisable.

❧ *Medicines and You: A Guide for Older Americans*
This complimentary booklet describes ways to take medication more safely and effectively.
The Council on Family Health   *Free*

❧ *Safe Use of Medicines By Older People*
Tips for using prescribed medications more safely and effectively are featured in this two-page publication.
National Institute on Aging   *Free*

❧ Food and Drug Administration booklets

A Doctor's Advice on Self-Care (528X) addresses the safe and effective use of over-the-counter drugs.

Food and Drug Interactions (529X) looks at the impact commonly used drugs have on nutritional needs.

Some Things You Should Know About Prescription Drugs (530X) provides tips for safe use of prescribed drugs.

When Medications Don't Mix (531X) emphasizes prevention of drug interactions. It includes questions to ask yourself and your doctor to ensure that medications are being used wisely.

Consumer Information Center   *Free*

🌿 *Worst Pills Best Pills: The Older Adult's Guide to Avoiding Drug-Induced Death or Illness*
Published by Public Citizen Health Research Group, edited by Sidney M. Wolfe, and available through a mail-order cooperative, this 532-page book details the 287 drugs prescribed most often to people over 60. It's broken down into the 104 pills that older adults should avoid and the 183 safer alternatives. A drug worksheet is included for consumers to better prepare for discussions with their physicians.
United Seniors Health Cooperative   *$5 to $15*

🌿 *AARP Pharmacy Service Prescription Drug Handbook*
To better understand the drugs prescribed by a physician or become more knowledgeable about what's available, consider purchasing this resource guide. It profiles approximately 1,000 prescription drugs, over-the-counter medications, generic drugs, and vitamins used most frequently by persons 50 and older. It's available in bookstores (list price $17.95), but can also be purchased at a reduced price through an 800 number.
AARP Pharmacy Service   *$5 to $15*

🌿 **Booklets on drug use**
Among the many informative booklets prepared by professional pharmacists are the following:

You and Your Medicine

How to Select Your Pharmacy/Pharmacist

Your Nitroglycerin

Choosing the Right (Not Wrong!) Non-Prescription Medicine Questions You May Have About Generic Drugs

As We Grow Older: Aging and Your Response to Medications

Your Personal Medication Record Card

Eye Medications May Be More Than Meets the Eye

What's Really Inside Those Pills?

The Consumer's Quick Guide to Using Medications Correctly
Medications and Travel

Elder-Health Program   *Free*

❦ The Smart Consumer's Guide to Prescription Drugs
This booklet presents information about generic drugs and on selecting a pharmacy that offers competitive prices. It includes a list of questions to ask the physician or pharmacist whenever a new medication is
prescribed.
AARP Fulfillment (D13579)   *Free*

❦ 900-number drug information
Fifty registered pharmacists provide information about drug side effects and interactions with other medications and foods. They can also
advise callers about the best way(s) to take medication (such as with
food).
Ask the Pharmacist   *under $5/minute*

❦ Mental Alertness

Forgetfulness and confusion are not a normal consequence of aging.
By keeping mentally active, you can retain your intellectual abilities.
Many researchers feel that mental gymnastics (such as solving puzzles and playing memory games) helps stimulate nerve-cell connections in the brain and keeps the central nervous system pliable. The
French even have mental gymnastics clinics in which older men and
women work with challenging games and puzzles. Although older
Americans typically do not have similar mental gymnasiums available
to them, there are a number of resources for learning about and preventing memory loss as well as for obtaining mental stimulation at
home.

(See also the section on Alzheimer's Disease in this chapter.)

❧ *Games*
This bimonthly magazine features a wide range of visual and word games.
Games   *$15 to $35 a year*

❧ **Three-dimensional puzzles**
Puzzles from all over the world, both modern and traditional, in wood, metal, glass, and plastic can be purchased through a mail-order catalog.
Ishi Press   *$5 to $75*

❧ **Jigsaw puzzles**
A wide variety of jigsaw puzzles (ranging from 500 to 6,000 pieces) can be ordered through the mail. Subjects include antique maps of the world, waterfalls, animals, candy bars, flowers, stained glass windows, and famous art work. Some three-dimensional puzzles are also available.
Bits & Pieces   *$5 to $75*

❧ *Maze Magazine*
This bimonthly magazine features at least 30 mazes for adults (and a couple for children) in each issue.
Maze Magazine   *$15 to $35 a year*

❧ **The Contest Center**
In addition to the obvious benefit of potentially winning prize money, older persons who enter puzzle contests improve their vocabularies, stay alert, and enjoy a sense of competition and participation. One of the oldest play-by-mail contest sponsors publishes six regular word puzzle contests in each bimonthly issue of *Contest Center News*. Each contest pays out $400 to $800. About once or twice a year special contests with much larger prizes are held.
$5 to $15 annual subscription;
$5 to $15 to enter contests

❧ **MasterMinds**
Another contest organization publishes three word puzzles (crosswords and word building, like Scrabble) every other month. Each has

a $1,000 payoff ($400 for first place, $200 for second place, $100 for third, and six prizes at $50 each) for the participants with the highest score. There is no membership fee; instead, there's an individual entry fee per puzzle. A newsletter that reveals the correct solution and lists the winners is available.

$5 to $15 entry fee;
$5 to $15 for annual subscription

❧ Confusion and Memory Loss in Old Age: It's Not What You Think

This two-page publication provides information about the causes of mental dysfunction and ways of coping with it.

National Institute on Aging   *Free*

❧ Now Where Did I Put My Keys?

Memory loss is briefly discussed in this pamphlet.

AARP Fulfillment (D13829)   *Free*

❧ Mental Health

Many older persons feel that their later years are the happiest and most fulfilling they've ever known. But others experience mental health problems as they grow older. Depression, the most common disorder, can be biochemical in origin, or it may be a reaction to changes or losses in a person's life. As with any medical condition, it must be diagnosed before it can be treated. Because older persons tend not to recognize when they're experiencing depression and many physicians fail to diagnose the condition in their aging patients, it's important to know the symptoms:

· feelings of sadness or irritability

· fatigue/listlessness/lack of energy

· feelings of guilt, hopelessness, or worthlessness

· restlessness or decreased activity

· changes in weight or appetite

· loss of interest in pleasure in activities previously enjoyed

- changes in sleeping pattern

- difficulty in concentrating, remembering, or decision-making

- complaints of physical aches and pains for which no medical explanation can be found

- thoughts of death or suicide

❧ Psychiatry/counseling
To locate a psychiatrist who has a special interest in the mental health of older persons, contact the **American Association for Geriatric Psychiatry.** The **American Association for Marriage and Family Therapy** helps people locate marriage and family therapists for consultations. Both referral services are free.

❧ Mental health
Ways to improve mental health and options for treating problems when they arise are discussed in four self-help booklets, *Mental Health Brochures.*
AARP Fulfillment (D13833)   *Free*

❧ *Depressive Disorders: Treatments Bring New Hope*
This comprehensive booklet discusses the types, causes, and treatment of depression and distinguishes depressive disorders of different age groups.
National Institute of Mental Health (86-1491)   *Free*

❧ *If You're Over 65 and Feeling Depressed . . .*
This booklet from the National Institute of Mental Health (NIMH) contains a checklist of the major symptoms of depression and encourages persons with symptoms to obtain professional help.
NIMH   *Free*

❧ *Answers to Your Questions About Clinical Depression*
This general-interest booklet is not specifically geared for older persons, but it does provide a helpful overview of causes, symptoms, and treatment approaches.
National Mental Health Association   *Free*

❧ *Nutrition*

You can forget what you learned about nutrition years ago because nutritional needs change with age. A 30-year-old has different requirements than someone in his or her sixties. Research has also led to changes in nutritional guidelines over the years. What was considered the healthy way to eat 40 years ago is quite different from what is currently thought to be the optimal diet.

The U.S. Senate Committee on Education and Labor reports that the vast majority (85 percent) of older Americans have chronic diseases whose symptoms could be decreased or eliminated by better nutrition. With poor nutrition, vitamins are lost, bones soften, and the immune system starves. Learn all you can about food and your nutritional needs to stay as healthy as possible.

❧ Fluid intake

The sense of thirst declines with age. It is very important to drink enough fluids to flush out wastes. Approximately eight glasses of water a day is helpful.

❧ Fat intake

According to the Tufts University Human Nutrition Research Center on Aging, the older a person gets, the longer it takes for fat to move out of the bloodstream into the cells. The longer the fat circulates in the blood, the more it contributes to the formation of plaque deposits. The plaque can block arteries and cause cardiac disease.

❧ Salt intake

Maturing kidneys can have problems with an overload of salt and lead to high blood pressure.

❧ Vitamins

Older persons may need supplemental vitamins because they can't absorb nutrients as well from their digestive tracts.

❧ Caffeine

Caffeine can have adverse effects, especially in older persons. It may increase the output of urine; stimulate the central nervous system, causing mild irritability to severe insomnia; and increase blood pressure and disturb cardiac rhythms. Older persons should limit their intake of coffee to two cups or less per day.

FOOD PREPARATION

✹ Salt monitor
By slipping the salt monitor into any moist food or beverage, you can get an instant reading of the food's salt content. It runs on three button cell batteries.

$15 to $35

Maxi Aids (13011)
Promises Kept (1069)

✹ Stovetop grill
The name is deceptive; this is actually a new type of frying pan for gas or electric stoves. Using it is as simple as placing it over a burner and turning on the heat. Fat is drained away from foods while cooking, and the grease is collected in an easy-to-clean, water-filled drip pan. Virtually anything can be cooked on it: chicken, fish, burgers, bacon, vegetables, and even "fried" eggs.
SelfCare Catalog (2051)   *$15 to $35*

✹ Fat skimmer
The fat in soup, stock, sauce, and gravy can easily be removed with this unique ladle. As soon as it is immersed into the pot, the ladle fills with the surface liquid while filtering out large food particles. When the fat separates, the trigger in the handle is pulled to release the stock back into the pot. The remaining fat and grease in the ladle can be discarded.
Colonial Garden Kitchens (660282)   *$15 to $35*

✹ Steamer
This steamer allows vegetables, meats, poultry, and seafood to be cooked healthfully without adding fats or oils. Its three separate compartments allow an entire meal to be cooked at once.
Solutions (60009)   *$35 to $75*

✹ Weight loss
A free booklet, *A Guide to Losing Weight*, offers a six-point plan for starting and sticking with a diet program. It provides a number of help-

ful hints on food selection. Send a self-addressed stamped envelope
when requesting the guide.
American Heart Association   *Free*

⚘ Balanced diets
Most older persons grew up hearing about the basic four food groups.
Now that the U.S. Department of Agriculture is recommending the
Food Guide Pyramid instead, it can be helpful to read more about it.
Balancing Meals and Money is a booklet that discusses the planning
and preparation of economical, healthful, tasty meals.
Healthy Dialogue   *Free*

⚘ *Thrifty Meals for Two*
Developed by the U.S. Department of Agriculture especially for the
older couple on a limited budget, this 69-page booklet describes how
to shop for and prepare economical and nutritious meals.
Consumer Information Center (122X)   *under $5*

⚘ ADA Hotline
The American Dietetic Association (ADA) offers a toll-free hotline
manned by dietitians during business hours. Personalized information
on nutrition can be provided. Recorded messages about the food pyramid can be obtained at any time.
ADA Hotline   *Free*

⚘ Consumer nutrition hotline
Registered dietitians will give advice and answer questions during
business hours on this toll-free line. Recorded information is also available 24 hours a day. Topics change monthly and can range from food
safety to weight control.
National Center for Nutrition and Dietetics   *Free*

⚘ Bibliographies, resource guides, and interlibrary loans
Among the topics covered are fad diets, nutrition and dental health,
vegetarianism, diet and nutrition for older Americans, nutrition and
cancer/hypertension/diabetes.
Food and Nutrition Information Center   *Free*

❧ NIA Age Pages Publications

These two-page publications include the following titles:

Be Sensible About Salt

Dietary Supplements: More Is Not Always Better

Hints for Shopping, Cooking, and Enjoying Meals

Nutrition: A Lifelong Concern
National Institute on Aging   *Free*

❧ *How Does Your Nutrition Measure Up?*

Techniques for assessing nutritional health and ways to improve it are presented in this helpful booklet. The focus is on the special needs of older adults: what we should eat, how much, and how often as we age.
AARP Fulfillment (D12994)   *Free*

❧ Cancer prevention

Send for the following free booklets from the **American Cancer Society** on eating smart:

Nutrition, Cancer and Common Sense (2096.00)

Eat to Live (2047.00)

Eat Smart with Fresh Fruits and Vegetables (2510.00)

Cooking Smart: Planning Meals (2642.01)

Cooking Smart: Menu Suggestions (2642.00)
American Cancer Society   *Free*

❧ *A Word About Low Sodium Diets*

Tips on reducing sodium intake are accompanied by recipes using salt substitutes.
Consumer Information Center (519X)   *Free*

❧ DietCoach

This hand-held computer provides nutritional information for virtually any food you might want to eat. In addition to providing the cholesterol, fat, calorie, sodium, and protein content, it can also provide daily totals and weekly averages of the calories, fats, and cholesterol that have been eaten. It comes with its own cookbook and runs on two AA batteries.
The Safety Zone (344183)   *$35 to $75*

❧ DINE software

The *DINE Right* program for IBM-compatible computers and the *MacDINE Perfect* program for Macintosh computers provide an easy way to analyze recipes, meals, and your daily diet. Its complete nutrient database contains 25 food components, such as vitamins, minerals, animal fat, plant fat, animal protein, plant protein, fiber, alcohol, caffeine, and aspartame (for artificially sweetened foods). Every food or recipe you consume each day can be analyzed. At the end of the day, DINE computes the nutrient values of the entire daily diet. The program helps to modify favorite recipes by suggesting healthier substitutions. By recording your food intake and daily exercise/activity level, you can reach and maintain your ideal weight and improve your overall health.

Center for Science in the Public Interest   *$125 to $200*

❧ *Osteoporosis*

While women are more likely to experience thinning of their bones (half of all women over 65 have osteoporosis), men can also be affected by this disease. You are at increased risk if one or more of the following characteristics apply:

- thin

- smoker

- heavy drinker

- take cortisone

- family history of osteoporosis

- diet low in dairy products and other sources of calcium

- early or surgically induced menopause

- postmenopausal woman

- don't exercise regularly

Both women and men need to engage in regular weight-bearing exercise and to maintain an adequate calcium intake (two or more glasses of milk or the equivalent each day). Caffeine, smoking, and high-protein diets should be avoided, as they tend to aggravate osteoporosis.

Maintaining bone requires calcium and vitamin D. Unfortunately, most older persons don't get a sufficient amount of D because they don't eat enough dairy products and don't spend much time outdoors where the ultraviolet sunlight synthesizes vitamin D in the skin. To adequately produce vitamin D, 15 to 30 minutes of sun are necessary.

While milk and dairy products (such as skim milk, low-fat yogurt, and low-fat cheese) are the best sources of calcium, other foods contain high levels of calcium, including broccoli, collards, turnip greens, tofu, almonds, oysters, canned sardines with bones, and canned pink salmon with bones. Calcium-enriched orange juice is another possibility.

Vitamin D (up to 400 International Units daily) can be used as a supplement.

Calcium Information Center
Oregon Health Sciences University and Cornell University jointly run a Calcium Information Center. By calling the toll-free line, people can ask specific calcium-related questions, listen to recorded messages about bone loss in postmenopausal women, and obtain booklets on calcium nutrition and osteoporosis. One of their helpful publications, *Calcium Close-Ups: Every Woman's Guide to a Vital Nutrient*, has a worksheet to calculate whether you're getting enough calcium in your diet and discusses ways to increase calcium intake.

Calcium Information Center   *Free*

Stand Up to Osteoporosis
This booklet provides information about the diagnosis, prevention, and treatment of osteoporosis.

National Osteoporosis Foundation   *Free*

Osteoporosis: The Bone Thinner
This two-page publication provides valuable information about this bone disorder.

National Institute on Aging   *Free*

Osteoporosis: Prevention, Management & Treatment
The disease process of osteoporosis and its risk factors are detailed in this 160-page book. Management of the disease is stressed through

proper diet, exercise, lifestyle, and medical treatment. Written by Harris H. McIlwain and published by John Wiley & Sons, the book can be specially ordered through bookstores or purchased through a mail-order cooperative.

United Seniors Health Cooperative   *$5 to $15*

⚜ Parkinson's Disease

More than one million people in the United States are affected by this progressive disorder of the central nervous system. It occurs more frequently in the over-50 age group than in younger people. The disease limits spontaneous movements, causing tremors, rigidity, and difficulty in walking, talking, or performing self-care activities. Drugs can relieve some of the symptoms, but there is not yet any cure. The toll-free hotline refers callers to local chapters around the country that provide information about community services, physicians experienced in treating patients with Parkinson's disease, and current treatment methods. A number of publications (such as *A Manual for Patients with Parkinson's Disease, Home Exercises for Patients with Parkinson's Disease,* and *Speech and Swallowing Problems in Parkinson's Disease*) are available.

American Parkinson's Disease Association   *Free*

⚜ Respiratory (Breathing/Lung) Concerns

We expect and need our lungs to serve us well over a lifetime, but we also tend to mistreat them over the years. We expose them to many pollutants and allergens. We may compromise them by smoking or by a lack of exercise. This can lead to problems such as emphysema, bronchitis, lung cancer, hay fever, allergies, and infections. But it's never too late to learn more about taking care of your lungs.

⚜ Better Breathing by Henry Hrehorow
Practical advice on exercises and other measures to improve breathing in people with respiratory conditions is provided in this 64-page book.

Enrichments (8451)   *$5 to $15*

⚰ Materials on lung disease and related subjects

A variety of free publications is available through the **American Lung Association,** including the following:

Home Control of Allergies and Asthma (3512)

About Emphysema (0375)

Around the Clock with Chronic Obstructive Pulmonary Disease (1230)

Chronic Bronchitis (0139)

Help Yourself to Better Breathing (4001)

Pneumonia? Not Me (1326)

Flu High-Risk Patient Brochure (1262)

Air Pollution and Exercise (0578)

Air Pollution in Your Home? (1001)

Q & A About Smoking and Health (0930)
American Lung Association   *Free*

⚰ *Understanding Emphysema*
This six-page booklet discusses the causes, complications, and relief of symptoms of emphysema so its sufferers can lead a fuller life.
National Jewish Center for Immunology and Respiratory Medicine   *Free*

⚰ *The Chronic Bronchitis and Emphysema Handbook*
Written by Francis and Sheila Haas and published by John Wiley & Sons, this 256-page book teaches techniques on self-managing chronic pulmonary disease so that a productive life is possible. It can be special ordered through bookstores or through a mail-order cooperative.
United Seniors Health Cooperative   *$5 to $15*

⚰ Respiratory information
Pulmonary nurses are available to answer questions about lung problems and diseases via a toll-free number run by the National Jewish

Center for Immunology and Respiratory Medicine. They can provide some literature as well.

Lung Line Information Service   *Free*

⚜ *Chronic Obstructive Pulmonary Disease*
This comprehensive brochure profiles all aspects of emphysema and bronchitis.

National Heart, Lung, and Blood Institute   *Free*

⚜ Information about allergies
Allergy and asthma sufferers can learn more about what causes their symptoms and how to treat them by calling a toll-free number to receive an information packet.

Allergy Information Center and Hotline   *Free*

⚜ Colds, viruses, and infections
With age, the immune system loses its vitality in warding off viruses and bacteria. Nutritional deficiencies, stress, and inactivity can weaken the immune system. To guard against this happening (and treat colds when they do occur), make sure to do the following:

· Get adequate sleep.
  Sufficient sleep is whatever it takes to leave you feeling well-rested for the entire day.

· Reduce stress.
  Meditation and exercise are great ways to get rid of stress. Lifestyles can also be changed so that daily routines seem less pressurized.

· Maintain a positive attitude.
  Learning to accept what can't be changed and laughing about the inconsistencies and frustrations of life can lead to improved mental *and* physical well-being. The *Immunity and Longevity* audiotape from **Effective Learning Systems** ($5 to $15) can help influence immunity through the development of a positive attitude.

· Exercise regularly.
  Studies at North Carolina's Appalachian State University have shown that women who walked briskly for 45 minutes 5 days a week throughout the winter and spring decreased the number of days they suffered from colds and flus by 50 percent.

- Get enough vitamins and minerals.
Vitamin C has still not been definitively proven to prevent colds, but it usually is safe to take unless you have kidney disease.

- Eat yogurt with active cultures.
Research at the University of California at Davis has found that these cultures may boost the immune system by increasing production of gamma interferon.

- Get a yearly flu shot.
The Centers for Disease Control in Atlanta recommends this for everyone 65 and older. Older persons with heart and lung problems are especially at risk for serious problems resulting from the flu.

- Use a humidifier.
Heating systems cause indoor air to be dry, which irritates tissue in the nose and throat. This irritation can make the upper respiratory system vulnerable to infections.

- Use a steam inhaler.
People have long been aware that steam can relieve stuffy noses and congested sinuses. Instead of using the old-fashioned method of covering your head with a towel and holding it over a pot of boiling water, consider a more modern device. The new systems have a clear vinyl hood that fits over the nose and mouth. Steam is controlled so that there is no danger of getting burned. Over-the-counter medications can be added if desired. Steam inhalers range in price from $35 to $475 and can be ordered from **Lifestyle Resource** (3870) and **Solutions** (5674).

- Use decongestant drops or sprays sparingly.
If they are applied too frequently, rebound congestion can aggravate a stuffy nose and actually make it worse.

- Wash your hands frequently.
This is especially important after touching someone who is sick or after touching something that has been handled by that sick person. Because the nose, mouth, and eyes are especially susceptible to viral transmission, unwashed hands should never touch these body parts.

- Avoid environmental pollutants.
  Toxins in the air (like cigarette smoke) can be especially irritating to sinus membranes that are already irritated from a cold.

- Send for *The Common Cold*.
  This six-page book published by the Food and Drug Administration profiles the effectiveness of a variety of cough, cold, allergy, and asthma remedies. It's available at no charge from the **Consumer Information Center** (535X).

- Request *What to Do About Flu*.
  In two pages, this informative publication looks at the ways older persons can deal with the flu. The free booklet can be obtained from the **National Institute on Aging.**

How to Create a Dust-Free Environment

Persons with breathing difficulties can find relief when dust levels in the home are reduced. Since approximately 8 hours a day are spent in the bedroom, it's especially important to keep this room as free of dust as possible. Ways to do this include minimizing clutter (by getting rid of dust-collecting objects), covering mattresses with plastic pads, and substituting wood, tile, or linoleum for carpet. A fact sheet providing tips on how to do this will help.

National Institutes of Health   *Free*

Clean mist humidifier

This is a quiet, vaporizing mist humidifier that sterilizes water straight from the tap without additional expensive solutions. It runs for sixty hours on easy-to-fill two gallon tanks and can handle rooms up to 800 square feet.

Brookstone (14653)   *$75 to $125*

Personal air purifier

Electronic air ionizers plug into any wall socket and can clean the air over a small portion of the room (such as over the bed). They silently emit negative ions that attract dust, smoke particles, pollens, allergens, and airborne bacteria and eliminate them from the immediate environment. They're usually available wherever small household appliances or health care aids are sold, or can be ordered through a catalog.

SelfCare Catalog (2009)   *$35 to $75*

❦ Home air purifier

A good purifier contains several filters that clear 120 cubic feet of air per minute and eliminate pollen, dust, animal dander, bacteria. and tobacco ash. They use the HEPA filtration recommended by allergists. The HEPA filter cartridge lasts up to five years while it removes particles as small as 3/10 of a micron; the charcoal prefilter lasts three months and removes larger particles like animal hair and lint.

$200 to $350

Promises Kept (D2050)
Sears HealthCare
SelfCare Catalog (1118)
The Safety Zone (122083)

❦ Purity air filters

These filters may be more expensive than ordinary ones, but they only need to be replaced one to four times a year, depending on the environmental conditions. The manufacturers claim that the filter is 97 percent effective in removing pollen from the air and 50 times more effective in controlling dirt, dust, and smoke than the standard fiberglass filter. They're available in sizes 16″ × 20″ × 1″, 16″ × 25″ × 1″, 20″ × 20″ × 1″, and 20″ × 25″ × 1″.

The Alsto Company   *$5 to $15*

❦ Materials on lung cancer and smoking

The **American Cancer Society** can furnish you with a number of free booklets about smoking and lung cancer.

Facts on Lung Cancer (2628.00)

If You Smoke Take This Risk Test (2656.00)

How to Quit Cigarettes (2604.00)

The Smoke Around You (2060.00)
American Cancer Society   *Free*

❦ *Clearing the Air: A Guide to Quitting Smoking*

The 45 pages of the National Institute of Health publication is filled with practical suggestions for kicking the habit.
Consumer Information Center (520X)   *Free*

❧ *Smoking: It's Never Too Late to Stop*

Older smokers can get advice about quitting in this two-page publication.

National Institute on Aging   *Free*

❧ *Stop Smoking*

This audiotape provides techniques and encouragement to stop smoking permanently.

Effective Learning Systems, Inc.   *$5 to $15*

❧ **Freedom from Smoking**

The **American Lung Association** provides audiotapes, manuals, and support groups for quitting smoking. Contact your local chapter for specific information.

❧ *Skin Health*

Because skin is the largest organ of the body, keeping it healthy is an important component of physical and psychological well-being.

❧ *Preventing Dry Skin and Other Skin Problems*

Prepared by professional pharmacists, this brief pamphlet focuses on the essentials of skin care.

Elder-Health Program   *Free*

❧ **Sunwatch**

Gardeners, golfers, and sunbathers need to monitor their time in the sun. The Sunwatch can be clipped onto a belt, sleeve, or hat, or worn like a watch. The wearer's skin type and sunscreen's SPF are programmed into the Sunwatch. A buzzer is sounded when it's time to come in out of the sun.

Promises Kept (1090)   *$35 to $75*

❧ *"Healthy Tan"—A Fast-Fading Myth*

Because excessive tanning can lead to skin cancer, its symptoms are detailed, along with techniques for protection.

Consumer Information Center (523X)   *Free*

✦ Skin cancer booklets

The **American Cancer Society** has several free booklets on skin cancer.

Facts on Skin Cancer (2049.00)

Why You Should Know About Melanoma (2619.00)

Fry Now, Pay Later (2611.00)
American Cancer Socirty   *Free*

✦ Psoriasis

This chronic skin condition, characterized by scaly, itchy patches on the scalp, elbows, knees, and shins, is not life-threatening, but it can be extremely uncomfortable and unsightly. The national organization for this disorder makes referrals to physicians who have expertise in treating the condition, provides a number of booklets on psoriasis, offers over-the-counter and prescription psoriasis medicines through the mail at a reduced cost, and operates correspondence networks across the United States to break down the isolation of people with psoriasis.
National Psoriasis Foundation   *Free*

✦ *Sleep*

Older persons don't necessarily require 8 hours of continuous sleep each night. But for optimal mental and physical health, elderly individuals do need to ensure that they get sufficient sleep (both in terms of quantity and quality). A variety of factors, including the normal aging process, medical conditions, and personal habits, can cause sleep problems. Even so, there are still a number of things that you can do to get the sleep you need.

✦ Sedatives

These may produce dependency and mental confusion. Even over-the-counter drugs to induce sleep can slow the heart rate and exacerbate the cycle of nighttime restlessness and daytime drowsiness.

✦ Best temperature

For sleeping, set the thermostat in the mid-sixties. If air conditioning is not available during the summer, place a fan by the head.

⚘ Adjusting sleep cycle with light

The sleep laboratory at Brigham and Women's Hospital has discovered that dysfunctional sleep patterns in older persons can be changed through doses of bright light in the evening. It appears that aging causes the low point in the circadian cycle to be reached earlier, resulting in most 70-year-olds awakening before dawn (typically about 2 hours earlier than the average 30-year-old awakens naturally). By limiting light exposure in the early morning (by using light-darkening window shades) and by increasing it in the evenings with outdoor walks and brighter indoor light, you can reset your internal body clock.

⚘ Silk eye pillow

If you like to take naps during the daytime, it may be helpful to use this eye pillow to block out the light.

SelfCare Catalog (1289)   *$15 to $35*

⚘ White noise sleep machine

It can be stressful and difficult to sleep in a noisy environment (spouse snoring, traffic, television, neighbors). This machine makes a soothing whooshing sound that blocks out other noise. The more expensive ones re-create sounds from nature (such as the surf and rain) and allow the user to adjust the sound (tone, volume, rate, and intensity) to suit his or her personal preferences.

$35 to $125

Aids for Arthritis (C-33)
Comfortably Yours (2959)
Promises Kept (8031)
Solutions (60013)

⚘ *The Nature of Sleep and Its Disorders*

The booklet addresses the effects of aging on sleep, as well as such disorders as insomnia (difficulty falling or staying sleep), sleep apnea (disordered breathing during sleep), narcolepsy (excessive daytime sleepiness), restless legs syndrome (sensation of discomfort in the legs and the compelling urge to move the legs, preventing the onset or maintenance of sleep), sleepwalking (ranging from sitting up in bed to preparing a meal while at least partially asleep), sleep talking (words or sounds during sleep), nightmares (frightening dreams that usually awaken a person from the dreaming stage of sleep), sleep terrors (sudden arousal with a loud scream and physical behavior of intense fear), and sleep eating (preparing or eating food while sleeping). It includes a section on the proper use of sleep medications and when to see a doctor.

National Sleep Foundation   *Free*

❧ *A Good Night's Sleep*
This two-page publication contains a number of tips for better sleep.

National Institute on Aging   *Free*

❧ *If Only I Could Get a Good Night's Sleep!*
Changes in sleep patterns and some causes of sleep problems (stressful life events, chronic pain, medication, and alcohol abuse) are discussed in this self-help guide.

AARP Fulfillment (D14580)   *Free*

❧ *The Audio Guide to Natural Sleep*
This two-cassette set features dozens of tips to assist in easier and healthier sleeping, as well as sleep-inducing guided visualization and relaxation music. An illustrated guidebook is included.

Adventures in Cassettes (BB572)   *$5 to $15*

❧ *Restful, Revitalizing Sleep*
Falling asleep can be easier and dreams more pleasant when you listen to this audiotape at bedtime.

Effective Learning Systems, Inc.   *$5 to $15*

❧ Sleep hotline
When counting sheep doesn't seem to help, a toll-free hotline staffed by trained sleep-lab technicians can be called for advice on what to do to get a good night's sleep.

Indiana University Medical Center's Sleep Center

❧ Sleep disorder centers and clinics
If the preceding suggestions and tips aren't effective and sleep continues to be a problem, sleep-disorder specialists may need to be consulted. For a free list of accredited sleep-disorder centers and clinics, contact the **Association of Professional Sleep Societies.**

⚶ *Stroke*

More than 500,000 people suffer from cerebrovascular accidents (strokes) each year. The risk doubles with each decade after 65. The best way to deal with strokes is to prevent them from occurring. This can be accomplished by treating hypertension, lowering cholesterol, exercising, losing weight, not smoking. If a stroke does occur, the effects may be slight and temporary or permanent and very disabling.

⚶ Stroke hotline
To learn how to reduce the risk of stroke in yourself or a family member, call the toll-free number of the National Stroke Association to request their free information (such as the booklet *Stroke: Reducing Your Risk*) or to ask specific questions.
National Stroke Association   *Free*

⚶ Stroke support groups
Referrals to nearby stroke support groups are available through a network of stroke survivors, their family members, and professionals. The network also publishes the *Stroke Connection* newsletter.
Courage Stroke Network   *Free*

⚶ Stroke information
Two additional brochures are available through a pharmaceutical manufacturer: *Know the Warning Signs of Stroke* and *Stroke Risk Reduction.*
Syntex Labs   *Free*

⚶ *Stroke Prevention and Treatment*
This two-page publication profiles ways in which strokes can be prevented and treated in older Americans.
National Institute on Aging   *Free*

⚶ *Urinary Incontinence*

Loss of bladder control is not a normal consequence of the aging process, but it does occur in a sizable number of older Americans. While not an actual disease, it is a symptom of other medical conditions. It can typically be treated by pelvic muscle exercises, behavioral techniques, medications, and surgery. Unfortunately, it is estimated that more than half of all incontinent persons never seek medical help. Without effective management and treatment, the condition causes embarrassment, decreased self-esteem, depression, and social isolation.

⚘ Drugs
Some medications may interfere with bladder function. These include antidepressants and antihistamines. Consult your physician if you take these drugs and experience incontinence.

⚘ Excess weight
Being overweight by 10 percent or more can contribute to bladder control problems by causing intra-abdominal pressure. Losing weight can mimimize episodes of incontinence.

⚘ Kegel exerciser
If this padded vinyl exerciser is used for a few minutes each day, weakened pelvic floor muscles can be strengthened so that incontinency accidents are reduced. The user places the device between the legs and squeezes.

$35 to $75

adaptAbility (10050)
Comfortably Yours (5475)

⚘ Personal protection
If you experience only occasional problems with bladder control, you may not want to constantly wear a pad. A more appealing alternative can be underwear with three layers of security. Wetness is drawn away into a breathable, leakproof layer where it eventually evaporates. This underwear is available for women or men in four hip sizes: small (30 to 35 inches), medium (36 to 41 inches), large (42 to 47 inches), and extra-large (48 to 52 inches).
Comfortably Yours (G5410, panty; 5412, brief)   *$15 to $35*
Leakproof half slips which feature a vinyl-coated protective lining are also available. They're 25 inches long and come in four waist sizes: small (24 to 26 inches), medium (27 to 29 inches), large (30 to 32 inches), and extra-large (33 to 35 inches).
Comfortably Yours (2103)   *$15 to $35*

Special adult pads for men and women are available at all drugstores and medical-supply dealers. There are also disposable and washable pads for beds and chairs. While most drugstores carry a small selection of these products, mail-order supply houses offer many more choices.
Shields Mail Order Medical Supply   *Free catalog*

❧ Support groups
I Will Manage is an educational/support group that meets in many hospitals throughout the country.
Simon Foundation for Continence   *$15 to $35 annual membership*

❧ Educational materials
A large number of newsletters, books, videos, and pamphlets are available. Among the best is a 33-minute video featuring a leading urologist. *Bladder Control* explains how the urinary system works, common causes of bladder control problems, and simple techniques to improve control.
Help for Incontinent People   *$15 to $35*

❧ *Urinary Incontinence*
This two-page publication describes the causes of diminished bladder control in older persons and ways to deal with it.
National Institute on Aging   *Free*

❧ Vision

Of all the changes that occur with aging, loss of vision may be the most difficult to accept. Failing eyesight can prevent older persons from participating in the activities they enjoy (such as reading, watching television, and driving). Do everything you can to preserve and improve your vision.

❧ Visual care for the needy
By calling the toll-free hotline sponsored by the American Academy of Ophthalmology, persons who qualify for the special vision project will be given the name of a participating eye doctor in the area. Eligibility requirements are not based so much on financial need as on the lack of

> **EYE EXAM**
>
> Because persons over 60 are at high risk for glaucoma (increased fluid pressure, which can cause progressive optic nerve damage and result in gradual visual loss without any perceivable pain or pressure), they should have a professional eye exam at least every 2 years. Diabetics should have an exam at least once a year to detect diabetic retinopathy (damage to the delicate blood vessels of the retina, causing blurred/distorted vision or a total loss of sight). A full eye exam with dilated pupils is necessary for detecting the visual changes that may occur with aging.

access to an ophthalmologist (either because an eye doctor used in the past is no longer available or no eye doctor was ever consulted). Volunteer ophthalmologists bill Medicare or other insurance and accept this payment in full (or provide volunteer services at no cost to patients over 65 without insurance or the ability to pay).
National Eye Care Project

🖋 **Informational pamphlets**
Seeing Well As You Grow Older provides general information about presbyopia, spots or floaters, cataracts, glaucoma, macular degeneration, and diabetic eye problems (the pathology and available treatment). More detailed information is available in individual pamphlets (*Macular Degeneration, Diabetic Retinopathy, Cataract,* and *Glaucoma*).
American Academy of Ophthalmology   *Free (with self-addressed stamped envelope)*
Vision in the Second Fifty Years, Sunglasses, Ultraviolet Radiation, Medication Effects on the Eyes, and *Contact Lenses After 40*
American Optometric Association   *Free (with self-addressed stamped envelope)*
Vision Problems of the Aging, Cataracts, Sunglasses, and Care of Your Eyeglasses
Better Vision Institute   *Free*
Cataract in Adults: A Patient's Guide
Agency for Health Care Policy and Research Publications Clearinghouse   *Free*

The Eyes Have It reviews general principles of eye care for older adults, with an emphasis on symptoms and treatment of common eye diseases.

AARP Fulfillment (D12460)   *Free*

Large-print list of resources on vision and aging:

The Lighthouse National Center for Vision and Aging

Free (with self-addressed stamped envelope)

Aging and Your Eyes describes the ways in which vision changes with aging.

National Institute on Aging   *Free*

⚘ Protective sunglasses

Younger people may be more concerned with fashion, not function, in their sunglasses. But older persons may have eye conditions that demand sunglasses that really screen out the light. NOIR sunglasses control ultraviolet, visible, and near infrared light. One style is made to be worn alone; the other is worn over other eyeglasses. Each color has a different function.

· Amber: These general-purpose lenses, which permit 10 percent total light transmission, heighten contrast and detail, especially in flat light conditions like snow and fog.

· Gray-green: This general-purpose color allows 18 percent total light transmission. They are especially good for aphakics (persons who lack a lens after cataract removal).

· Yellow and orange: Yellow lenses have 65 percent visible light transmission, whereas orange allows only 49 percent. They protect eyes from computer glare and fluorescent light. Persons with retinitis pigmentosa, macular degeneration, or night blindness can benefit from these glasses.

· Medium gray: This color is similar to that of many less functional glasses, but permit only 32 percent visible light transmission. They help persons with macular degeneration deal with bright light.

· Dark gray: Persons who have glaucoma or who have had surgeries such as corneal transplant, radial keratomy, and cataract removal will benefit from this color, which permits 13 percent visible light transmission.

Independent Living Aids (amber, 541540; wear alone; 541550, over other eyewear; gray-green, 541542, alone; 541555, with other eyewear; yellow, 541720; orange, 541725; medium gray, 541730; dark gray, 541735)   *$5 to $15*

✿ Macular disease support network

As the leading cause of legal blindness in persons over 50 years of age, macular degeneration interferes with almost every activity of daily living (such as reading or driving a car or even recognizing faces and colors). Individuals who are trying to adjust to the restrictions and changes brought about by macular disease need support. Through a nonprofit national organization, they can keep in touch with each other by mail, if able, or by telephone. The organization's newsletter issues updates on medical advances as they occur and advises readers on the newest developments in low-vision aids.

Association for Macular Diseases, Inc.   *$15 to $35 a year*

✿ *Glaucoma*

Testing and treatment of glaucoma are discussed in this 10-page booklet prepared by the National Institute of Health. Diet, drugs, and laser surgery are profiled as viable methods of dealing with the eye condition.

Consumer Information Center (416X)   *under $5*

✿ Glaucoma support groups

The **Foundation for Glaucoma Research** can put persons with glaucoma in touch with a support peer network.   *Free*

✿ *Miscellaneous*

The following items can't be readily categorized into any of the preceding sections but are nonetheless worthy of consideration.

✿ Light

Humans need balanced full-spectrum light to live and thrive. Most people spend more than 23 hours a day indoors, where illumination rarely exceeds twilight levels. Daylight deprivation is especially common among homebound individuals, night-shift workers, and those who live in northern latitudes (where daylight hours are shorter) or in cloudy or overcast areas. Individuals who are daylight-deprived may experience trouble with their sleeping patterns (in falling and staying asleep or becoming drowsy during the day), moodiness, low energy levels, and decreased alertness.

Special light boxes, used for 20 to 60 minutes a day, can provide light of daytime intensity (early morning/late afternoon springtime levels) to put and keep internal body clocks regulated. Body clocks can be reset by carefully timed exposure to strong, bright light. Light boxes offer intense light (100 times brighter than other indoor lights) that is equivalent to standing 1 inch away from a window on a sunny summer day. The box is turned on while the person reads or watches television close by.

$350 to $600

Medic-Light, Inc.
OTT Light Systems, Inc.
SelfCare Catalog (2012)
Ordinary fluorescent lights produce only a narrow color spectrum of energy wavelengths. Full-spectrum fluorescent lights simulate natural daylight without the sun's inherent dangers. Full-spectrum bulbs, as the closest thing to natural sunlight, have been shown to alleviate the depression associated with endless winter nights in Finland. The National Institutes of Mental Health recommends a dose of sunlight in the morning and late afternoon to combat seasonal affective disorder. The 60-100-150-watt bulbs do cost more than regular incandescent bulbs but last five times longer.
OTT Light Systems, Inc.   *$5 to $15*

ꙮ Health Book
This personal health organizer enables you to keep track of your medical history. It provides sections for office visits, medicines, exams, and tests.
Promises Kept (5018)   *$15 to $35*

ꙮ The Self Audit Analyzer
Much like an accounting book for the body and mind, this organizer/diary tracks everything that affects physical and emotional health: foods, medications, exercise, sleep, mood changes, weather, and daily

events. It helps users become aware of what lifestyle changes may need to be made and can also be shared with physicians for diagnostic purposes.

B. Young   *$5 to $15*

❧ HealthDesk

Keeping track of your personal health history can be a little over-whelming. This computer program makes it easier to maintain medical records on a daily or weekly basis concerning illnesses, medications, exercise, diet, expenses, and so on. Progress in exercise, weight loss, cholesterol monitoring, and stress reduction strategies can be planned or monitored. It can be used on IBM-compatible PCs running Microsoft Windows.

HealthDesk   *$75 to $125*

❧ Home Medical Advisor

This computer software program does not replace care by physicians, but it can limit unnecessary trips to the doctor. The program begins by asking for a selection of the chief complaint from a list of 70 ailments. Then related symptoms can be entered. For example, if difficult breathing is the major complaint, other symptoms such as a cough, fever, or nausea can be added. The program asks additional questions and incorporates a patient history to help determine a diagnosis and evaluate the necessity of a visit to the doctor. Other features include a drug file with 800 prescription and nonprescription drugs and their side effects and interactions with other drugs, a poison file with anti-dotes to 500 toxic substances, an injury file detailing 130 injuries and accidents, and a disease file listing 450 illnesses and their symptoms. Versions are available for IBM-compatible and Macintosh computers.

Pixel Perfect   *$75 to $125*

❧ Nutrition, health promotion, and physical fitness programs

Special programs for older adults are offered by Area Agencies on Aging. The **National Association of State Units on Aging** can refer you to local programs in addition to sending you free publications such as *Where to Turn for Help for Older Persons* and *Nationwide Network of State and Area Agencies on Aging*.

❧ Cosmetic Surgery
Seven common cosmetic surgery procedures and their risks are pro-filed, along with questions to ask the doctor and yourself before decid-ing on surgery.
Consumer Information Center (411X)   *under $5*

❧ Cosmetic surgery information
In addition to verifying a particular physician's certification in plastic surgery and providing names, addresses, and phone numbers of 10 physicians in the caller's geographic area who perform the desired pro-cedure, the national organization of plastic surgeons has a number of pamphlets available. These include *How to Select a Plastic Surgeon; Using Cosmetics to Camouflage the Aftereffects of Surgery; An Over-view of Cosmetic Procedures; Tummy Tuck; Eyelid Surgery; Breast Enlargement and Reconstruction; Chemical Peel; Dermabrasion; Facelift; Forehead Lift; Liposuction; Nose Reshaping;* and *Tissue Ex-pansion.*
American Society of Plastic and Reconstructive Surgeons
Free

❧ Medical care while traveling
There's never a good time to become ill, but it's especially unnerving to get sick while away from home. Many older persons hesitate to travel because they don't know what they would do if they needed a physician in a strange city. A special service connects travelers with local MDs across the country for nonemergency care. The operator at the toll-free line will put a doctor in touch with the caller. Some of the physicians will even make house calls at hotels.
Medical Assistance Passport Plan (MAPP)   *$15 to $35/year*

❧ *Seeking a Second Opinion*
Before you put your health into the hands of any surgeon, obtain a second opinion to make sure that surgery is absolutely necessary. It also pays to interview more than one doctor so you have a choice in terms of personality and qualifications. A pamphlet on when and how to seek a second opinion is yours for the asking.
American College of Surgeons   *Free*

❦ *Facing Surgery? Get a Second Opinion*

This five-page booklet by the Health Care Financing Administration details the procedure of obtaining a second opinion.

Consumer Information Center (536X)   *Free*

❦ Tremors

Slight tremors of the hands or head (and occasionally the voice) tend to occur with age, but these symptoms don't necessarily indicate Parkinson's disease. More than 4 million people are affected by essential tremors. Hands shake when performing activities such as writing or eating but don't tremble when resting as they do with Parkinson's. Movement occurs at regular speed, without the muscle stiffness seen in Parkinson's. The disease cannot be cured, but it can be treated by drugs and surgery. A differential diagnosis between this disorder and Parkinson's is essential so that proper treatment can be prescribed. Referrals to neurologists and movement-disorder specialists as well as information about essential tremors are available free of charge.

International Tremor Foundation   *Free*

MEDITATION

People who meditate are well aware that the practice helps relax them, but scientists have discovered that, in addition to reducing blood pressure, meditation boosts the immune system and helps ward off bacteria, viruses, and tumors. Studies have shown that older residents of a retirement home significantly increased the strength of their immune systems when they meditated, and experienced less illnesses. Blood glucose levels can also be regulated through the practice of meditation. Schools, colleges, Y's, and health clubs teach simple but effective techniques.

3

A Safer and More Secure Life

LIFE DOES not come with any guarantees. Wish as we might for never-ending security, there are problems and pitfalls that can threaten even the best-planned and most cautious of lives. Technology, advanced though it may be, still can't control circumstances such as natural disasters like earthquakes and hurricanes.

Happily, though, there *are* some risks and dangers in our personal lives that can be minimized. It's especially important that older persons take advantage of every possible opportunity to ensure their safety. Too many senior citizens wind up in hospitals or nursing homes after being injured in accidents around the house. (Nearly 1 million people over age 65 are treated in hospital emergency rooms each year for injuries sustained at home.) Some commonsense precautions and adaptations can prevent most mishaps from occurring, so it's certainly worth some time, effort, and money to implement a number of the safety suggestions in this chapter into daily living.

While safety is generally associated with physical well-being, security has psychological implications. Older individuals need to feel that they have at least some protection against changes and hardships that would be difficult to cope with. Great wealth is probably not a major desire at this point in life, but enough money to take care of both routine and extraordinary needs (such as medical care for a major illness) is crucial. Emotional security is extremely important; peace of mind is of utmost concern as people face the challenges of the later years.

❧ Emotional Security

Peace of mind arises from the knowledge that adequate measures have been taken to ensure personal safety and financial security. But to really feel emotionally secure, older persons need to take some measures to assure their protection and well-being in case they become incapacitated. They also need to know that their wishes concerning dying and death will be carried out.

❧ Carrier Alert

Mail carriers are often willing to check on older persons to make sure that all is well when they deliver the mail 6 days of the week. You may be able to arrange for your carrier to do this. There is also a special Carrier Alert program sponsored by the Postal Service and the National Association of Letter Carriers (NALC). This is a free program for infirm seniors who live alone. An unobtrusive sticker is placed on the older person's mailbox to remind the carrier of his or her participation in the program. When the carrier makes the daily delivery, he or she checks to see if the mail from the day before has been picked up from the box. If it is still there, the cooperating Carrier Alert agency (such as a senior center or Red Cross) is notified. The agency then will attempt to contact the older person by phone or contact a friend or relative to make a visit to the home. Call the local post office to see if a Carrier Alert program is operating in your neighborhood. If it is not available where you live, call your local Area Agency on Aging to suggest that they initiate one. (The number is in the phone book, or call the **Eldercare Locator** number.) A free kit on the program's history and guidelines for implementation is available from the NALC.

National Association of Letter Carriers   *Free*

❧ Vial of Life

The American Red Cross sponsors this simple but effective program in many communities. Information about an older person's medical condition, physician, closest relative, and preferred hospital is written down and placed inside a small vial or bottle. A Vial of Life sticker on the front door alerts paramedics to look for the vial inside the refrigerator. Look in the White Pages of the phone book for the local branch and contact them to see if they run the program.

Free

✱ Emergency response services

Older people who live alone need to ensure that help will quickly be available if they should experience a bad fall, accident, or sudden illness. Several companies offer 24-hour-a-day communication services. They feature portable units that are easily installed by plugging into a modular telephone jack and an electric outlet. If help is needed, the user presses the waterproof personal help button (a 1-ounce transmitter constantly worn around the neck or the wrist). An automatic call for help is activated, placing the user in two-way voice contact with a service representative who has fast access to the individual's medical records and designated "responders" (nearby relatives, neighbors, doctors, hospital, ambulance service, police and fire departments). They immediately dispatch the needed help.

$35 to $75 a month

Lifeline Systems
MedicAlert
This © PhoneCare System requires no membership or monthly fees but does provide round-the-clock activation as needed. PhoneCare plugs into the phone like an answering machine. In an emergency, the button is pressed on the remote control device worn around the neck or carried in the pocket. When the button is pressed, the machine dials one of five previously programmed phone numbers (a neighbor, family member, or 911) and plays a prerecorded message in the user's own voice requesting assistance. When PhoneCare encounters a busy signal, gets an answering machine, or doesn't get an answer, it keeps dialing the next number on the list until a connection is made. The built-in speakerphone enables two-way conversations. It runs on a 9-volt battery and operates with a 300-foot range.
The Safety Zone (344148)   *$200 to $350*

✱ Wireless personal pager

Even persons who live with a spouse, friend, or roommate may not feel entirely safe. If they become ill or hurt in another room or outdoors, it can be difficult to summon help from the other person. An inexpensive wireless pager with a 150-foot range eliminates the need to yell for help or attention. The push-button transmitter can be clipped to the belt or pocket. The receiving unit has a belt clip as well or may be mounted on the wall or placed on a table.
ID Marketing (WPP-1)   *$35 to $75*

⚜ MedicAlert bracelet or necklace

In a medical emergency, needed care may not be rendered and fatal mistakes can be made if paramedics and physicians don't know about the patient's special medical conditions. MedicAlert provides a bracelet or neck chain engraved with MedicAlert's 24-hour hotline, the wearer's ID number, and critical medical facts (such as allergies to specific drugs, asthma, Alzheimer's, cataracts, deafness, diabetes, hypertension, pacemaker, and prescribed medications). The emergency team can quickly read the vital information and begin treatment. They can call MedicAlert once the condition is under control to obtain details of the wearer's medical records, including the phone numbers of physician, pharmacist, and family. MedicAlert also provides a wallet-sized copy of the medical records (updated each year). As a nonprofit foundation, it provides a lifetime service for a very reasonable one-time fee.

MedicAlert   *$15 to $35*

⚜ Emergency medical data card

When a sudden illness or accident occurs, the injured or ill person isn't always in a position to provide his or her medical history. Paramedics and emergency room physicians aren't able to provide the best or quickest care until they know more about existing medical problems, allergies, and medications. It would be impractical to carry your complete medical chart around with you at all times in case of an emergency, but you can easily furnish health care providers with the essential highlights of your medical history when you carry a Lens-Card. This plastic card looks like a charge card and can easily be carried in a purse or wallet. To access the medical information, the caregiver simply bends the card in half and holds it up to any light source. Your personalized microfilmed medical history can then be read with the powerful magnifying lens on the opposite side of the card. Information that can appear on the card includes allergies, medical conditions, a partial EKG tracing, emergency contacts, donor information, preferred hospital, personal physician, emergency contacts, and family members to notify.

LensCard Systems   *$5 to $15*

⚜ Implant registry

Modern medical technology has saved many lives, but it doesn't always lead to peace of mind. Many persons with implants (including pacemakers, heart valves, and artificial joints) worry about the safety and efficacy of these replacement parts. To make sure that you're immediately notified if the implant is ever recalled, sign up with a national registry that will alert you to any new developments.

International Implant Registry   *$15 to $35 enrollment; $5 to $15 annual renewal (free memberships to those who can't afford the fees)*

⚘ Living will

If you become terminally ill, you may not want to be kept alive by heroic measures such as feeding tubes, mechanical respiration, chemotherapy, kidney dialysis, blood transfusions, electrical or mechanical resuscitation, and diagnostic tests. Many states have "living will" laws stipulating that hospitals find out a patient's wishes when he or she is admitted. But even if you live in one of these states, many state living wills come into effect only when the patient is actually dying (which excludes advanced Alzheimer's or vegetative patients). Other state living wills do not allow individuals to refuse tube feeding. To ensure that your wishes can be known and followed, it is recommended that you fill out a general living will drafted by the Choice in Dying, a state living will, and a durable power of attorney for health care authorizing someone else to make decisions for you when you can't. These documents are easy to fill out and do not have to be drafted by an attorney. They can be personalized according to your own wishes, noting what you don't want in terms of life-prolonging treatment and what you *do* want (such as pain medications, even if they dull consciousness and indirectly shorten the remaining life, and the choice of dying at home). Once filled out, copies should be kept in several safe places and given to your physician.

Choice in Dying   *Free—all three forms available (contribution encouraged)*

⚘ Legal rights

Lawyers who specialize in "elder law" can ensure that an older person's rights are protected when appointing someone to act as a durable power of attorney, as well as in other legal matters. *Questions & Answers When Looking for an Elder Law Attorney* is a brochure that can be obtained by sending a self-addressed stamped envelope to the association of these specialized attorneys.

National Academy of Elder Law Attorneys   *Free*

Free legal services are available to persons over 60 who are unable to pay for an attorney. Contact your local bar association (find it in the White Pages of the phone book listed under your city, county, or state) and ask about *pro bono* services from attorneys who volunteer their time. Local area agencies on aging can also provide names of lawyers who can help with public benefits, housing, consumer fraud, elder abuse, conservatorship, and health care problems.

❧ Values history form
This supplements (but does not replace) traditional advance directives such as living wills and durable power of attorney. Whereas a living will asks how you would like to die, the values history asks how you want to *live.* It explores individual attitudes toward illness, independence, living environment, finances, personal relationships, dying, and death. The answers you give can help someone else make decisions for you based on what you would want if you cannot make decisions for yourself or express your wishes. The document can be given to your lawyer or attached to your medical records or durable power of attorney.

Institute of Public Law *under $5*

❧ Medical directive
A medical ethicist and physician designed this thought-provoking method for exploring the type of medical care an individual would want if he or she became disabled. Because there are no easy answers and actual situations can be extremely complex, a wide range of choices are provided, including one that concludes "I am undecided." Filling out the medical directive enables older persons and their families to become aware of each other's feelings and desires. It can assist in determining how a living will should be filled out.

Harvard Medical School Health Letter *$5 to $15*
(plus self-addressed stamped envelope)

❧ Hospice
Terminally ill patients and their families often feel more comfortable, both emotionally and physically, when the patient is cared for at home. Hospices provide medical care for dying patients as well as counseling and supportive services for the patient and family members. Hospice

Hotline, a toll-free, referral line, directs callers to hospice services in their area.

National Hospice Organization *Free*

❧ Funeral planning

You may wish to plan and prepay your funeral. Talk candidly with your relatives so they become aware of your wishes. You may wish to choose hymns or write your own epitaph. **AARP Fulfillment** offers a free booklet on pre-need funeral planning, *Product Report: Prepaying Your Funeral?* (D13188), as well as on planning for and buying *Cemetery Goods and Services* (D13162). The **Council of Better Business Bureaus'** booklet *Tips on Planning a Funeral* is another helpful resource. The cost is under $5.

❧ Organ donation

Body parts (such as corneas, lungs, and blood vessels) can be donated for use in medical research or transplantation. You can obtain a uniform donor card free of charge that will enable them to designate your wishes. This will register you as a donor. Specific organs and tissues can be designated, or the entire body can be willed to medical science.

The Living Bank *Free*

❧ *Planning Ahead*

Change is a fact of life. Planning for major changes can make them easier to deal with when they do occur. This booklet provides helpful information on preparing for illness or injury; divorce or death of a mate; financial setback.

AARP Fulfillment (D14579) *Free*

❧ *Tomorrow's Choices*

This comprehensive guide helps individuals and families plan now for important decisions that may need to be made in the future. Living arrangements, health care, finances, and legal needs are addressed.

AARP Fulfillment (D13479) *Free*

❧ *Financial Security*

Most older persons have worked hard all their lives so they could be financially secure in their old age. But even the most careful planning and scrimping doesn't guarantee a trouble-free retirement. Inflation, health problems, and unexpected expenses can make it difficult for you to maintain the lifestyle you enjoyed in your earlier years or which you hoped to attain in your later years. Take advantage of the following suggestions to increase your financial security to make these years as worry-free as possible.

❧ Income tax information
You may be entitled to certain tax breaks. Call the toll-free number for the **IRS** to receive their free publication (#554) *Tax Information for Older Americans.*

❧ Income tax preparation
The Tax-Aide program run by volunteers from the American Association of Retired Persons provides tax counseling and preparation at no charge to senior citizens. Both federal and state tax returns can be completed at the tax centers, which are set up in approximately 9,000 shopping centers and community facilities (such as libraries) around the country. They operate February 1 through April 15. The local IRS office can refer you to the nearest Tax-Aide center or call the toll-free **IRS** number.

❧ VITA program
Free tax assistance is also available through the IRS. Professional and student accountants assist older individuals in filing their returns from January through the April deadline. Call the IRS tax hotline for the location of the nearest Volunteer Income Tax Assistance (VITA) program.
IRS tax hotline   *Free*

❧ Verifying a bank or S&L's health
To ensure that your bank, savings and loan association, or credit union isn't about to go under, there are two 800 numbers that, for a nominal

fee, will provide written information about an institution's rating and fiscal health. It's especially important to learn more about an institution's financial stability when it's offering a high interest rate.

$5 to $15 per rating

Veribanc
Bauer Financial Reports

⚴ Questions or complaints about banks

Call the **FDIC** consumer hotline if you have any concerns about your bank. All information is provided free of charge.

⚴ Checking on the health of an insurance company

For a small fee, you can call an 800 number that will provide information on the stability and prosperity of your insurance company.

Weiss Research   *$15 to $35 per report*

⚴ Credit unions/organizations

If you belonged to a credit union while you were employed, you know that they are an excellent source for lower-cost loans, as well as for investing money. But membership in the credit union may have lapsed. At no cost to you, the National Association for Retired Credit Union People (NARCUP) will help you rejoin the original credit union or locate one close by.

Membership in NARCUP is limited to retirees 50 and older who were or currently still are credit union members. Among the benefits of belonging are

- subscription to *Prime Times* (quarterly magazine)

- subscription to *NARCUP Newsletter*

- access to MediMail (discount mail-order pharmacy)

- accident insurance

- reduced rate on Car/Puter (computerized car pricing service)

- travel services, including discounted travel packages tours, hotels, and car rentals

- eye care plan

- emergency cash service

· eligibility to purchase Medicare, supplemental, and whole life insurance through the organization

National Association for Retired Credit Union People   *$5 to $15 a year*

❧ Charity scams
Too many older people donate money to disreputable charities. Be sure to make informed decisions about who really deserves your money. Contact the **Philanthropic Advisory Service** to find out whether the charity you're considering is legitimate.

Free

The **Council of Better Business Bureaus** will also provide free philanthropic advisory reports (information on the fundraising practices of national nonprofit charitable organizations).

❧ Social Security
For answers to questions, solutions to problems, or just an explanation about benefits, the **Social Security Administration** has a toll-free number for you to call. It can also be beneficial to have your Social Security check directly deposited into your bank or savings and loan account. After filling out Form SF-1199 at the financial institution, you won't have to worry about cashing or losing your checks.

Information about Social security is also available from the following sources.

$5 to $15

Social Security Manual, from **National Underwriter Company**

Consumer's Guide to Social Security Benefits Including Medicare, from **Consumer Education Research Center**

Your Social Security Benefits, from **Retirement Living Publishing**

The Social Security Book: What Every Woman Absolutely Needs to Know, from **AARP Fulfillment** (D14117)   *Free*

Social Security: Crucial Questions & Straight Answers, from **AARP Fulfillment** (D13640)   *Free*

Social Security Medicare and Pensions, from **Nolo Press**

Understanding Social Security, from **Social Security Administration**   *Free*

❧ Supplemental Security Income

SSI payments are made to people who are blind, persons with disabilities, and people 65 years of age or older who have limited income and resources. A free booklet (*Social Security Income*) in either English or Spanish explains SSI, eligibility, and the application procedure.

Social Security Administration   *Free*

❧ Medicare

Basic information on Medicare eligibility, benefits, and those services and products not covered are detailed in *Medicare* (#05-10043). Another booklet, *Guide to Health Insurance for People with Medicare* (#02110), provides hints for shopping for private health insurance as well as an explanation of Medicare coverage. *Your Medicare Handbook: A Comprehensive Guide to Your Medicare Hospital and Medical Insurance Benefits* (#10050) offers a detailed description of Medicare benefits.

Health Care Financing Administration   *Free*

Additional free information is available from **AARP Fulfillment.** There are three booklets that address Medicare, Medicaid, and Medigap:

Knowing Your Rights (D12330)

Medicare: What It Covers, What It Doesn't (D13133)

Medigap: Medicare Supplemental Insurance—A Consumer's Guide (D14042)

❧ *Managing Your Health Care Finances: Getting the Most Out of Medicare & Medigap Insurance*

In 88 pages, this guide explains Medicare, its gaps in protection, and what to look for in supplemental coverage. It also provides a system for organizing medical bills, tracking them through the reimbursement system, and appealing Medicare denials.

United Seniors Health Cooperative   *$5 to $15*

❧ Medigap hotline

The toll-free hotline answers questions about Medigap insurance (health insurance to supplement Medicare). It also takes reports of

suspected Medigap and Medicare fraud. A Medigap booklet is available for the asking.
Health Care Financing Administration   *Free*

⚹ National Insurance Consumer Helpline
Information is provided on the toll-free helpline on a wide range of health insurance issues, including continuation of group health benefits, major medical, Medicare supplements, and long-term care insurance. Consumer complaints are referred to appropriate sources. Among their publications are *A Consumer's Guide to Medicare Supplement Insurance* and *A Consumer's Guide to Long-Term Care Insurance*.
Health Insurance Association of America   *Free*

⚹ *Health Care and Finances: A Guide for Adult Children and Their Parents*
This 21-page booklet by the United States Department of Agriculture reviews various health care choices and financial considerations for older adults.
Consumer Information Center (440X)   *under $5*

⚹ Revocable living trust
This is a very flexible means of managing money and property that relieves you of the day-to-day duties of monitoring your assets. All or part of your assets can be placed under the control of the trustee. If you choose, you can remain in control of your assets as the initial trustee for as long as you're able. You can put money in or take it out, change it, or revoke it while it is in effect. When you're no longer capable or when you die, the person named as the trustee takes over. A relative can be named as the trustee or a professional trustee such as a bank can be named (for an annual management fee of about 1 percent of the value of the trust's assets). One of the major advantages of a revocable living trust is the avoidance of probate, saving time and money as opposed to transferring assets under a will. Contact an attorney for help in drawing up a living trust.

⚹ Power of attorney
You may want to grant power of attorney to your children so that they have access to your bank account and can deposit and write checks for

you if you can't. You can go to a lawyer to file for power of attorney, but most stationery stores have forms for general or limited power of attorney. The **American Association of Retired Persons (AARP)** can provide information and copies of power-of-attorney forms. Ask for a free copy of publication D13895.

⚘ AARP benefits

Joining the American Association of Retired Persons for a minimal fee will enable you to receive travel discounts, generic prescriptions through the mail, and insurance (auto, health, homeowners) bargains. Membership is available to anyone 50 or older. More than 32 million older adults belong to the organization and one of its 3,700 local chapters. Membership also includes the bimonthly magazine *Modern Maturity*.

AARP Membership   *$5 to $15 a year*

⚘ Association of Retired Americans

This organization's goal is to enhance lives through group benefits. Persons 50 and older may take advantage of any of the following:

· reduced price accidental health insurance

· discounts on eyeglasses

· discounts on hearing aids

· reduced prices of home health care products

· low-interest charge cards

· discounts on travel (hotel, airfare, cruises)

                                                          $15 to $35 a year

⚘ Mature Outlook

Sponsored by Sears and open to people over 50, membership entitlements include discounts on products and services in Sears stores, access to a mail-order pharmacy, no-fee traveler's checks, discounts on hotel rooms/car rentals/accident insurance, and discounted travel opportunities. Members also receive the *Mature Outlook* magazine and newsletter in alternating months.

Mature Outlook   *$5 to $15 a year*

❧ Freebies

Using just a few of the many suggestions in Linda Bowman's book, *Freebies (& More) for Those Over Fifty*, will more than recoup the price of the book. A great number of money-saving opportunities are available in the travel and entertainment fields. The book can be ordered through the publisher's toll-free number. It can also be special ordered at bookstores.

Probus Press   *$5 to $15*

❧ On Your Own: A Widow's Passage to Emotional and Financial Well-Being

Written by Alexandra Armstrong and Mary R. Donahue, this hardcover book enables women (especially widows) to take charge of all aspects of their finances.

Dearborn Trade   *$15 to $35*

❧ Finances After 50—Financial Planning for the Rest of Your Life

Your entire financial situation can be organized and managed with the help of this self-study guide. Income, expenses, insurance (health, life, and property), taxes, investments, and estate preservation are addressed in a comprehensive manner.

United Seniors Health Cooperative   *$5 to $15*

❧ How to Stretch Your Retirement Dollar

This 40-minute VHS video and 116-page book provide instruction on cutting taxes, increasing income, boosting savings, dealing with medical costs, protecting assets from inflation, reducing living costs, tapping home equity, and avoiding high estate taxes and probate costs.

United Seniors Health Cooperative   *$15 to $35*

❧ Investing

Investing needs change as people age. A 60-year-old person invests differently than someone who is 30 or 40. A free booklet, *How to Invest: A Guide for Investors Aged 50 and Over*, provides more information. The booklet is a product of the AARP's investment services program.

Scudder   *Free*

✥ Staying Independent: Planning for Financial Independence in Later Life

If retirement is still a number of years away, this guide can help evaluate the feasibility of retirement at that time. Prepared by the U.S. Department of Agriculture, it suggests some ways to prepare for retirement.

Consumer Information Center (440X)   *under $5*

✥ Financial planners

Stockbrokers can provide investment advice, but it's not always part of a cohesive plan for financial security. All too many brokers call up with a "hot tip" or new product without looking at the total picture. Because they earn variable commissions on the products they sell, some brokers are more likely to recommend those products that pay them the highest commissions.

For a complete financial plan that takes your best interests into account rather than those of the person selling the investment, consider having a detailed financial plan drawn up by a certified financial planner. Fee-only planners (as opposed to those who earn commissions only or a combination of fees and commissions) may charge fees of up to $3,000, but they will develop a plan of action for saving and investing money that is fully personalized. This plan will enable you to successfully manage your money for the rest of your life. Either of the two professional associations for financial planners can provide referrals to local practitioners.

Institute of Certified Financial Planners (ICFP)   *Free*
International Association of Financial Planners (IAFP)   *Free*

✥ Investing newsletters

There is no shortage of newsletters that each tout their own theories and suggestions for investing, but only one is specifically geared for the older investor.

Mature Investor   *$5 to $15 for 3 months*

✥ Learning about investing

Many adult education programs offer basic courses about investing. It's also possible to study at home with a 10-lesson course that examines investment risk and return; investment alternatives; common stock analysis; options; bonds; mutual funds; currencies, metals, and gems; futures and commodities; real estate; and collectibles. There are investment fundamentals video courses as well, which provide 6 hours of instruction in basic investment concepts; the language of investments; investment choices; stock analysis and research; pooled investment products such as mutual funds; and developing a personal financial plan.

American Association of Individual Investors   *$75 to $125*
home study course or video course

❧ Investing clubs
More than 50 local chapters meet in metropolitan areas to discuss a variety of investment topics.

American Association of Individual Investors   *$35 to $75*
annual dues

There are also 9,400 investment clubs affiliated with the National Association of Investors. In each club, 10 to 20 members meet to discuss investments, and each contributes $20 or more every month for investing in securities as a group. Contact the national association to learn about a group near you.

National Association of Investors Corporation

❧ Home equity conversion
Over 80 percent of homes owned by persons 65 and older are "free and clear," with no outstanding mortgage. Persons who are "house rich and cash poor" can improve their cash flow by borrowing on the equity. A 5- to 10-year loan for this reverse mortgage can be arranged through a bank or savings and loans. Interest is charged at the market rate. You receive a monthly income. At the end of the loan period, you can sell the home or refinance the loan. Most loans require no repayment as long as you remain in your home. If the owner(s) dies before the loan is paid back, the estate becomes responsible for repaying the loan and any charges. Contact the American Association of Retired Persons for their bulletin *Home-Made Money—A Consumer's Guide to Home Equity Conversion* and a list of FHA-approved lenders.

AARP Home Equity Information Center   *Free*

The **National Center for Home Equity Conversion** (NCHEC) offers a free booklet, *A Financial Guide for Reverse Mortgages,* and a comprehensive guide, *Retirement Income on the House: Cashing in on Your Home with a "Reverse" Mortgage.*

Free (booklet)/$15 to $35 (book)

⚸ Tax implications of relocation

Many older persons relocate out of state to be in a warmer climate or to live closer to their children and grandchildren. Before you make such a move, you should consider the tax implications. A free guide (*Relocation Tax Guide: State Tax Information for Relocation Decisions*) provides state-by-state information on a variety of taxes: sales, property, estate, inheritance, and personal income.

AARP Fulfillment (D13400)   *Free*

⚸ Senior Community Service Employment Program (SCSEP)

Part-time employment is a financial necessity for some older persons who need to supplement their Social Security. SCSEP provides part-time opportunities in community service employment for persons over 55 who are unemployed and low-income (as determined by a Department of Health and Human Services formula). All 50 states, the District of Columbia, and Puerto Rico have SCSEP projects in public or private nonprofit agencies (dealing with education, legal services, health, welfare, social services, public protection, and so on). After training, participants are paid minimum wage or better for about 20 to 25 hours of work a week. A maximum of 1,300 hours can be compensated each year. Whenever possible, participants are eventually assisted into transitioning to private, unsubsidized employment. The local Area Agency on Aging or the State Department on Aging can provide more information. Use the **Eldercare Locator** number sponsored by the National Association of Agencies on Aging to find a local agency.

⚸ Penny-pinching newsletters

Older persons on fixed incomes often have to watch their spending. Even when it's not an absolute financial necessity, it can still be psychologically and fiscally rewarding to save money on necessities and luxuries. Monthly newsletters can provide many valuable tips. Send a postage stamp with a request for a sample before purchasing a year's subscription.

$5 to $15

Cheapskate Monthly
Skinflint News
The Tightwad Gazette

❧ Couponing/refunding newsletters
Shoppers of all ages can appreciate the money that coupons and re-fund offers save on food and consumer good purchases. Newsletters can suggest ways to maximize the savings. They include information on current rebate, sample, and coupon offers.
Refundle Bundle   *$5 to $15 for six issues*

❧ Bartering
A bartering system is a terrific idea for senior citizens who have limited money but plenty of time and talent. In exchange for lawn care or plumbing services, older persons can cook, babysit, run errands, or help business owners with mailing or bookkeeping. Time Dollars are a special system of tax-exempt credits that are earned by performing work for others and that can then be used to buy other services. Write for a brochure which explains the system in detail.
Time Dollar Network   *under $5 (plus self-addressed stamped envelope)*

❧ Direct deposit
Direct Deposit: A Consumer's Guide explains why direct deposit can be advantageous. It also describes legal protection in the event of an error. The four-page guide is prepared by the National Reserve Board.
Consumer Information Center (432X)   *under $5*

❧ Consumer scams
It's an unfortunate fact of our times that there are a lot of people who would like to take your money without giving you what you thought you'd be getting. Whenever you're contacted by mail or phone with offers that seem too good to be true, you can call a toll-free line for clarification of the offer and information about current scams.
National Consumer League   *Free*

There are also a couple of brochures that instruct on recognizing a scam, dealing with attempts at fraud, and reporting swindles. Ask for *Swindlers Are Calling* from the **National Consumers League** or *Consumer Information* from the **American Telemarketing Association;** both are free with a self-addressed stamped envelope. Local **Better Business Bureaus** provide information about consumer satisfaction and dissatisfaction with individual businesses in the community. They also investigate consumer complaints. Their services are free.

❧ Personal and Household Safety

A lot of us have a false sense of security in our homes. We convince ourselves that home is the *one* place where we're truly safe.

Statistics show a different story. Many accidents occur at home; some are serious enough to cause permanent injury or even death. The kitchen, bathroom, and stairs can be especially dangerous for older people. And no community is immune from crime. Unwanted intruders can invade any home and may target the elderly in particular. Personal protection is also needed when we leave home and go out into the community.

ALARMS AND SIGNALS

You may not understand much about modern technology, but that doesn't mean you shouldn't take advantage of it. A variety of devices can make your home a safer place. These include smoke detectors, security alarms, and gas leak detectors. Portable personal protection devices are profiled in the Personal Protection section later in this chapter.

❧ Smoke detectors

Every floor of your home should have a smoke detector, installed either on the ceiling or on the wall 6 to 12 inches below the ceiling. It's especially important to place them in or near the bedroom. The instructions that come with the smoke detector will advise you on how to install it, but it should be located away from air vents. Make sure the batteries are checked and replaced regularly. A good rule of thumb is to replace the batteries when you set your clocks for daylight savings time. Detectors should also be vacuumed once a month so that dust and cobwebs don't damage their sensitivity.

⚶ Smoke detectors for the hard-of-hearing

A smoke detector doesn't do much good if a hard-of-hearing person doesn't notice it. But there are some special detectors that use visual (a flashing light) as well as auditory cues.

$35 to $75

Hear You Are, Inc. (SM0757)
Maxi Aids (11347)
TTY of Carolina, Inc.
Another alert system for the hearing-impaired uses a bed shaker simultaneously with a bright strobe light and loud buzzer when the smoke detector alarm is activated. The Alert Plus also alerts users to ringing of the phone, knocking at the door, and sounding of the alarm clock.
TTY/TDD Store   *$200 to $350*
There is also a smoke alarm that sounds twice as loud as conventional alarms to provide a greater warning.
Hear You Are, Inc. (SM0756)   *$15 to $35*

⚶ Home safety drill

Change Your Clock, Change Your Battery is a free booklet which describes how to make sure that all safety equipment (especially smoke detectors) is functioning properly.
Energizer Batteries   *Free*

⚶ "Watchdog" security alarm

This sensitive electronic alarm can be placed on the inside metal doorknob of any nonmetal door. A piercing alarm (to wake up anyone inside the home and scare off the prospective intruder) is triggered when anyone outside touches the knob or tries to insert a key. It runs on a 9-volt battery.
Enrichments (9936)   *$15 to $35*

⚶ Barking dog alarm

Most burglars won't break into homes with barking dogs. Rather than risk getting bitten or waking up the home's occupants or neighbors, they'll move on to another house that seems less threatening. But many people don't want the expense or responsibility of a dog, particularly as they advance in years. This alarm system provides an electronic alternative to man's best friend. The motion detector is installed on the outside of the home. A wire connects the sensor to the master unit plugged into a wall outlet inside the home. When someone gets within about 50 feet of the house, the infrared motion sensor is triggered and the "dog" starts barking. Detection is possible through wood, brick, glass, or plaster walls. The system can be put on an automatic timer to be activated at a set schedule or it can be turned on and off as desired.

$75 to $125

Home Automation Laboratories (7210)
The Safety Zone (234007)

❧ Motion detector and speaker
The wall-mounted Telko S002 Motion Activated Alarm and Chime features an infrared sensor that detects motion and heat up to 60 feet away (within a 110-foot arc). An alarm is sounded when the device is triggered. A shield allows small pets to roam freely in certain areas of the house without activating the alarm. A keypad allows users to turn the alarm on and off when entering and exiting. The system runs on a 9-volt battery. An auxiliary 120-decibel speaker can be mounted outside the house to alert neighbors while the alarm is going off inside the house.

The Safety Zone (233012, alarm)   *$35 to $75*
                      (SY052, speaker)   *$15 to $35*

❧ Vox II emergency alert system
Once this motion sensor alarm is placed in an entrance hall, stairway, or other potentially hazardous spot in the home, any motion within 6 feet will automatically trigger the user's personally recorded message (up to 60 seconds). This is helpful for the visually impaired or those who aren't very alert when getting out of bed in the middle of the night for a trip to the bathroom. It can prevent a fall down the stairs or bumping into something that could be dangerous.

Maxi Aids (39500)   *$350 to $600*

⚐ Doorstop alarm

This portable doorstop prevents any door at home or in a hotel from being opened *and* sets off a piercing alarm if someone tries to enter. It runs on two AA batteries.

Maxi Aids (94697)   *$5 to $15*
The Safety Zone (324161)

⚐ Mini window alarm

The same magnetic sensor technology used in expensive alarm systems is utilized in this window alarm—at a fraction of the cost. Once the sensor is attached to the window and the small alarm to the window or patio door frame, opening the window breaks the magnetic seal and sets off an 80-decibel alarm. It can be turned on and off with a switch so that the window can be used without activating the alarm. The alarm easily installs with double-backed tape and runs on two button cell batteries.

The Safety Zone (234008)   *$15 to $35*

⚐ DoorScope

Most peepholes provide a very distorted view of the person on the other side of the door, often making it impossible to identify who it is. DoorScope offers a large-scale undistorted view even when the person is standing up to 7 feet away from the door (without revealing your presence). It installs easily on doors up to 2 inches thick.

The Safety Zone (233034)   *$35 to $75*

⚐ Observation system

Most doors have peepholes, but it can be difficult to really see who's outside. This system provides full protection through clear video and audio monitoring. The compact camera with built-in microphone is installed in the yard, driveway, or at the door so that visitors can be screened and intruders prevented from proceeding any further. The monitor can be switched to view up to four areas consecutively. Two-way conversation is possible with an additional special intercom.

The Safety Zone (243058)   *$350 to $600 (includes monitor,
camera, outdoor intercom, camera stand, cable, and connectors)*
(243065, two-way intercom: $15 to $35)

❧ Scarecrow simulated alarm control system

An expensive alarm system isn't always necessary to deter would-be burglars. Many security experts feel that it's sufficient just to give the impression of having a professional system. This can be simulated through warning decals that the premises are protected by an electronic security system and a control panel with a flashing LED. The system runs on two AA batteries and mounts readily on any surface. It can be turned on and off with a key.

Home Automation Laboratories (7351)   *$15 to $13*
The Safety Zone (233046)   *$35 to $75*

❧ Emergency flashing light

Police, ambulance, and fire departments can more quickly locate your home with this flashing light. It easily screws into any outside light fixture and works with all regular bulbs and switches. It works as a regular light when the wall switch is turned on one time. When the switch is turned on twice, the outside light flashes on and off continuously. It may be helpful to put a note by the light switch as a reminder to turn the switch on two times in an emergency.

$15 to $35

Aids for Arthritis (H-16)
Maxi Aids (12911)

❧ Gas-sniffer alarm

An 85-decibel alarm sounds if gas levels fall below their lower explosive limits in the home. People with all-electric homes obviously don't need this, but it is important for those who heat or cook with natural gas, propane, or butane. The alarm shuts off automatically when gas levels fall below detection range, and then resets itself. It's installed simply by plugging it into a standard AC wall unit.

The Safety Zone (122161)   *$75 to $125*

BATHROOM

Bathtubs can be one of the most dangerous places in the home for the older person. Many broken hips have been caused by slipping in the tub. An alternative to using the tub or shower is a sponge bath in bed or on the toilet, but this is never as satisfying or as cleansing as a real bath or shower. Happily, there are a number of ways to make bathing safer.

Using the toilet is a very basic self-care activity, but it can be unsafe and uncomfortable for older people with arthritis, muscle weakness, and other problems.

ℳ Small electrical appliances

Hair dryers, shavers, and curling irons should be unplugged when not in use. Always unplug the appliance after using it, or consider an alternative means of securely storing the appliance (such as an overhead shelf or hook on the wall). Don't forget that a lethal shock can be caused by a plugged-in appliance falling into water in the sink or bathtub, even if it isn't turned on.

ℳ Hot water heaters

Water heaters are routinely set at 150°F, but such hot water can cause burns (especially in older people who may not be able to move quickly enough to adjust the water). Check your water heater and set it at a lower temperature, such as 120°F.

ℳ Shower Gard Anti-Scald Shower Valve

To guard against hot-water scalding, this special valve can be easily installed on any showerhead or faucet. The valve instantly reacts to scalding hot water by cutting off the spray to a trickle when the temperature reaches 110°F and before it reaches 120°F.

$15 to $35

Home Trends (E801)
Maxi Aids (13420)

ℳ Aqua Shield Anti-Scald Shower Products

In addition to offering an anti-scald valve, the company also has a hand-held shower that offers fail-safe scald protection while bathing. Extreme hot water is reduced to a slight trickle until the hot water is readjusted by the user. Shut-off temperatures can be set at 110° or 120°F. The device can be easily installed at home.

Showersafe, Inc.   *$15 to $35 valve; $35 to $75 hand-held shower*

ℳ Bathmat or safety treads

People of all ages should always use these in their tubs and showers to prevent slipping. They're available at all discount department and

> **GLASS SHOWER DOORS**
> Accidents may happen if glass doors are grabbed for stability in getting in and out of the tub or shower. They can easily pop out of their tracks and shatter or crush a bather who has fallen. Replace these doors with a shower curtain or folding plastic door.

home improvement stores. Some mats are extra-size so they cover the entire tub and grip tight with hundreds of suction cups.

$15 to $35

Home Trends (H804, shower; H805, bath)
Joan Cook Housewares (7157, tub; 7156, shower)
The Safety Zone (132124, bath; 132123, shower)

⚘ Ultra-Safe bathtub finish
This invisible finish takes just 9 minutes to apply. It makes a porcelain tub nonslippery for 10 years. (The finish does not work on fiberglass or resurfaced tubs.)
Solutions (A784363)　　　　　　　　　　　　　　*$5 to $15*

⚘ Slip-X Splash Control
Bathroom floors can be very slippery when wet. This device attaches to the top ends of the shower curtain and wraps the curtain within the shower enclosure or bathtub to prevent leakage onto the floor outside the tub or shower.
Enrichments (9964)　　　　　　　　　　　　　　*$5 to $15*

⚘ Tub/shower splash guards
This white plastic guard fits in the outer corners of the tub to prevent water from getting on the floor and causing slippery conditions. Eleven inches high, it installs easily without tools.
Home Trends (F803)　　　　　　　　　　　*$5 to $15 a pair*

⚘ Bathtub bumper cushion
The rim of a tub is a hard, unforgiving surface when a person falls in the tub. To prevent bathroom bumps in getting in or out of the tub, this slip-resistant vinyl pad can be placed over the rim.

$15 to $35

Aids for Arthritis (J-39)
Taylor Gifts (459)

⚜ Bathtub transfer benches

Two legs of the bench rest on the bathroom floor outside the tub, while two rest inside the tub. Instead of stepping directly into the tub, you can sit down on the bench and then slide over.

$75 to $125

Aids for Arthritis (D-17)
Cleo, Inc. (83-1056)
Sears HealthCare (11750)

⚜ Tub seat

Featuring an anodized aluminum frame and padded vinyl seat slats and back, this seat allows the older person to sit while showering.

$35 to $75

Comfortably Yours
Enrichments (6547)
Sears HealthCare

⚜ Quick clamp tub grab bar

This bar easily clamps onto the edge of the tub without tools. Made of textured coated steel, it assists the older person in getting into the tub safely. These bars are available at medical supply stores or in catalogs.

$35 to $75

Comfortably Yours (3492)
Enrichments (6500)
Sears HealthCare (10246)

⚜ Grab bars

The built-in soap dish was never intended to be used for support. Too many people have grabbed onto these soap dishes attempting to break a fall and wound up pulling them out of the wall. Install straight or angled bars on the wall of the bathtub/shower so that you may safely enter and exit.

$15 to $35

Cleo, Inc. (84-1002 to 1008)
Enrichments (6285)
Sears HealthCare

Install them yourself, or hire a handyman to put them up. There are also grab bars that easily install over the 5- to 7-inch rim of the tub. Some have a high section (18 inches) to provide a safety grip while standing and getting in or out of the tub, as well as a low section (6 inches) to assist when sitting in the tub and rising.

$35 to $75

Access to Recreation (NC28380)
Cleo, Inc. (83-1149)
Sears HealthCare (1180)
Custom grab bars may be needed for tubs of special dimensions. Send the dimensions and a description of any physical limitations. The company will provide referrals of professional installers upon request.
Adaptations   *prices vary*

⚘ Little octopus
These rubber pads have 68 suction cups that can hold soap securely on the wall or in a soap dish and make sure that it doesn't fall onto the floor, where it can cause you to slip. They're available at discount stores, some pharmacies, and catalogs.
Enrichments (1259)   *under $5 for three*

⚘ Magnetic soap holder
Another way to avoid any mishaps with a bar of soap is to place it in a magnetic holder. This holder has many advantages over a soap dish. Once the metal clip is attached to the bar of soap, it holds the soap more securely and completely eliminates any mess; the soap dries in minutes as it's suspended in the air by a powerful magnet.

$5 to $15

Home Trends (L805)
Maxi Aids (11180)

⚘ Soap/shampoo/conditioner/lotion dispenser
To avoid an accident from dropping a bottle or spilling a slippery liquid in the shower or tub, consider a dispenser, which can easily be installed on the wall and filled with your favorite products. Up to 14 fluid ounces can be held in each of the four sections. A touch of a button dispenses the liquids.

$15 to $35

Promises Kept (2041)
Solutions (4866)

⚘ Safety facial hair trimmer
Even if you have poor eyesight or unsteady hands, you won't cut yourself while trimming hair from the nose, ears, and eyebrows with this

precision trimmer. Unlike sharp scissors and tweezers, the safety groomer has a tiny inner blade that rotates within a protective chamber and never touches tender skin. It's cordless and runs on one AA battery.

$15 to $35

Promises Kept (1477)
Solutions (5542)
The Safety Zone (340334)
The Vermont Country Store

❧ Raised toilet seat

These white enameled seats securely clamp onto standard and elongated toilet bowls and add from 3 to 6 inches of extra height, enabling you to get on and off the toilet more easily. Some have armrests attached to the seat. They're available at convalescent aid stores and through catalogs.

$35 to $75

Aids for Arthritis (J-16)
Solutions (A784371)

❧ Toilet safety rails

The rails make sitting down or rising from the toilet much safer and easier in the presence of knee or hip problems. They can be quickly installed by unbolting the toilet seat and placing the bracket between the seat and the bowl, giving something to hold onto on either side.

$35 to $75

Aids for Arthritis (B-33)
Enrichments (5269)
Sears HealthCare (1181)

BEDROOM

Beds are usually considered to be very safe places. Even so, there are some hazards and accidents that can occur in bed. Take the following precautions to ensure that your bedroom is as safe as possible.

❧ Fire-resistant mattress covers and pillows

These are available wherever linens are sold.

❦ Smoker's robot

Smoking is no healthier for you than it is for your children or grand-children. But if you are a confirmed smoker, at least eliminate the dangers of smoking in bed. The smoker's robot eliminates the possibility of fire by collecting the ashes and securing the butt. The smoke goes through a long 38-inch tube connected to a mouthpiece.

Cleo, Inc. (87-1063)   *$5 to $15*

❦ Electric blankets

If you enjoy using an electric blanket, make sure you understand how to use it as safely as possible. To avoid an excessive heat buildup, these blankets should not be "tucked in," nor should additional coverings (like other blankets, comforters, or pets sleeping on top of the blanket) be placed on top of them. Electric blankets should not be set so high that they could cause a burn while you are sleeping. Ideally, you should use yours just to warm up the bed before getting into it and turn it off before you turn out the light to go to sleep.

❦ Heating pads

Never to go to sleep with a heating pad, even when it is on a low setting; serious burns have resulted from this practice.

DRIVING

As a mature driver, you are unlikely to get a speeding ticket or take daredevil risks behind the wheel. But older drivers are not necessarily the safest drivers. Delayed reflexes, impaired vision and hearing, and medication can make older drivers a danger to themselves and others on the road. Take the following steps to ensure your driving safety.

❦ Driving safety tips

Have your eyes examined professionally each year to make sure that your vision is adequate for driving. Proper vision correction for both day and night driving is essential if you are driving during these different times.

If you have some doubts about your (or a loved one's) ability to drive, a professional can make an objective determination as to whether or not driving is safe. Many hospitals with well-equipped rehabilitation medicine departments have occupational therapists who use driving simulators to evaluate vision, hearing, reflexes, and cognition as they relate to driving. A trained driving instructor can also assess the situation. You can locate these resources through the phone book.

A helpful guide to evaluating driving ability is available from the American Automobile Association (AAA). *Concerned About an Older Driver? A Guide for Family and Friends* can be obtained from local AAA clubs or its national foundation.

AAA Foundation for Traffic Safety   *$5 to $15*
A self-assessment booklet entitled *Drivers 55 Plus: Test Your Own Performance* can also be obtained through AAA.

AAA Foundation for Traffic Safety   *under $5*
Getting Around enables readers to evaluate their driving capabilities. The booklet suggests transportation alternatives when driving is no longer feasible.

AARP Fulfillment (D13849)   *Free*
Send for *Your Health and Your Driving*. This booklet, compiled by safety experts, details ideas on what can be done to avoid becoming a traffic fatality statistic.

Metropolitan Life Insurance Company   *Free*
Driving Tips for Older People brochure:

American Optometric Association   *Free (with self-addressed stamped envelope)*

· A restricted driver's license may be appropriate. This could stipulate that the driver can drive no farther than 6 miles away from home or is only allowed to drive during the daytime.

· Avoid rush hour.

· Restrict night driving if night vision is less than optimal.

· Keep windshield, rearview mirrors, and headlights clean and properly adjusted.

· Avoid tinted windshields, which reduce the amount of light entering the eyes and can be a handicap at night for older persons.

- Wear quality sunglasses during the day to control glare.

- Be aware of any side effects of medications (such as antihistamines, antihypertensives, and sedatives) that could impact driving safety by causing blurred vision or sleepiness.

- Reduce distractions, such as the radio and conversation.

- Increase the distance between your car and the car ahead of you.

- Keep up with the flow of traffic so that faster-moving cars with impatient drivers don't dart in front of you and cut you off.

- Resist the temptation to be relaxed on short trips; most accidents occur within a few miles of home.

- Wear seatbelts.

- Drive a car equipped with an airbag.

- Look for other features to make driving easier and safer, such as antilock brakes, power steering and brakes, rear-window defroster, large rear-view mirrors to minimize the need to swing the head around, and controls that are easy to see, reach, and operate.

❦ Driving safety products

❦ Anti-reflective lens coating and glasses
A special coating is available for eyeglass lenses that can greatly reduce the glare of oncoming headlights. Inexpensive night-driving glasses can be helpful. The special plastic lenses cut out glare from headlights and overhead road lights.

One size fits all.

under $5

Dr. Leonard's Health Care Catalog (8330, glasses; 8331, clip-ons)
Miles Kimball Company (0722, glasses; 0729, clip-ons)

❦ Visor extender
This green plastic visor extender clips onto the regular visor to provide more protection against glare.
Miles Kimball Company (1393)   *under $5*

❦ Doze alarm

To help stay awake when driving, especially at night or on long trips, this device can be worn around the ear. It emits a loud alarm if the head drops forward. A button cell battery is required.

$5 to $15

Miles Kimball Company (1423)
The Safety Zone (526083)

❦ Enlarged rear-view mirror

Until auto makers provide this as standard equipment on their vehicles, it's well worth paying a few extra dollars for the added safety. It eliminates blind spots by providing a 300-percent wider angle view than the average rear-view mirror. As an extra safety feature, the glass is treated to reduce nighttime glare. It easily clips over the existing rear-view mirror. The standard mirror is for compact or small cars; the large size is made for medium or large cars and vans.
Solutions (60001, standard; 60002, large)   *$15 to $35*

❦ Blind spot mirror

Regular side- and rear-view mirrors can't detect the "blind spot" on each side of the car. This makes changing lanes or pulling out from the curb hazardous. This pair of 2-inch circular mirrors attach to the side-view mirrors (with self-adhesive backing) to increase the visibility of that dangerous area.
The Safety Zone (520501)   *$5 to $15*

❦ Slanted seat cushion

Use a slanted seat cushion that prevents the user from sinking into the car seat and raises him or her at least an inch for a better view. It eliminates the need for short persons to strain their necks trying to peer over the wheel.

$5 to $15

Dr. Leonard's Health Care Catalog (8172)
Miles Kimball Company (1408)
Taylor Gifts (9533)
The Vermont Country Store (19805)

❦ Back Up Alert

Install this device to warn children, shoppers, joggers, and pets that the car is backing up. One of the brake lights is replaced with the alert.

The alarm sounds automatically when the car is in reverse. Every driver has at one time or another forgotten to check to see what's behind the car; this can prevent tragic accidents when such instances occur.

$15 to $35

Promises Kept (1703)
Solutions (4862)

❦ Deer alert
The risk of collision with animals (such as deer, dogs, cats, and raccoons) can be reduced by attaching these tiny units to the front bumper of the car with adhesive-backed mounting plates. Wind pressure through the units at speeds over 30 mph create a high-frequency whistle that, although inaudible to human ears, repels animals up to ¼ mile ahead of the car.
The Safety Zone (550440)   *$15 to $35*

❦ Easy Stop
It's not just older persons who have trouble pulling into their garages at home. Younger drivers have also had their share of mishaps, such as running into the wall or over bicycles on the ground. But since aging can affect depth perception, the Easy Stop is especially helpful for older drivers. The mat is placed on the floor of the garage so that the driver knows it's time to park when the wheel meets the 3-inch-high rubber curb. Only one Easy Stop (3″ high × 18″ long × 13″ wide) is needed per vehicle.
The Alsto Company   *$15 to $35*

❦ Defensive-driving courses
The American Association of Retired Persons offers the 55-ALIVE program (an 8-hour course that teaches older people how to become safer, better drivers). In two 4-hour sessions, participants learn how to handle adverse driving conditions and traffic hazards, as well as how to recognize the effects of aging and certain medications on driving. Persons who complete the course may qualify for lower auto-insurance rates. Send for the free brochure (D0748) about this re-education course for older drivers.
55 Alive/Mature Driving   *$5 to $15 for 8 hours*
Local **AAA (American Automobile Association)** clubs and the **National Safety Council** can also refer you to defensive-driving courses

for mature operators. These generally cost $35 to $75 for a 6- or 8-hour course.

✇ 40 Channel Emergency CB

Getting stranded on the road can be extremely scary. It's best to wait in the car for help to come, but sometimes this can be a while in coming. This CB two-way radio allows help to be contacted much like a car phone would, but at a fraction of the price. Its channel 9 button gives instant access to the Emergency Band monitored by many police and highway patrols. It operates on even weak car batteries and is so compact that it can be easily stored in the glove box or under the seat.

The Safety Zone (546063)   *$35 to $75*

ELECTRICAL CORDS AND APPLIANCES

Electricity is an essential part of our everyday lives. Although we couldn't do without it, we tend to take it for granted. This is unfortunate because safety does need to be considered when using electrical cords and appliances.

(See also the Bathroom, Kitchen, and Lighting sections of this chapter.)

✇ Lamp, extension, and telephone cords

Even if you have lived in your home for many years, you may sometimes forget to watch out for electrical cords. It's all too easy to trip over cords that lie across walkways. To prevent a fall, try to arrange furniture, lamps, and phones so their cords are out of the way. Make sure that furniture doesn't rest on the cords; the damage could create fire and shock hazards. And don't be tempted to get cords out of the way by running them under carpeting or nailing/stapling them to the wall; a fire could be the end result. Instead, use tape to attach cords to walls or floors. Another technique is to use Cord-A-Way to store up to 8 excess feet of lamp-size cord. The cord wraps around the reel, which holds it securely until the tension is adjusted.

$5 to $15

Comfortably Yours (6527)
Home Trends (G116)
Check regularly to make use that cords are not damaged or cracked and replace them immediately if they are.

❧ Pull-a-plug

To avoid struggling with pulling electrical plugs from the wall socket and avoid electrical shock, secure each end of this device into the two prongs of the plug to form a strap that adds ease and safety.

Aids for Arthritis (J-26)   *under $5*

❧ Safety electric wall plate/plug ejector

This plate can be used instead of a conventional wall plate. It has levers that insert and remove the plugs, eliminating the need to touch the actual plate.

under $5

Independent Living Aids (673300)
Maxi Aids (73300)

❧ Automatic shut-off iron

To prevent an accident if you forget to turn appliances off, purchase an iron with an automatic shut-off feature. Some models beep when the temperature is reached or the iron is not moved for 10 minutes and automatically shut off anywhere from 2 to 12 minutes later if not used. They're available by mail or wherever small appliances are sold.

Maxi Aids (44000)   *$35 to $75*

❧ Iron safety guard

This device prevents the hands from being accidentally burned by the iron. The guard consists of two plastic rods that surround the bottom plate of the iron. It's excellent for older people with poor coordination or limited vision.

$35 to $75

Independent Living Aids (285357)
LS&S Group (136-75464)
Maxi Aids (19106)

KITCHEN

Frying an egg and cutting up some vegetables don't seem like high-risk activities, but many accidents do occur in the kitchen. Cooking is a necessary and often pleasurable activity, so you shouldn't be restricted from the satisfaction and independence of preparing your own meals, but you need to make sure that potential safety hazards are minimized.

⚜ Fire extinguisher

One-third of all home fires start in the kitchen, so it's essential to have an extinguisher that's readily accessible in the kitchen. Fire extinguishers are available at all hardware and home improvement stores, as well as through mail-order catalogs. Be sure to check the pressure gauge once a month. The owner's manual gives the correct reading. The most versatile fire extinguisher is a multipurpose A-B-C model, which can be used on all three classes of fire (ordinary combustibles such as wood, cloth, paper, rubber, and plastics; flammable liquids such as oil, gasoline, grease, tar, oil-based paint, lacquer, and flammable gas; and electrical equipment, including wiring, fusing, circuit breakers, and appliances).

The Safety Zone (112165)   *$15 to $35*

⚜ Flammable materials

Towels, curtains, and pot holders should not be kept on or near the range. Make sure to store these items properly. Curtains can be shortened or removed to avoid brushing against heat sources. The location of the towel rack can be changed as well. Remember to roll back long, loose sleeves or fasten them with pins or elastic bands to avoid sleeves catching on fire while cooking.

⚜ Giant tongs

These 15-inch tongs safely pull hot dishes to the front edge of the oven rack, minimizing the chances of getting burned while reaching into the oven. The serrated jaws securely grip the container or food.

Enrichments (3072)   *$5 to $15*

⚜ Toast tongs

To safely remove toast, muffins, or bagels from the toaster, broiler, or toaster oven, use these wooden tongs instead of your fingers. Small magnets allow you to hang the tongs on the side of the toaster when not being used.

Home Trends (J703)   *$5 to $15*

❧ Hot/cold grip

Both hot and cold dishes can be moved safely with this plastic-handled grip. It clamps securely onto cookware, pans, cookie sheets, and casserole dishes from the oven, range, or freezer.
Enrichments (3070)   *$5 to $15*

❧ Appliance cords

Cords and appliances need to be placed away from the sink to prevent shock or electrocution by their coming into contact with water. They should also not be kept on hot surfaces (such as on the toaster or the range) because cords can be damaged by excess heat.

❧ Automatic shut-off appliances

A toaster oven that automatically turns off after 60 minutes increases kitchen safety for anyone who has ever forgotten about something in the oven. Models are available wherever small appliances are sold.

❧ Unplugging appliances

Because coffeepots, toaster ovens, and other appliances can overheat if left on and cause a fire, they should be turned off and unplugged when not being used.

❧ Electric kettle

Unlike stovetop tea kettles, which can be damaged or create a fire hazard by boiling dry, this 1500-watt electric kettle has an auto-stop switch which shuts it off automatically as soon as the water boils. Made of polished stainless steel with a black handle, it holds up to a half-gallon of water and comes with a detachable cord. If you've ever forgotten a kettle or pot on the stove, you'll appreciate this item because it's much safer than boiling water on the stove and much faster than boiling in the microwave.
Solutions (800)   *$35 to $75*

❧ Cool-wall deep fryer

Frying in an open pan can be dangerous, but it is possible to enjoy fried foods with an ultra-safe electric deep fryer. The food is fried inside a 2½-quart sealed chamber with locking lid and viewing window. The Cool Wall exterior lives up to its name at all times. A special feature is the self-timer, in which a buzzer rings after the preset frying time is completed, the unit is automatically shut off, and the basket is raised from the oil.

The Safety Zone (142059)   *$125 to $200*

⚘ Super stuffer for garbage disposal

To safely stuff garbage into the disposal while it's running, use this special plastic stuffer instead of your fingers. It allows water to run freely around it.

$5 to $15

Home Trends (G702)
The Safety Zone (142038)
Williams-Sonoma (568386)

⚘ Safety can opener

Most electric openers pierce the surface of the lid, but this special hand-held opener applies pressure to the rim and removes the lid smoothly. There's no chance of getting cut on sharp, jagged edges. Another safety feature is that neither the opener nor the can's lid ever touches what's inside, ensuring that food can't be contaminated. The opener plugs into a wall outlet.

The Safety Zone (142060)   *$35 to $75*

⚘ Pot handles

Pot handles sticking out over the edge of the stove can be dangerous if bumped into, causing the contents to be overturned and possibly burning the cook. To prevent any chance of this, a pan holder can be used. The frame of this device prevents the pot handle from moving. It mounts to the stovetop with suction cups and stabilizes the handle of the pot in the vertical slot.

$5 to $15

Enrichments (3011)
Independent Living Aids (571480)

LIGHTING

Proper lighting is one of the most basic factors in home safety. If you have difficulty seeing when making your way around your home during the day or night, your safety will be compromised. Here's how to light up your home.

⚞ Lighting safety tips

· Choose bulbs of the appropriate wattage. An 85-year-old needs three times more illumination than a 15-year-old. This does not mean, however, that high-wattage bulbs should immediately be installed in your current fixtures. Exceeding the recommended wattage can lead to fire through overheating. If the correct wattage isn't known, the bulb should be no larger than 60 watts.

· Consider installing additional lighting where safety hazards exist, such as overhead in the bathtub and shower and in stairways.

· Install fluorescent lights over the stove to provide extra lighting for meal preparation.

· A cordless battery-operated light can provide additional lighting in areas where electrical outlets are not available, such as closets or cabinets.

· Control glare by using matte-finish paint, wallpaper, and countertops.

· Make sure that you have adequate window treatments such as miniblinds, since these can control glare.

· Maximize the available light in your home by using light-colored wall coverings and work surfaces such as countertops.

⚞ Lighting safety products

⚞ "Daylight" light bulbs

These glare-free halogen bulbs have a special composition that reduces the yellow tint of regular incandescent bulbs, enhancing the contrast of colors and showing the true spectrum of colors. Eyestrain and accidents caused by impaired vision are reduced, as are energy costs. The bulbs last more than four times longer than regular bulbs. The 52-watt bulb provides as much light as a 75-watt bulb; the 72-watt bulb gives the equivalent of 100 watts.
Brookstone (14366-52W; 14367-72W)   *$5 to $15*

⚞ Automatic power failure light

When storms or accidents interrupt electrical power, a room can still be brightly lit with this light. It turns itself on automatically (through permanent nickel-cadmium batteries) the instant power fails, and it shuts off when power is restored. It also has a night-light and can be used as a rechargeable flashlight when unplugged. The bedroom, hallways, and kitchen are ideal locations for the light.

$15 to $35

Frontgate (1827)
Aids for Arthritis (B-71)
Sporty's Preferred Living Catalog (7812L)

🔆 Night-light

Most older persons feel more secure with a night-light in their bedroom, bathroom, and hallways. Inexpensive night-lights are available at grocery stores, drugstores, and discount department stores, as well as through catalogs. The best ones have built-in photosensitive switches that automatically turn the light on in the dark and turn it off when the room is light. They plug into any 110-volt household outlet.

$5 to $15

Aids for Arthritis (E-28)
Enrichments (3215)
Independent Living Aids (090075/pair)

There's also a night-light with a motion sensor that turns on when movement is detected (up to 20 feet away within a 90-degree arc). The light activates only in the dark. An adjustable dial allows the light to remain on after activation, anywhere from 5 seconds to 15 minutes.

The Safety Zone (152178)   *$15 to $35*

The Sonar Lite has a photosensing cell that activates the light at nightfall *and* an adjustable sound-sensitive lever that turns on the light upon hearing either low-level sounds like talking and walking or louder sounds such as clapping, depending on how it's set. The light stays on for 2 to 5 minutes after the user leaves the area.

The Alsto Company   *$15 to $35*

🔆 Automatic night-light

One night-light, the Security Light, comes on automatically after dark. If the power goes out, it can be left in place or unplugged and carried as a flashlight. The rechargeable battery provides up to 50 minutes of light. When left plugged in an outlet, it keeps a full charge.

Solutions (5670)   *$15 to $35*

❧ Security guard automatic lamp control

The compact module is plugged into a socket and then a standard lamp is plugged into it. The light sensor activates the lamp when it gets dark, avoiding fumbling in the dark for the lamp switch.

$5 to $15

Independent Living Aids (683729)
The Safety Zone (150110)

❧ Plug-in sound-activated security lamp switch

To use, just plug the switch into an electrical outlet and plug any lamp into the switch. Sound turns the light on automatically (but a light sensor prevents the light from being turned on in the daytime). The sound needed to activate the system can be adjusted to varying sensitivity settings. Similarly, the length of time the lights stay on can be programmed (from a few minutes to 8 hours) before they turn off automatically. This helps deter burglars and also ensures that a light is quickly turned on when entering a dark room.

Independent Living Aids (615622)   *$15 to $35*

❧ Sonar Socket

A variation of the sound-activated lamp switch is the sound-activated socket. Any incandescent bulb up to 100 watts can be used in this special socket. The photosensitive cell activates the socket for nighttime use only and the sound-sensitivity lever can be adjusted to react to low-level sounds such as walking or louder noises such as shutting a door or clapping. The light stays on for 3 minutes after leaving the area. Appropriate locations for the socket are basements, stairways, garages, and entranceways.

$15 to $35

The Alsto Company
The Safety Zone (150932)

❧ Remote light control system

Any preselected lamp can be turned on from a distance of up to 50 feet when this compact transmitter is used. The transmitter can be carried in a pocket or purse. The receiver plugs into a standard wall outlet where the lamp is plugged in. You will never have to walk into a dark house again with this device.

$35 to $75

Independent Living Aids (657634)
Home Trends (J915)

⚡ Wireless remote control system

Lights can be turned on inside the house with this system even when no one is home. The telephone responder enables the user to turn lamps on (or off) from any touch-tone phone in the world. The system is easily installed without wires. Up to 10 lights or other household appliances can be controlled.

Home Automation Laboratories   *telephone responder 2540, $35 to $75; lamp module, 2010, $5 to $15*

⚡ Automatic sensor porch lamp

With the help of this special lamp, you'll never need to worry again about turning on or off an outside light. Because the light automatically goes on at dusk and off at dawn, you'll always be assured of having the front entrance of your house lit up at night when you need it (and off in the morning when you don't). It's also good by the garage door, porch, pool, or patio. Available in black or white, the lamp works with a 60-watt bulb and mounts easily on the wall.

Taylor Gifts (772)   *$35 to $75*

⚡ Electronic lamp dimmer

Not only does this device allow you to select any light level desired, from bright to dim, in one touch, it also has a delay feature which keeps the lamp lit for 30 seconds after it's turned off. This can prevent accidents by ensuring that the room is still safely lit up while you exit. It fits any lamp in the house and has an 8-foot cord for remote operation.

For Convenience Sake (5219)   *$15 to $35*

LOCKS

It's been said that a professional burglar who wants to break into a home will be able to do so regardless of whatever locks and security systems are used, but this doesn't mean you should make it easy for would-be thieves. Sliding glass doors and windows especially place you at risk. Consider the following devices to deter criminals from entering your home or hotel room. The extra time and work required to break in may cause them to go somewhere else or may increase the chances of their getting caught.

❦ Safe-T-Lock
Windows and patio doors can be secured with this clamp-on lock. The screws are twisted into place, holding the lock so that it allows the sliding glass door or window to be opened partially, but not all the way.
Home Trends (J117)   *$5 to $15*

❦ Door Jammer
Any door with a regular hinge at home or in a hotel can be intrusion-proofed in seconds. The Jammer adjusts from 25 to 42 inches and can be used on hardwood floors or carpets. It's simple to use: one end rests against the door and one on the floor. Forced opening of sliding glass doors is also prevented when the device is placed in the frame.
The Safety Zone (231010)   *$15 to $35*

❦ Sliding door and window lock
This aluminum bar deters burglars by preventing forced opening of sliding glass doors or windows. Full use of the door or window is restored by lifting the bar into its vertical storage position; the bar is easily dropped back into the horizontal locked position for protection. It adjusts from 27½ to 50 inches to fit most sliding doors and windows.
The Safety Zone (230144)   *$5 to $15*

❦ Security bar/alarm
Intruders can't slide glass doors open with this electronic security bar. It blocks the track and withstands up to 5,000 pounds of force. If any attempt is made to open the sliding glass door, a piercing siren sounds. It fits openings 6 to 8 feet and uses a 9-volt battery.
Mature Wisdom (561720)   *$5 to $15*

MOBILITY

You probably don't worry much about your safety as you walk around inside and outside your home, but you should. In most cases, there isn't much to worry about. But slick conditions (from waxed, polished floors or ice) or impaired balance can cause a fall. Take some precautions to prevent a fall from happening.

⚬ Standing up
Caution should be used in getting up after eating, lying down, or resting. Low blood pressure may cause faintness or dizziness when you are rising to a standing position.

⚬ Socks and slippers
Avoid wearing socks (without shoes) or smooth-soled slippers to walk around the house (and especially while using the stairs). You need to wear something with a rougher surface that provides more friction.

⚬ Nighttime temperature
At night the temperature inside needs to be at least 65°F. Prolonged exposure to cold temperatures may cause a drop in body temperature, which can lead to dizziness and falling.

⚬ Safety-grip boots and overshoes
You will have sure footing on ice when you slip these black rubberlike overshoes and boots over your shoes to keep feet warm and dry. The soles have a special aluminum oxide grit originally developed for mail carriers. The size nearest the actual shoe size should be ordered: women's 6, 7, 8, 9, or 10; men's small (6 to 7½; medium (8 to 9½); large (10 to 11½); extra-large (12 to 13½); extra-extra-large (14 to 15).
The Alsto Company   *$35 to $75*

⚬ Ice safety treads
Putting these rubber treads over boots or shoes is an easy way to avoid a spill on the ice. They're like wearing studded snow tires. The grippers adjust to fit any width shoe or boot. They come in two sizes (medium for women's shoes 4 to 9, men's 6 to 8; large for women's shoes 9½ and up, men's 8½ and up).

$5 to $15

Ann Morris Enterprises (GITW, small; GITM, large)
Maxi Aids (25639)
The Vermont Country Store

✒ Snow boots for canes

Placing these nonslip "boots" over the end of a standard cane could prevent you from slipping on ice or snow. They fit most 2-inch-diameter canes.

$5 to $15

Cleo, Inc. (40-1168)
Sears HealthCare (1074)

✒ Ice pick

The pick gives an older person surer footing when walking on icy surfaces. Even if you don't normally use a cane, this device is still worth purchasing because it's an easy way to help avoid a broken hip from falling on the ice.

Cleo, Inc. (40-1170)   *$5 to $15*

There's also a single-prong ice grip that easily attaches to all standard-sized canes with two screws. The grip flips up, out of the way, when not needed. It provides effective gripping action on icy surfaces.

Maxi Aids (94598)   *$5 to $15*

✒ Sole grips

Self-adhesive egg-shaped grips can be placed on the soles of new or slippery-soled shoes to prevent slipping indoors or out, even on wet floors.

under $5

Maxi Aids (59215)
Miles Kimball (A011)
The Vermont Country Store

✒ Nightwalker Slippers

These are the only slippers that have little "headlights" built into the toes to prevent bumping into furniture or tripping over sleeping pets when getting up in the middle of the night. When the switch on the heel is pressed, the krypton bulb is activated to shed a broad beam of light up to 12 feet away. The slippers are black terry cloth and have nonskid rubber bottoms. Four AA batteries are included. They come in men's sizes extra-small (5 to 6½), small (7 to 8½), medium (9 to 10½), and large (11 to 12½).

Signals   *$35 to $75*

PERSONAL PROTECTION

In an ideal world, no one would have to worry about protecting himself or herself at home or out in the community, least of all an older person. But this is not an ideal world. You may need to use a self-protection device to ensure your safety.

❧ Alarms

A lightweight alarm can be carried when you go out. To scare someone away or summon help, just pull the pin so that a loud 110-decibel siren is emitted. The siren sounds for up to 3 hours or until the pin is replaced. A belt clip (included) makes it easy to wear when walking. The alarm uses one 9-volt battery.

$15 to $35

SelfCare Catalog (2071)
The Safety Zone (334182)
Another device attaches to a purse with Velcro straps. When danger appears, the button on the Echo (Emergency Call Help-Out) can be pushed to emit a 115-decibel alarm that can be heard for two city blocks. It can't be turned off unless the 9-volt battery is removed.
Echo Corporation   *$35 to $75*
It may not be technologically advanced, but a whistle can drive away would-be attackers. Special whistles of 120 decibels are available; these can be heard over noisy crowds, airplanes, traffic, trains, and howling wind. They attach to a key ring and can easily be used, even upside down.
Solutions (60049)   *$5 to $15*

❧ Mace

Avoid carrying and using Mace. It can easily be grabbed by the perpetrator and used against an older person.

❧ Guns

If you own a gun or are contemplating using one, make sure you can handle it safely. A firearms instructor can evaluate your ability. Look in the Yellow Pages under "Rifle and Pistol Instruction/Ranges" for local classes.

❧ Lights for walking at night

To walk safely at night, walkers need to be sure that they're visible to traffic. Sporting goods stores sell fluorescent vests and jackets for this purpose. Another possibility is the Cue Light, which can be strapped to the arm. Its flashing red lights are visible up to 2,000 feet and last up to 500 hours. It runs on two AAA batteries.

The Safety Zone (314119)   *$15 to $35*

Still another option is to use a reflective stick. In addition to providing added support and balance while walking, the stick is highly reflective in the lights of a car. The 8-ounce stick has a soft grip for a comfort as well as a hand strap.

SelfCare Catalog (2069)   *$5 to $15*

❦ Dog repellent

Encountering an unfriendly dog can spoil anyone's walk. It can be especially threatening to older persons who may not be able to move fast enough to escape from attacking canines. One solution is to carry a pepper-based aerosol to repel dogs. The spray won't harm dogs but is effective in stopping an attack (spraying up to 12 feet). It's approved for use by postal workers on their delivery routes.

$5 to $15

Promises Kept (1059)
Solutions (A785501)

❦ Dazer

To stop an aggressive dog with the push of a button, this hand-held device emits a sound that discourages but doesn't harm dogs (and can't be heard by humans). It deters animals up to 15 feet away, allowing the user to escape. The device runs on a 9-volt battery and weighs just 4 ounces, so it can be slipped into a pocket or clipped onto a belt.

$15 to $35

Solutions (5306)
The Safety Zone (330206)

❦ Safety Steps for Pedestrians

Procedures and products that can help pedestrians are described in this booklet.

AARP Fulfillment (D12757)   *Free*

SAFES

A deposit box at the local bank is your safest bet for storing valuables, but getting to and from the bank every time you want access to money or jewelry or important documents can be inconvenient.

❦ Can safes

Actual product containers (such as Campbell's vegetable soup, STP oil treatment, Ajax, Pledge, and Colgate instant shave) have been modified with weights added so they feel like the real thing. The bottom screws on and off invisibly so that valuables can be placed inside to be hidden from view and later retrieved.

$15 to $35

Frontgate (1792, furniture polish; 1799, shaving cream; 1806, hair spray; 1813, deodorant; 1820, soup; 3919, beer; 3926, engine cleaner)
Promises Kept (3330, specify desired container)
Solutions (6423, specify desired container)

❦ Book safe

Money and jewelry can be placed in this cleverly designed book safe. Made from an actual book, the center is cut out for storage.

$5 to $15

Promises Kept (3601)
Sporty's Preferred Living Catalog (1129L)
The Safety Zone (728051)

❦ Flowerpot safe

This plastic flowerpot with a faux-granite finish is also a safe. The base of the pot unscrews to allow access to a 3½- by 4-inch secret compartment for cash, jewelry, and other valuables.
The Safety Zone (20651)   *$15 to $35*

❦ Wall outlet safe

Although it looks like just another electrical outlet, this one is actually a wall safe where jewels and cash can be stored. It locks and unlocks with a turn of a screw. It easily installs in regular Sheetrock walls with template and saw (which are included in the kit).
The Safety Zone (720748)   *$5 to $15*

❦ Waterproof minisafe

Valuables are at risk of being stolen while swimming at the pool or beach. This waterproof white plastic safe allows jewelry, money, or even a passport to be taken into the water with you. The cotton belt holds the safe securely around the waist. The safe is 5½" x 4" x 1⅛".
The Safety Zone (476008)   *$5 to $15*

STAIRS

Stairs can be highly treacherous for older persons. Almost a quarter of all falling accidents in the homes of older people involve stairs. The safest housing is on one level and eliminates the need to climb up or down any steps. But if your home has stairs and you want to remain in it, at least take precautions to make the stairs (both indoors and outside) as safe as possible.

✿ Handrails

You should always use a handrail when climbing up or going down the stairs. If you don't have one, have at least one handrail installed on the right side facing the stairs. Make sure any existing handrails are tightly affixed to the wall. Replace a short handrail with a longer one that extends the full length of the stairs so that you don't forget that there is still another step or two and fall by misjudging the last step. If the handrail curves into the wall at the last step, you'll always be aware that the steps are ending. Nonskid tape can be wrapped around the bannisters to increase the grip security.

✿ Extendable handrail

Persons with impaired balance, decreased vision, weakness, or pain in their joints feel more secure ascending and descending a staircase when they have something to hold onto on both sides. Unfortunately, most staircases have only one handrail or have two rails that are spaced too far apart to grasp at the same time. This safety device functions as a standard railing when in the wall position. When pulled out from the wall so that it extends to within 22 inches of the fixed rail on the other side, it allows the user to grasp the railing with both hands while moving up and down the stairs. The possibility of head-over-heels falls is greatly minimized when the user holds onto the railing on both sides. This stained wooden rail attaches to an aluminum mounting and pivoting system that locks into place to prevent accidental closure. The system requires less than 5 pounds of pressure for easy opening and closing. The company will send instructions for measuring and will custom-make railings when a ready-made system won't fit.

St. Croix Railings   *$350 to $600, depending on length of railing*

❧ Carpeting on the stairs

Whenever possible, stairs should not be carpeted. Deep-pile or dark-colored carpeting can be especially hazardous because it's difficult to see the edges of the steps clearly. If you can't bear to have the stairs uncarpeted, consider putting on treads in a contrasting color.

❧ Rubber stair and step treads

The molded pattern provides safe footing and helps prevent stairway falls when wood, tile, or concrete is slippery. The treads can be installed with a staple gun, adhesive, or heavy carpet tacks. Each tread (sold individually) is made 10¼ inches deep to wrap over the nose of each step.

The Vermont Country Store   *under $5*

❧ Gritty paint

Textured paint can also provide a nonslip surface for the stairs.

❧ Adequate lighting

Bright lights in the stairway can prevent accidents.

❧ Ice melter

The salt-free chemicals in the shakers melt ice quickly on stairs, driveways, and walkways, yet they don't harm plants, grass, skin, shoes, or carpet.

The Vermont Country Store   *$5 to $15*

❧ *Miscellaneous*

The following entries can't be readily categorized into any of the preceding sections but are nonetheless worthy of consideration.

❧ *Home Safety Checklist for Older Consumers*

This excellent booklet can alert you to safety problems in your home. It details possible hazards and ways to avoid them.

Consumer Product Safety Commission   *Free*

❦ The Perfect Fit: Creative Ideas for a Safe and Livable Home

Techniques for making homes safer are included in this booklet, along with ways to make them more comfortable and easier to maintain.
AARP Fulfillment (D14823)   *Free*

❦ Decals on sliding glass doors

To prevent "walk-in" injury, which can occur when people don't realize that a sliding glass door isn't open, use decals as a reminder that the glass is there. A variety of stickers is available. For people who don't care to use brightly colored ones, clear plastic circles with a 4-inch diameter give a prism effect and subtly but effectively alert people to the presence of the glass. These Safe-T-Spots instantly affix to the glass.
The Safety Zone (182201)   *$5 to $15 (set of four)*

❦ Voice-changing phone

To prevent would-be burglars and robbers from calling your number and hearing an elderly voice (whom they might consider an easy target), you might want to have this phone, which disguises the user's voice. It has a built-in modifier that can change a male voice to female, female to male, adult to child, or child to adult. It operates like a standard telephone, but has 16 programmable voice-masking levels. The device runs on four AAA batteries and is compatible with any phone that has a detachable handset. It's plugged into the base of the phone and the handset is plugged into the Voice Changer. It can be turned on or off as desired. If you're female and live alone, this would be especially valuable because it would give the illusion of a male presence in the home.

$75 to $125

Home Automation Laboratories (5205)
Joan Cook Housewares (7148)
The Safety Zone (334122)

❦ Safety marking tape

The phosphorescent tape can be used to mark light switches, stairs, doorknobs, and hallways.
Independent Living Aids (673307)   *$5 to $15*

❧ Dycem nonslip netting

This can be placed under area rugs to prevent them from slipping and sliding. It comes in a 6-foot roll that can be trimmed to the desired length or shape with scissors.

Enrichments (6616)   *$15 to $35*

❧ Super Grip nonskid spray-on coating

Lasting 3 to 6 months, this substance stops throw rugs from skidding.

Independent Living Aids (732342)   *under $5*

❧ Rug gripper

PVC-covered polyester scrim can be placed under any type of rug to make it skid resistant. One package secures rugs up to 24 by 38 inches; larger rugs require two or more packages.

Independent Living Aids (480876)   *under $5*

Another gripper, Hide-A-Rug, holds area rugs in place so that dangerous slipping, sliding, and wrinkling are eliminated. It can be cut for a custom fit and is available for either hard-surface or carpeted floors.

Solutions (5553 for carpets; 5550 for hard surfaces)   *$35 to $75*
for a 6- by 9-foot piece

❧ Safety step stools

Standing on a chair or flimsy stool or box to reach faraway objects is not safe for anyone. It's especially not safe for an older person. Avoid accidents by using a high-quality step stool. It should lock in place and not move until the person gets off. Ideally, it should have a handrail to grip onto. They're available wherever housewares are sold, as well as in mail-order catalogs.

Aids for Arthritis (C-31)   *$15 to $35*

❧ Ladder with safety handle

This three-step aluminum ladder is extra safe because of an elongated support handle that helps maintain balance when climbing or reaching. It folds easily, weighs less than 7 pounds, and can safely support up to 330 pounds.

The Alsto Company   *$35 to $75*

❦ First-aid chart

A chart for hanging on the wall of the kitchen or bathroom details first-aid procedures in case of an accident.

Council on Family Health   *Free*

❦ Emergency exit plan

Develop an emergency exit plan, with two exits to escape from a fire. Post it in a strategic place so you can review it periodically and refer to it if needed.

❦ *In Time of Emergency*

The Federal Emergency Management Agency provides a wealth of information about protecting life, health, and property from floods, hurricanes, snow and ice storms, tornadoes, earthquakes, and fires in a 41-page booklet.

Consumer Information Center (463X)   *under $5*

❦ *The Hartford House*

Although only 77 pages long, this booklet includes a number of valuable tips to help make homes safer for older adults. Featured sections include lighting, fire safety, and getting around the house (including use of the bathroom and kitchen).

Hartford Insurance Group   *Free*

❦ Crime prevention seminars

The **American Association of Retired Persons** (AARP) sponsors crime prevention training for older adults. Contact the national head-quarters of the AARP to get the number of your local chapter and find out what's being offered in your area.

AARP National Headquarters

❦ Safety tips for travelers

A folder with a variety of safety information for staying in hotels and motels features such tips as not leaving room keys at the swimming pool and not answering the door without calling the front desk to make sure that the person at the door is a member of the staff who is authorized to have access to the room.

American Hotel and Motel Association   *Free*

4

A HAPPIER LIFE

LIFE SHOULD be more than mere survival. Once the basic needs for food, clothing, and shelter are satisfied, human beings have the capacity to add meaning and pleasure to their lives. How they go about doing this is highly individualized, but the basic goal is the same.

Happiness knows no age limits. Older people can—and should— strive for fulfillment and enjoyment in their lives. But because the ways in which happiness is sought and found can change as a person ages, some older people aren't very successful at making life happy for themselves (or the people who care about them). Living can become a burden rather than a joy.

Ultimately, the responsibility for personal happiness lies within each individual. For most of us, this can be accomplished by engaging in activities and experiences that

· provide meaning and purpose to life;

· offer a connection with other people;

· furnish opportunities to stay busy and actively involved in the process of being alive.

Adding Meaning to Life

The demands of daily living may consume a good deal of our time and energy, but most of us need something more to feel fulfilled. We want

✵ AARP Crime Prevention booklets

Practical tips are presented in five publications:

How to Conduct a Security Survey (D396), featuring two checkl
assessing home security (how attractive the home is from a burgl
viewpoint and how secure the home is from the inside)

How to Protect Your Home (D395), describing methods to red
burglary

How to Protect Your Rural Homestead (D12244), offering sugg
tions for reducing crime against rural property

How to Protect Your Neighborhood (D397), discussing the build
of a neighborhood watch network on the block

How to Protect You and Your Car (D393), providing techniques
protection while traveling in an automobile and in securing it whe
is unoccupied

AARP Fulfillment

✵ Safety publications

The following two-page publications are yours for the asking:

Accident Prevention

Crime and Older People

Heat, Cold, and Getting Old

Preventing Falls and Fractures

National Institute on Aging

life to have some meaning that goes beyond mere existence. A meaningful life is especially important as we grow older. We need to feel that we're still contributing to the world and that our lives have some value. Helping other people, even in small ways, can provide purpose and satisfaction in the later years of life. By leaving our communities or the world in a better condition than we found it, we make a difference and leave a little of ourselves behind in the process. Ensuring that part of ourselves will live on after death as a link in the human chain of life can be accomplished through a number of ways.

CONNECTING WITH GRANDCHILDREN

Establishing deep bonds with grandchildren can be difficult these days because so many families live far apart and don't see one another very often. But a relationship with your children's children is definitely worth trying to cultivate and can add meaning and joy to the lives of both generations.

⅏ Grandparents' Little Dividends

For information on improving relations between grandparents and grandchildren, write to **Grandparents' Little Dividends** and send a self-addressed stamped envelope. They'll send you free information about a number of books and resources on the subject.

⅏ *A Grandpa's Notebook*

This is a book for older adults containing how-to ideas, anecdotes, and stories to encourage communication and interaction between grandparents and grandchildren (or older adults and unrelated youth). While the emphasis is on writing fictional stories and personal anecdotes, it also details other projects such as a family history scroll on which each family member adds a hand-scribed note or picture to a long sheet of paper (mailed to those who cannot contribute to the scroll in person); two-way interviewing in which both grandparent and grandchild ask each other questions; audiotaping explanations and descriptions of family photo and records albums; compiling an heirloom catalog with details about and the history behind family treasures and relics. It even discusses the writing of an "ethical will" in which the writer acknowledges what was accomplished and left undone during his or her lifetime, what was learned, and what ultimately was viewed as being important. Just as a last will and testament guides survivors on dealing with the distribution of material things, the ethical will instructs survivors in carrying out the deceased's spiritual and emotional thoughts and hopes.

Mike Moldeven   *$5 to $15*

⚜ The Write Connection

Keeping in touch with grandchildren is easy and fun with this special kit. It includes stationery, stickers, suggested topics, and stamped postcards for the child to reply back. Ample materials are included for 6 months of weekly correspondence. It's aimed at children 4 to 12 years old.

Positive Parenting Inc.   *$15 to $35 (refills $5 to $15)*

⚜ GRANDTRAVEL

When grandparents and grandchildren travel together, they become closer, strengthen their relationship, and create lasting memories. But there can be special needs and considerations for intergenerational travel. Standard trips geared for adults can be inappropriate for children. GRANDTRAVEL is a special vacation program designed and run by teachers, psychologists, and leisure counselors. Summertime travel experiences throughout the United States (Washington, D.C., Maine, New York City, New England, the Southwest, the Grand Canyon, western parks, California, Hawaii, and Alaska) and Europe, Australia, and Kenya can be enjoyed by old and young alike. Most activities are shared by both generations, but occasional separate activities are also scheduled. Children have the opportunity to be with peers (generally age 7 to 17) while also spending quality time with their grandparents (or surrogate grandparents such as aunts, uncles, and friends) during their 1- to 3-week vacation. Accommodations are first class, so the tours tend to be on the expensive side.

GRANDTRAVEL   *$2,500 to $5,000*

⚜ *Grandparents' Book*

A lasting family history can be created when grandparents provide simple answers to the questions asked in this hardcover book. Childhood, marriage, travel, and family celebration experiences can all be detailed so that grandchildren have a deeper understanding and lasting record of their grandparents' lives.

The Right Start (D067)   *$15 to $35*

LEAVING YOUR LEGACY

A piece of you will always remain on this earth when you leave behind your memoirs, autobiography, family tree, or video portrait.

❧ Yarns of Yesteryear Project
Make a contribution to your family and society by writing about your life. This will preserve your historical and cultural legacy. A special project at a Wisconsin university can assist you with writing your memoirs through correspondence courses.

Free

❧ *Lifeline: A Guide to Writing Your Personal Recollections*
Autobiographies are commercially viable only when they're written by celebrities. But although the life stories of people who aren't famous may never land on the best-seller list or even end up in a bookstore, they are still worth recording. Children, grandchildren, greatgrandchildren, and nieces and nephews want to know all about the relatives who came before them. The act of writing about personal challenges and achievements can be highly therapeutic for the autobiographer, allowing him or her to put a lifetime of events and relationships in perspective. But getting started can seem overwhelming to people who aren't professional writers. *Lifeline* is a comprehensive book that enables nonliterary types to begin and complete their life stories.
Betterway Publications   *$5 to $15*

❧ *Recording Your Family History*
This book is another helpful resource for setting down your life story. It asks hundreds of questions about every phase of a person's life, from childhood to involvement in historical events. Answers to the questions can be written down or answered orally on audio or video tape.
For Convenience Sake (1901)   *$5 to $15*

❧ Memories software
For all those persons who hated English composition, the "Memories" computer software program offers a simple, no-fuss way to put together an autobiography. The computer compiles responses to more than a thousand questions about special events and all the relation-

ships experienced throughout a lifetime and organizes them into an autobiographical format. The finished product reads and looks like a book but doesn't take the skill or effort to complete that a book usually does. The program is IBM-compatible.

Senior Software Systems   *$75 to $125*

✿ Video portrait

Family memories are preserved forever on video film. Special events, parties, and family gatherings can all be taped by amateur videographers. Video autobiographies are also wonderful, allowing descendants to hear the life stories of their ancestors and learn their wisdom. Hiring a professional can be expensive, but the results can be very impressive. A unique service produces hour-long broadcast-quality video portraits that include music and photographs from different times in the subject's life. The video features an in-depth interview with the subject. The result is a tape that can be treasured by future generations.

Lifescope Videos   *$1,000 to $2,500*

MAKING A VIDEO

If you live far away from your grandchildren, obtain a camcorder to make a video of yourself talking and singing or giving a guided tour of your home and community. (Camcorders can be rented at many stores that rent videotapes.) You can also read a storybook on tape and send it with the book to the grandchildren to follow along.

✿ Genealogy

Tracing family roots can be a rewarding activity for both young and old. You may enjoy playing the role of the family historian as you complete the family tree. Obtain books, charts, and aids to make this task easier.

Genealogists Bookshelf   *under $5 for catalog*

VOLUNTEERING

Anyone who volunteers will tell you that giving your time, money, and energy to someone or something other than yourself is extremely rewarding and meaningful.

❧ Referrals to volunteer opportunities

A list of more than 40,000 opportunities is yours for the asking.

Commission on Voluntary Service and Action   *Free*

❧ Special Olympics

You don't need to be athletic to be a Special Olympics volunteer. All you need is a warm heart and enthusiasm to help encourage a developmentally disabled child or adult to achieve success in sports training and athletic competitions. Activities suitable for older "coaches and friends" include swimming, bowling, and wheelchair events. Volunteers receive much satisfaction as they help the athletes develop a sense of mastery and self-esteem. Events are held on a local and national basis during the year.

❧ Schools

School volunteers don't need advanced degrees to make a difference in the lives of elementary and secondary school students. All they need is an interest in children. Working with youngsters gives older people a renewed enthusiasm for life and a chance to pass on their skills and learning. They can work directly with students, tutoring, reading to them, chaperoning field trips, helping with homework or special projects. Or, if they prefer, they can work behind the scenes and help teachers, librarians, and administrators. Even homebound persons can contribute at home by making holiday decorations or costumes for plays. Some programs use seniors to be special telephone friends to latchkey children who are home alone for several hours after school. To volunteer in a school, you can contact the principal of a nearby school, the volunteer coordinator of the local school district (look in the phonebook for your city or county school superintendent's office), or the **Retired Senior Volunteer Program.** Send for the **AARP's** free booklet, *Becoming a School Partner* (13527). The **National Association of Partners in Education** can also provide information about volunteer programs in your area.

❧ Make-A-Wish Foundation

As the nation's largest and strongest wish-granting charity, Make-A-Wish Foundation has granted more than 18,000 wishes since its beginning in 1980. More than 11,000 volunteers help turn dreams into reality for children under 18 who have terminal illnesses or life-threatening medical conditions. Wishes are limited only by a child's imagination. The most requested wish is going to Disney World, but wishes may also include meeting celebrities, traveling to other places, receiving something like a computer, or doing something like riding with a policeman or throwing out the first ball at a baseball game. All wish expenses are fully covered for the child and his or her family, including any travel and spending money. Volunteers from the 79 local chapters form wish teams to create the wish. After visiting with the child and family, they go to work raising the money and making the arrangements for the wish to come true. Older adults have many talents to offer the organization: fund-raising, public relations, office skills, and problem-solving.

❧ AARP Volunteer Talent Bank
You can register for AARP volunteer projects in such areas as the widowed persons' service, tax-aid assistance, health advocacy, environmental concerns, and criminal justice.

❧ Literacy Volunteers of America
Teaching an adult to read or to speak basic English as a second language is an extremely rewarding volunteer activity. The largest literacy organization has 450 local groups and welcomes new volunteers. Most volunteers work individually with their students in public libraries.

❧ Block volunteer
A meaningful civic project is the establishment of a block nurse/volunteer program. In addition to the intrinsic rewards of helping the elderly remain at home, it also ensures that such services will be available for older volunteers who are currently well and independent but may themselves need assistance in the future. The St. Anthony Block Nurse Program in St. Paul, Minnesota, is the model for this type of program. It delivers services to neighbors 65 and older, regardless of their entitlements or ability to pay for services. In addition to block nurses (public health nurses who live in the neighborhood, assess client and family needs, and perform nursing care) and block companions (neighborhood residents who are trained at local vocational-

technical institutes to provide basic home health and homemaker services), the program also uses block volunteers (neighbors near the same age who are trained to provide counseling and emotional support to their elderly peers). Other volunteers run errands and provide transportation and other services. The program has succeeded in keeping many older individuals from having to go to a nursing home. It has proven to be a much less costly alternative to institutional care. Although the program is based in Minnesota, it could just as easily be replicated elsewhere. The **Living At Home/Block Nurse Program** can provide further information.

℘ Friendship Force

While Friendship Force involves travel to a foreign country, it's much more than just a vacation. It's actually a unique way to contribute to world peace. By sharing the lifestyle of a foreign host family or by acting as a host to persons from other countries, participants quickly learn that people are more alike than different, regardless of where they live. Members of 110 Friendship Force clubs throughout the United States are matched up with persons from other countries. More than 1.5 million friendship matchups have occurred since 1977. Participants (many of whom are retirees) are screened for motivation, adaptability, and sense of humor. These unofficial diplomats have to pay expenses for their trip abroad, but the expenses are much less than comparable trips overseas spent in hotels rather than in local citizens' homes.

$1,000 to $2,500 (average 2-week stay)

℘ International Development

No matter where we live or what our age may be, we're all part of the global community. Older persons who want to get involved in making a difference in other parts of the world can volunteer for humanitarian projects sponsored by the AAIA. Opportunities can range from teaching in Costa Rica to setting up a livestock breeding program in Belize. There are also research projects (in fields like archaeology and zoology) and work camps in Europe, North Africa, Canada, and the United States at which small groups of individuals from a variety of countries come together to learn more about one another and promote world peace. But volunteers don't necessarily have to trek off to remote places thousands of miles away. They can remain in the United States to help raise money, educate the public about the need for international programs, and host international students and visitors. The AAIA, in conjunction with the AARP, has a guide entitled *65 Ways to Be Involved in International Development.*

American Association for International Aging   *$5 to $15*

❧ International Executive Service Corps

Retired executives can share their technical and business expertise with persons in science, technology, and business fields in other countries. The average age of volunteers is 68. The average length of service is 2 months. Volunteers pay their own expenses.

❧ U.S. Peace Corps

There is no upper age limit for serving as a Peace Corps volunteer. Persons in their eighties have donated their time and talents for projects around the world. Possibilities may range from teaching sign language in an African country to working in eastern European orphanages to developing a factory in a South Pacific island. The major requirements are patience, flexibility, and a strong desire to serve. Individuals who have skills in science, technology, and business are especially needed. Participants are provided with 6 to 12 months of training, including very intensive instruction in the language of the country they'll be serving in. While serving, they receive a $200 to $350 monthly stipend. Travel and living expenses are paid. Specific countries may be requested but cannot be guaranteed; final assignments are based on needs at the time. If interested, you need to complete an application at least 9 months before the desired departure.

❧ Global Volunteers

Sixty volunteer trips are organized each year, enabling 6 to 12 persons to serve on individual projects in the Americas, Africa, Asia, and eastern Europe. Possibilities can range from laying water pipes in a Mexican village to building a community center in Romania. Volunteers pay $1,000 to $2,500 to cover lodging, land travel, and food (airfare is extra).

৵ Amnesty International

As a worldwide movement of people acting on the conviction that governments must not deny individuals their basic human rights, Amnesty International works impartially to

- free prisoners of conscience (men, women, and children imprisoned solely for their beliefs, race, or ethnic origin, who have neither used nor advocated violence);

- ensure fair and prompt trials for all political prisoners;

- abolish torture and executions.

Members send letters, cards, and telegrams on behalf of individual prisoners to government officials in any part of the world where human rights are being denied. They also organize public meetings, collect signatures for petitions, and arrange publicity events, such as vigils at appropriate government embassies. Since the organization was founded in 1961, Amnesty International has worked on behalf of more than 43,000 prisoner cases.

$15 to $35 a year

৵ RESULTS

This grass-roots organization believes—and has proven—that individuals can make a difference in the world. They help create the political will to end hunger throughout the world. By lobbying their elected representatives, writing letters, publicizing the issue, and educating the public, they've acted as the impetus to major legislation and programs being passed and funded. Active partners commit to attending three local meetings a month for learning and taking action. Other members who can't make this time commitment can still make a difference through monthly meetings or financial sponsorship.

৵ Earthwatch

Earthwatch is a nonprofit institution that sponsors scholarly field research by finding paying volunteers to help scientists on research expeditions around the world. The focus is on studying the natural and human environment. Destinations have ranged from the Pacific Northwest (studying the spotted owl) to upstate New York (exploring the unique French architecture of Jefferson County) to Kenya (identifying and observing birds and aquatic plants in Lake Naivasha) to Mexico (excavating Mayan ruins) to Australia (working to preserve native Aboriginal culture). Participants assist scientists in the work projects, in addition to sharing cooking, dishwashing, and other chores. Each research project uses 10 to 20 volunteers for 2-week stints. Volunteers in this EarthCorps (a Peace Corps–like organization for the environment) do not need special skills or training to serve. Anyone age 16 or older is eligible to apply. (One-third of all participants are over 55, and a number have been in their eighties.) Some projects are quite rigorous, involving hiking, climbing, or rising before dawn, while others are less physically challenging and more cerebral. Volunteers share the costs of research expeditions. These fees, which cover basic living expenses but do not include transportation to and from the site, are tax-deductible.

$350 to $5,000

National Wildlife Federation

The National Wildlife Federation works to protect wildlife and the habitat needed for its survival. Membership in the organization entitles you to its magazines and newsletters, as well as other information such as the *Citizens Action Guide* (which describes actions to protect such resources as water and air) and the *NWF Activist Kit* (containing booklets such as *Making Congress Work for Our Environment* and *Use the News to Protect Your Environment).* The National Wildlife Federation's Washington Action Workshop is held in Washington, D.C., every spring. The workshop teaches participants about the most pressing environmental issues and helps them acquire the skills to lobby lawmakers and work effectively on environmental issues in local areas.

$15 to $35

Friends of the Earth

This global environmental advocacy organization focuses on how environmental policies affect people. It strives to stop environmental hazards that threaten the health and safety of our families (everything from ozone-depleting chemicals and toxic chemicals to polluted drinking water). It fights for environmental justice so that poor people don't bear the brunt of environmental hazards, and challenges corporate polluters. Activist members can become involved in attending local environmental briefings and helping lobby their legislators.

$15 to $35 a year

❧ Sierra Club

Since its beginnings more than a century ago, the Sierra Club has expanded its focus beyond the preservation of the Sierra Nevada range and now acts to protect the natural environment throughout the nation and the entire planet. The Sierra Club educates, lobbies, and legislates on any issue that impacts the environment. They also sponsor local, national, and international trips and outings (hiking, bicycling, or canoeing). Among their many publications are *How to Become an Environmental Activist*, *Environmental Protection Begins At Home*, *Socially Responsible Investing & Influencing Corporate Behavior*, *National Conservation Organizations*, and *What You Can Do* (solving the garbage crisis, saving tropical rain forests, stabilizing world population, protecting our coasts, and keeping the Great Lakes great). The free *Sierra Club Sourcebook* lists all these publications (most available for under $5 and at a discount to members).

$15 to $35

❧ Recording for the Blind

There are more than 24,000 individuals with visual impairments and physical disabilities who cannot use regular textbooks and reference books. Recorded books enable them to participate in school and professional careers. Anyone with a clear speaking voice and good reading ability can help record the 3,300 titles needed each year. Volunteers (who record at local studios) receive satisfaction from knowing that they're enabling someone to access important information that wouldn't otherwise be available.

❧ Lions Clubs International

By joining a local Lions Club, you'll meet lots of new friends while helping people in your community and around the world. Their Sight-First program is dedicated to eradicating preventable and reversible blindness worldwide. They run eye banks and raise funds for research, training, and rehabilitation of the visually impaired. Other projects include vocational training of the disabled, relief work for flood, earthquake, hurricane, and tornado victims, and services for youth (such as programs in school to increase self-esteem, scholarships, and youth leadership camps), There are 15,000 clubs in the United States with 510,000 members. Most clubs meet twice a month. Membership is open to anyone of "legal majority and excellent reputation in the community."

Dues vary from club to club

Kiwanis International

The men and women of the Kiwanis Club improve their communities, encourage international understanding, and assist youth, the aging, and the needy. More than 325,000 members in over 8,500 clubs perform voluntary community service through participation on committees that meet for breakfast, lunch, or dinner. While the purpose of Kiwanis is not to be a social club, fellowship and lasting friendships are natural by-products as members work closely together. Anyone of good standing in the community is eligible to join.

Dues vary from club to club

Civitan International

Civitans believe that living a full, rewarding life must include giving a portion of our time and talents to help others. Historically, Civitan clubs help the mentally retarded, physically handicapped, and youth, but projects can vary from club to club, depending on the local community's needs. More than 57,000 members belong to one of the 1,800 local clubs. Any person 18 years or older of good reputation and character is eligible to join. Social events are planned in addition to the work projects and business meetings.

Dues vary from club to club

Making blankets for the homeless

Anyone who can knit or crochet can join a nationwide effort to provide warmth for people living on the streets. Rectangles (7 by 9 inches) are sewn together to make blankets. They should be made from worsted weight acrylic blend or wool yarn. Knitters should use size 7 needles to

obtain five stitches to the inch. The squares should be mailed to the fabric store that is coordinating the project.
House of Fabrics

❦ Prison Pen Pals
Men, women, and teenagers in prisons are without home, family, and friends. A voluntary organization helps them keep in touch with the outside world through letters written by concerned citizens. Nearly 2 million citizens and prisoners have been matched through the mail. Writers select the prisoner(s) they wish to write to from listings that profile sex, age, and interests. The organization (begun in 1974) believes that correspondence with law-abiding citizens who care can help turn prisoners' lives around and ultimately reduce crime. However, writers do need to be cautious about any attempts at exploitation or abuse by prisoners. Nothing should be exchanged except letters. Face-to-face visits are not a part of this program.

Free listing with self-addressed stamped envelope

❦ America Remembers
U.S. troops stationed overseas appreciate receiving mail from home. Once you obtain the name of a serviceman or servicewoman, you can send regular letters to show your support (and may receive some in return).

❦ International Mailbag Club
The lives of homebound and disabled adults are brightened by letters and cards. Volunteers receive names and addresses of persons who would like to receive mail.

❦ Operation Green Plant
As part of the America the Beautiful Fund (ABF), Operation Green Plant operates as a clearinghouse of ideas for community projects by civic and other groups of interested citizens who want to protect and beautify the land, as well as help the needy. Volunteer groups choose such gardening projects as growing food for the poor, beautifying neighborhoods, starting educational programs, improving ecologic

conditions, and using plants therapeutically with the handicapped, ill, and older population. If you love gardening but want to make more of a contribution than just arranging flowers with a garden club, one of these projects could be just what you're looking for. See if you can get a group together through your church, library, school, senior citizen group, or charitable organization or contact ABF to learn of a group operating near you. ABF will provide direction and support, as well as furnish free seed packets for flowers, herbs, and vegetables.

America the Beautiful Fund (ABF)   *under $5 handling*
(for the first 50 packets or
each additional 100 packets)

⚘ ACTION programs

ACTION is the equivalent of a domestic Peace Corps, providing volunteer services across the country. They sponsor three Older Americans Volunteer Programs.

· **Retired Senior Volunteer Program (RSVP)**
Anyone who is 60 or older and retired qualifies. There are no income or educational requirements. Volunteers may choose from assignments (usually involving some sort of social service, such as in schools, courts, libraries, day-care centers, hospitals, and community centers) compiled by the local RSVP office. Transportation is reimbursed to and from the volunteer site.

· **Foster Grandparent Program**
Low-income persons 60 and older are assigned to work in schools and community programs with children with special needs (usually mental or physical handicaps). Participants receive a transportation allowance, are provided with hot meals and accident insurance while in service, and are furnished with an annual physical exam. They also receive a small tax-free stipend.

· **Senior Companion Program**
Requirements and benefits are the same as for the Foster Grandparent program, but volunteers work with the homebound elderly as companions and advocates.

❧ 20/20 Vision National Project

The 20/20 Vision National Project believes that 20 minutes a month and $20 a year can have a significant impact on public policy. They encourage citizen involvement and political activism through simple and convenient activities that take no more than 20 minutes a month to complete. Their vision of a better world includes global peace, reduced military spending, preserving and helping the environment, and addressing human needs. Every month the organization sends its members a postcard that recommends a specific action, such as writing a brief letter or leaving a phone message for a policymaker currently facing a decision about a particular issue. An update on the results of the action and any decisions that were made as a result is provided every 6 months.

$15 to $35 a year membership

❧ Gray Panthers

For more than 20 years, this national organization of people of all ages has fought to change attitudes and laws that hurt persons who are vulnerable. The Gray Panthers believe that everyone, regardless of age, race, sex, or lifestyle, should have the opportunity to lead productive lives. They work for reforms in health care, promote peace and international cooperation, and fight for environmental and economic justice. On a national level, they bring attention to these issues; on a local level, their social activism may be manifested in such projects as teaching inexpensive but nutritious recipes to persons in fixed incomes, developing training to organize nursing home visitors, sponsoring student essays on aging, and building coalitions to study and promote health systems. There are more than 45,000 members in over 60 chapters throughout the United States.

$15 to $35 a year

❧ International Senior Citizens Association

Senior citizens who are interested in nuclear disarmament, world peace, protection of the environment, and creation of a better world for their children, grandchildren, and generations to come may want to consider joining the International Senior Citizens Association. This nonprofit agency has consultative status with the United Nations and

is truly an international organization (with members in nine countries). Its quarterly newsletter offers some suggestions for individual
involvement, such as writing letters to persons in the United Nations
who can bring about human rights improvements. Delegates from the
ISCA attend annual international conferences on aging and social
change.

$5 to $15 a year

⚘ The Older Women's League (OWL)

As the first and only national grass-roots membership organization to
focus exclusively on women as they age, OWL is active on the local,
state, and national political scenes. Major goals are the achievement of
economic and social equity and the improvement of the image and
status of mid-life and older women. Members lobby Congress, hold
speak-outs on the issues, participate in local and national press conferences, and sponsor major conferences on important issues.

$15 to $35 a year

⚘ Service Corps of Retired Executives (SCORE)

More than 13,000 volunteers participate in this program sponsored by
the U.S. Small Business Administration. Most are retired business
owners, executives, accountants, attorneys, and military officers. They
provide free advice to new businesses that are experiencing some
problems, Volunteers receive no remuneration, but their expenses are
paid by SCORE.

⚘ American Society for the Prevention of Cruelty to Animals

There is a variety of tasks to be done in local animal shelters or their
outreach groups. Jobs may range from feeding the dogs and cats to
bringing the pets to hospitals and nursing homes for pet therapy programs. Behind-the-scenes jobs, such as fund-raising or clerical duties,
are also available. If you can't find a nearby shelter, you can contact the
national organization affiliated with most shelters.

⚘ National Coalition for the Homeless

Over 500 local groups have been organized across the country to help
the homeless. Volunteering may range from sitting on an advisory
board to fund-raising to serving food in a soup kitchen to visiting with

the homeless in shelters to helping unemployed individuals gain job search and work skills.

⚜ Habitat for Humanity

Safe, attractive, and affordable housing is made possible by this ecumenical Christian ministry. Volunteers may assist with house building or renovation in local projects or in sites across the country or around the world. Families chosen to receive the homes are employed but lack the income needed for commercial housing. Older persons who are handy and have some carpentry/homebuilding skills are especially welcome, but no volunteer is turned away. Other tasks such as fundraising and clerical duties are also performed by volunteers.

⚜ *Combatting Loneliness*

Loneliness is one of the most common problems of older persons. People who have outlived their siblings and friends may feel a great void in their lives. The loss of a spouse can be devastating. Living alone is obviously a major contributor to feelings of isolation, as is the inability to get out of the house and into the community.

Even in retirement settings filled with people around the same age, circumstances may preclude sufficient opportunities for companionship. Sometimes spouses are both alive, but one of the partners still feels very much alone because the relationship is impacted by illness or a lack of nurturing. When children, grandchildren, and other family members live far away, a feeling of loneliness can also result.

While constant companionship may not be realistic (or even desirable), there are many ways to feel less alone in the world.

DIVORCE

Divorce is always accompanied by powerful emotions. Depression and anger can cause mid-life and older persons to feel alone.

⚜ *Divorce After 50—Challenges and Choices*
This book provides suggestions on dealing with negative feelings, as well as financial and legal issues.
AARP Fulfillment (D12909)   *Free*

Hosting Visitors

Your home doesn't have to be a palace for you to open it to visitors from all over the country and the world. In doing so, you'll be providing travelers and students with economical housing while expanding your world and combatting loneliness by visiting with all different types of people.

✤ Evergreen Club

Strangers don't stay strangers long when they live under the same roof. It's easy for older persons to enlarge their circle of friends when they open up their homes to out-of-town guests. By joining the Evergreen Club, members can act as hosts and meet compatible persons over 50 from all over the country.

While hosting may initially sound a little overwhelming, keep in mind that no one is expected to become a professional innkeeper. Most guests stay only 1 or 2 nights. Hosts average three or four guests per year (and can accommodate more or less, depending on their wishes). If a prospective visit is not convenient, the would-be host can decline the use of his or her home. The 700 members make their own arrangements by contacting hosts from a list provided by the club. Guests pay $10 nightly if single and $15 as a couple.

Evergreen/Travel Club   *annual dues $15 to $35 (singles);*
                                  $35 to $75 (couple)

✤ U.S. Servas

This organization sponsors programs on a global basis. Its goal is to build world peace and goodwill through an international cooperative of hosts and travelers. As a nonprofit, nongovernmental, interracial, and interfaith organization, it is open to persons of all ages (once they send two letters of reference and are interviewed). A list of hosts in the United States and abroad is provided (with some background information, such as their interests and local recreational/cultural activities). Participants make their own arrangements, usually for a 2-day stay. No money is exchanged between travelers and hosts.

For persons who are not able to travel, Servas "brings the world

into your living room through the visits of friendly, enthusiastic people from every continent." Fancy accommodations and meals are not
expected; travelers just want to share the everyday lives of their
hosts. Those who can't open their homes to overnight visitors can still
participate by becoming "day hosts." If a prospective host does not
have the time or desire for a visitor, travelers do not have to be accepted; arrangements must be mutually agreeable between traveler
and host.

$35 to $75 annual membership

✿ American Field Service

Hosting a high school student from another country is a bit like parenting, but it lasts for only 6 months or a year. While not a lifetime
commitment, close bonds are formed as the young person and host
live as a family. Since its beginnings in 1947, the American Field Service (AFS) has encouraged families with teenagers to host, but they
also allow couples without children or even single people to serve as
hosts. Placements are made on a combination of interests, tempera-
ments, and lifestyles. A local AFS liaison helps to ease the initial and
ongoing adjustment by providing orientation and counseling. If a
placement does not appear to be working out, AFS will move the student out of the home.

Hosting a young person isn't difficult. The student will be involved
with schoolwork and extracurricular activities at the local high school,
so it's not necessary to constantly provide entertainment. The student
is treated as a family member. Emotional support needs to be provided, and basic needs must be met. Host families are not paid; they
volunteer their homes and time to nurture a young person from another country. (A $50 tax deduction may be taken for every month an
AFS student resides in the home.)

It's also possible to be an aunt/uncle family to a student hosted in
the community. Once a month, the aunt/uncle invites the student to
dinner, a movie, a ball game, or another fun activity. This allows the
aunt/uncle to spend some time with someone from another culture
without making as large a commitment as a host.

Yet another alternative is hosting a visiting teacher. Teachers from
Latin American or Asian countries are integrated into local schools

and reside in the United States for 6 months to a year. Older people who feel that they could have difficulty adjusting to the energy level of a high school student may want to consider sharing their homes with a mature adult. As with the student exchange program, hosts provide room and board; no reimbursement is received. Friendships and lasting memories are created as people from different cultures expand their world together.

INTERACTIVE COMMUNICATION ON COMPUTERS

The majority of computer users may be students and businesspeople, but that doesn't mean that senior citizens can't put a home computer to good use. Older persons may not want or need to learn complicated word processing, database, or accounting programs, but they can readily use a computer to electronically communicate with thousands of other people. The homebound elderly can keep in touch with relatives and make new friends from all over the country by using a commercial on-line forum.

✤ CompuServe

At all hours, lively conversation is available. You can also get involved in electronic games (adventure, role-playing, trivia contests, casino tables, word games, and spelling quizzes) or join a special-interest group in which information and opinions are exchanged on such topics as food, wine, gardening, health, and hobbies. A personal computer, modem, telephone, and communications software are needed to get started.

$5 to $15 per month

✤ SeniorNet Online

One nonprofit 24-hour national computer network is for seniors only (age 55 and up). Members form an electronic community on Senior-Net Online on which they "talk" to each other through computer messages. Evenings after 6 P.M. and on weekends, members enjoy general conversation as well as specific discussion forums relating to travel, health, writing, retirement, cooking, gardening, and science fiction. New discussion groups can be started at any time, depending on the interest of members. On Wednesday nights, a "cocktail party" is held. Participants bring a glass of wine to the computer, and all "talk" at once as if there was an actual cocktail party. SeniorNet Online members also have access to America Online, on which they can play interactive games together or communicate via electronic mail with faraway children and grandchildren who also subscribe.

(See also SeniorNet later in this chapter.)

SeniorNet   *$15 to $35 annual fee for SeniorNet membership, plus $5 to $15 per month for SeniorNet Online network (unlimited use on weekends and evenings after 6 P.M. local time and 1 hour per month of America Online's other services)*

LIVING WITH A SICK SPOUSE

Married persons who care for a spouse with a chronic illness or disability can still feel alone even though there's another person living under the same roof. The well spouse may feel guilty when she or he tries to live a relatively normal life and may experience pangs of loneliness living with a partner who may be too sick or disabled to provide companionship.

⚘ Well Spouse Foundation

This national organization is available for support to the 7 to 9 million well spouses who act as caregivers. Membership entitles the participant to networking with other well spouses through a pen-pal service and regional support groups, allowing persons in similar circumstances to develop friendships and share techniques to make coping easier. A quarterly newsletter and monthly bulletins are also included in the membership fee.

$15 to $35 a year

PEN PALS

Letter writing is somewhat of a dying art, but there are some older persons who still enjoy corresponding through the mail. Pen pals are a great way to make new friends and learn about other lifestyles.

❦ The Golden Years

This monthly newsletter provides a listing of mature individuals (names, mailing addresses, and interests) who want to connect with someone else.

$15 to $35 a year

❦ International Pen Friends

Other organizations match pen pals by using a questionnaire. These are not limited specifically to older persons; instead, they include individuals of all ages and from over 100 countries. The large number of participants (more than 300,000) ensures that compatible and interesting pen pals are always available. They do offer a service for people over 60 in which they can furnish 14 names. To learn more, send a self-addressed stamped envelope to IPF.

$15 to $35 annual membership

❦ The Letter Exchange

This is a truly unique service for persons who want to write and receive letters. Instead of being matched by a questionnaire, computer, or worker at a pen-pal organization or choosing someone from a brief general listing that doesn't reveal much about a person, you can select the person(s) who appeals most to you from listings that can be witty, poignant, or just plain weird. The listings are grouped according to category, such as art and photography, clippings (persons seeking newspaper and magazine clippings on specific topics), contemporary issues, education, family life, genealogy, ghost letters (in which correspondents assume fictional or imaginary characters), health, hobbies and games, holidays, humor, information (persons seeking specific answers of an informational nature rather than sustained correspondence), insights/religion/philosophy, literature, men's interests, metaphysics/new age, movies and TV, music, nature and gardening, pets, politics and history, postcard exchange, psychology, regional interests and travel, seniors, sports, tape exchange (audio and visual), and women's interests.

A free forwarding service enables persons to exchange letters without revealing their addresses (unless they later choose to). Letters are placed by the writer in an envelope addressed to the code number of the person they wish to correspond with, sealed, and stamped and then placed in a larger envelope and mailed to The Letter Exchange to be forwarded to its intended recipient. There is no limit to the number of letters that can be forwarded with this double-envelope, double-stamp procedure. More than 3,000 people subscribe to the magazine. More than 100,000 letters have been forwarded.

$5 to $15 single copy;
$15 to $35 for 1-year
subscription (three issues);
separate charge per word to be
listed in the magazine

✿ Long Distance Love

This is a highly specialized pen-pal service that connects people throughout the world who are afflicted with or who have overcome the same disease, illness, or handicap, or who have suffered a similar type of accident. Through a questionnaire and computerized file, persons are matched according to health problems, age, and other interests. These pen pals' special bonds enable them to provide support and encouragement to each other in a way in which persons who have not experienced the same health problem cannot.

$5 to $15 voluntary contribution plus
self-addressed stamped envelope

✿ The Voicespondence Club

Persons who have difficulty putting their thoughts and feelings on paper (due to visual limitations, physical disabilities, or writer's block) can still make new friends via the mail. All that's needed is a tape recorder and the membership directory of a tape correspondence club. "Voicespondents" can chat about hobbies, politics, and family affairs, and even exchange recordings of music and other performances. Each member is entitled to an annual directory of members (profiling ages and interests) and the quarterly club bulletin, which has news about the club and its members, as well as advice on buying and using tape machines. New members get a tape of welcome and help. Taped directories are available to the visually impaired. Members use the directory to select those persons they would like to voicespond with. Tapes (after they're listened to) must be returned to the sender. A tape visit with friends from the United States and abroad can alleviate loneliness and establish long-term friendships.

$5 to $15 annual dues

PETS

Research has shown that pets reduce depression, relieve anxiety, and help slow chronic disease. It's even been found that owning a pet lowers blood pressure, cholesterol, and triglycerides. The unconditional love that pets offer is especially therapeutic for older persons. Dogs and cats provide the most companionship, but birds, hamsters, and fish also have some value.

⚘ Purina Pets for People Program

If you would like a pet but are afraid that the upkeep is too expensive, you may want to investigate a special program offered through Purina and humane societies. Older homeless animals can be adopted at minimal costs (with Purina covering the adoption fees, shots, bowl, collar, leash, a starter supply of food, spaying or neutering, and initial veterinary costs).

⚘ Selecting the right breed

Some breeds are better suited to older persons than others. To make sure you buy the right type of dog, consider using the computer match-making service provided by Kalkan. With the answers to a multiple-choice quiz about lifestyle and personality (such as the size of the home or the amount of time that can be spent with the animal), the computer can provide the names of 2 to 4 breeds out of a total of 93 popular ones that would be suitable.

Pedigree Selectadog Service   *Free*

> **PET DOOR**
> Consider having a pet door installed so that you won't be bothered with the need to let the cat or dog inside and outside. They're available at home improvement stores.

SHARED HOUSING

Many older persons who live alone would benefit from the companionship, security, and help with household finances that a housemate could provide. There are more than 350 home-sharing programs across the country. Some coordinate small shared group residences with common living areas and private bedrooms; others match up homeowners with boarders. Compatible housemates can be of any age or either sex, depending on individual preferences. Intergenerational sharing has been shown to work out very well, especially between college students and older persons.

❧ Shared Housing Resource Center
As the foremost specialist in shared housing, this organization has a large number of publications available on the subject. Contact it for more information and for a listing of its publications.

❧ Making Home Sharing Work for You: A Planning Guide
This informative booklet lists issues to be discussed when interviewing for potential housemates and even includes a model contract.
Cornell University   *under $5*

❧ Shared Residences for Older Persons
A model home-sharing lease is included in this booklet, along with questionnaires for home providers and those considering moving into another person's residence.
AARP Fulfillment (D12774)   *Free*

SPECIALTY SINGLES GROUPS

You may tend to discount all singles groups as being for losers and certainly not something you would want to be involved with. But there are some organizations that go way beyond the awkward singles dances and parties that most people dislike.

❧ Singles for Charities
Volunteer work can alleviate loneliness for many older persons. Volunteers are able to interact with a variety of other people and to feel really connected to the human race. The work draws attention away from one's own problems (such as loneliness) by focusing on the needs of someone or something else. There is no shortage of possible volunteer opportunities to choose from. But one especially worth considering is the New York–based Singles for Charities. While the emphasis of the organization is on helping others, it has a social aspect as well. Individuals who normally would shy away from joining

typical singles organizations can feel more comfortable with this group because the sole focus isn't on meeting and mating. But it does offer a social outlet with compatible persons who want to make a difference. Activities include fund-raising, gathering food for the homeless, delivering meals to shut-ins, and cooking holiday dinners for residents of shelters. Similar organizations can be started elsewhere. Contact Singles for Charities to learn how to replicate their success.

⚘ Gourmets and Friends

Many older persons love good food, but don't enjoy it often enough because they don't want to eat in nice restaurants or do much cooking just for themselves. Membership in Gourmets and Friends can solve this problem and help singles meet other singles who share their culinary interests. A monthly bulletin provides brief descriptions of each member. When a reader finds someone of interest, he or she sends a more detailed biography (including address and phone number). Members exchange letters, calls, and recipes. Some travel many miles to meet up with each other and enjoy a meal together. Most members are in their fifties and sixties and are recently single.

$35 to $75 a year

TRAVEL

Traveling solo can be a lonely experience. It's much more fun to travel with someone else, and more economical as well. Too many would-be mature travelers restrict their trips because they don't want to travel alone or can't afford the expenses of traveling as a single.

(See also the Travel section later in this chapter.)

⚘ Golden Companions

This confidential travel companion network for those 45 years and older has helped more than 2,000 people find travel companions since 1987. Their members are from 45 to 89 years of age and live in all parts of the United States and Canada. Some are looking for same-sex companions, whereas others prefer companions of the opposite sex. (At least a dozen member couples married after meeting and traveling together!) Networking with potential travel companions is easy. Members write a description of their personal interests, travel wishes (anything from a weekend trip to the Grand Canyon to a 1-week Caribbean cruise to 6 weeks in Asia), and desired travel companion (sex, age, level of gregariousness, smoking/drinking habits) and are listed in the club's directory and bimonthly newsletter. Names, addresses, and phone numbers are never revealed in the printed material; codes identify each person. Members contact each other through the free mail-exchange service. They make their own arrangements to meet each other or to travel together. Club get-togethers are also held periodically across the country so that members can meet.

$75 to $125 a year (sample newsletter under $5)

⚸ Travel Companion Exchange

The company publishes a bimonthly newsletter with profiles of travelers looking for compatible companions. They operate a Hosting Exchange program in which members act as tour guides for singles visiting their hometown. The hosting program enables prospective travel companions from different regions to test their compatibility before making a commitment to share a room or a car for an extended period.

$35 to $75 for 6 months; $125 to $200 a year
(sample newsletter under $5)

⚸ Seniors Abroad

One way to eliminate the loneliness that can occur when traveling to a foreign country where you don't know anyone is to stay with a foreign host family. Seniors Abroad, as the only international home-stay program for persons over 50, enables travelers to have an authentic travel experience by sharing the lives of other active people over 50. The foreign hosts volunteer their time and hospitality. Travelers spend a week each in three different homes in different towns during their 3 weeks in a country such as Japan, Denmark, New Zealand, or Australia. Almost every traveler (and there have been more than 500 so far) has acquired long-term friends from at least one home visited. The only requirements for visitors are being over 50 and in good enough health to travel. At least one person in each host family speaks English. There is no obligation to be a host in return (although this is an equally rewarding experience).

$1,000 to $2,500 for 3 weeks
(includes round-trip airfare,
hotel accommodations for the first
2 to 3 nights, and
administrative costs)

VOLUNTEER COMPANIONS

Most churches and synagogues have visitation programs in which volunteers spend a few hours each week with older persons who are mostly confined to home. If you aren't involved with a religious group, there are civic groups that may provide the same service.

Little Brothers—Friends of the Elderly

One organization exists solely to match an older person with a volunteer who offers year-round friendship. Home visits are the predominant means of contact, but group outings, vacations, and emergency food and medical transportation can also be provided. Any older person over 60 is eligible if he or she feels alone and isolated, regardless of income, religion, race, sex, ability, or social status; the oldest and most isolated are considered priorities. Programs are currently offered in San Francisco, Chicago, Philadelphia, Boston, Upper Peninsula–Michigan, and Minneapolis/St. Paul. It's possible that new groups in other cities could be started.

WIDOWED PERSONS' SUPPORT

More than 1 million persons are widowed each year in the United States and Canada. The loss of a spouse results in emotional, psychological, and functional effects, such as shock, confusion, fear, anger, guilt, loneliness, depression, anxiety, social isolation, susceptibility to illness, and financial insecurity. Survivors need help in working through their grief and should take advantage of the available resources.

THEOS Foundation

Educational, emotional, and psychological support is provided by this nonprofit organization through monthly support group meetings, seminars, workshops, and conferences. More than 100 chapters are active in North America, with the possibility of new chapters forming when an interest is expressed. The foundation's publications also help widowed people rebuild their lives. These include *Survivor's Outreach* magazine (eight issues a year for $24), *Facing the Holidays* booklet for 20 cents, *The 12 Steps of Grief* card for 16 cents, and a bibliography for $4.

Local dues vary

Widowed Persons Service

Volunteers widowed at least 18 months listen to and support new widows and widowers on a one-to-one basis as they face the problems of widowhood. These volunteers are trained to make appropriate referrals to counselors and other professionals as needed.

AARP Widowed Persons Service   *Free*

International Association for Widowed People

Over 200 state groups offer self-help programs in hich widowed persons learn to cope with grief and loneliness while setting new goals for themselves. They also sponsor national travel programs, provide information about benefits, and lobby for changes in laws that could benefit the widowed.

Local dues vary

So Many of My Friends Have Died or Moved Away

This pamphlet provides a brief discussion on the loss of old friends and ways of finding new ones.

AARP Fulfillment (D13831)   *Free*

On Being Alone

This booklet helps the newly widowed deal with grief, housing concerns, finances, and adjustment to the loss of a spouse.

AARP Fulfillment (D150)   *Free*

Widowed Persons Service Bibliography

A variety of books relating to various aspects of widowhood are listed.

AARP Fulfillment (D435)   *Free*

⚜ *Keeping Busy and Involved in Life*

Too much time with too little to do makes life boring. People can become listless and depressed when they don't have enough to keep them busy. While health, finances, and a lack of transportation may make it impossible to pursue all the activities enjoyed in younger days, mature persons can—and should—strive to stay active and involved in life. All it takes is a little time, energy, and money to maintain some of those old leisure interests and incorporate new activities into the later years.

ACTING

The theater has a magic for both the audience and the actors. Older persons can participate in both roles through nonprofessional community theater groups. Acting is a terrific creative outlet at any age, but there often aren't enough roles for mature persons.

⚜ Ripe and Ready Players

A theater group in Chattanooga called the Ripe and Ready Players has solved this problem by performing skits about the problems of later life and retirement. They're willing to share information on starting similar groups in other areas.
Senior Neighbors of Chattanooga

ASTRONOMY

For a nocturnal activity, consider looking at the skies. Spotting and identifying the various stars and constellations can be an engrossing way to spend leisure time. You don't need a high-powered telescope to get started; there's quite a lot that can be seen with the naked eye.

⚜ Astronomy booklet

Stars in Your Eyes: A Guide to the Northern Skies offers helpful hints on finding the seven best known constellations. This booklet is published by the Department of Defense.
Consumer Information Center (155X)   *under $5*

BIRD WATCHING

People don't necessarily need to live in the country to enjoy bird watching. A windowsill feeder can be very effective in attracting birds. Information is available from a variety of sources.

🌿 Department of the Interior booklets

Two booklets published by the Department of the Interior provide guidance on feeding and housing birds. *Backyard Bird Feeding* (558X) discusses ways to attract different species with the right food and type of feeder. It even gives advice on where to place and how to clean the feeder. *Homes for Birds* (572X) details how to choose the right house for specific species and how to protect the houses against predators.

Consumer Information Center   *Free*

🌿 National Bird-Feeding Society

More information about attracting, feeding, and housing backyard birds is available from the organization dedicated to bird watching at home. Annual membership includes a quarterly newsletter.

$15 to $35 a year

🌿 Audubon Society

The 500 chapters of the **National Audubon Society** organize bird walks, give lectures, and offer useful information such as the booklet *A Beginner's Guide to Bird Watching*.

under $5

🌿 Mail-order supplies

Bird feeders, houses, baths, and seeds are available at many nurseries and plant stores, as well as through mail-order companies.

American Wild Bird Company   *Free catalog*

CLOWNING

Clowning is a fun hobby that brings joy and happiness to children and adults alike. Clowns may perform for free in hospitals, day-care centers, nursing homes, and fund-raising events for charities or for pay at parties and promotional events for businesses.

To learn more about clowning, attend a seminar or workshop, network with other amateur or professional clowns, and read the *New Calliope* (a bimonthly newsletter that contains information about props, makeup, costuming, and other aspects of the art of clowning).

Clowns of America, International   *$15 to $35 annual fee*
(includes subscription to the
New Calliope)

COLLECTING

Virtually anything is fair game for collecting as a hobby. Possibilities include antique spoons, angels, beer cans, antique and modern buttons, Coca-Cola memorabilia, cookie cutters, decorative plates, fishing lures, folding fans, frogs, hatpins, Howdy Doody memorabilia, miniature license plates, owls, pens, sugar packets, World's Fair memorabilia, and much, much more. To get started on something which will interest you, look through the hobby section in the *Encyclopedia of Associations*. This reference book is available at all public libraries. You'll find many listings for organizations that specialize in collecting certain objects.

⚞ Stamp collecting

Stamp collecting is a hobby enjoyed by young and old alike. It expands your horizons as you learn more about the stamps associated with other periods of time or exotic places around the world. You can spend as much or as little on collecting as you wish. You can specialize in American stamps or foreign stamps from a specific country. You can collect stamps of famous historical figures or of cats, butterflies, or ships. Membership in the foremost philatelic society includes a subscription to the monthly magazine *The American Philatelist*. The society offers a lending library of reference materials, stamps for sale, stamp insurance, seminars, and an appraisal service. Publications for beginners include *10 Low-Cost Ways to Start Collecting Stamps, How to Avoid Common Mistakes as a Beginning Stamp Collector*, and the *Beginning Stamp Collecting* correspondence course. Collecting can easily be done through the mail without ever leaving your home, but you may enjoy the companionship of belonging to one of more than 700 local clubs around the country.

American Philatelic Society *$15 to $35*

Coin collecting

Coin collecting is another major collecting activity. As with stamp collecting, you can specialize in a certain time in history or in a foreign country. Correspondence courses, research services, a lending library, and *The Numismatist* monthly journal are available through a national organization. This organization can direct you to one of their 600 local clubs.

American Numismatic Association *$15 to $35 a year*

Computing

There's no getting around the fact that we have truly become a computer-oriented society. Computer literacy is becoming a necessity for many of us. In additional to its functional benefits, a computer can also provide a lot of fun. (See also CompuServe and SeniorNet Online earlier in this chapter.)

SeniorNet

This nonprofit organization offers a wealth of opportunities for persons 55 and older to stay mentally active. Beginners can learn how to use computers through SeniorWorks tutorials. These step-by-step, self-teaching lessons enable even the most computer-shy senior to acquire basic computer skills at home at his or her own pace. There are also more than 40 SeniorNet Learning Centers around the country where instructors are provided for hands-on learning experiences. Once a member is able to use the computer, SeniorNet can suggest ideas for computer projects. The following are some of the possibilities:

- doing a spreadsheet to track finances
- using databases to organize a recipe collection
- writing a novel or autobiography
- publishing a family newsletter to stay in touch with distant relatives

- performing volunteer work for nonprofit organizations, such as re-cordkeeping and compiling mailing lists

- taking electronic classes through SeniorNet Online (such as Gene-alogy or Microsoft Works) in which an instructor provides lessons and communicates on-line by critiquing assignments

SeniorNet   *$15 to $35 annual membership*
(plus additional $5 to $15 a month
to participate in SeniorNet Online network)

CRAFTS

All kinds of craft work can be very fulfilling for older persons. Working with the hands can be intellectually stimulating, spiritually enriching, and psychologically rewarding. Sales of handicrafts can also become an additional source of income.

✵ Elder Craftsmen

The Elder Craftsmen program enables older persons to sell their crafts through a consignment shop in New York City. Samples can be mailed to the shop (although large or heavy samples should first be described in a letter, accompanied by a photo). Accepted crafts (in-cluding quilts, sweaters, rugs, clothing, baby gifts, folk art, toys, Christ-mas ornaments, and other household and decorative objects, but usually not paintings) are not purchased outright by the shop but are displayed for sale at a price determined by the craftsperson and/or the shop manager. When an item is sold, 50 percent of the selling price is paid to the craftsman. (The other 50 percent is retained by Elder Craftsmen for operation of the shop). Elder Craftsmen also publishes a helpful brochure, *Opportunities in Crafts for Older Adults* ($1), listing other shops and cooperatives throughout the country that also accept crafts on consignment.

✵ The Crafts Report

More information on the business aspects of crafts can be obtained from *The Crafts Report* (a monthly publication that advises crafters on market trends and business practices, in addition to listing shows and

fairs nationwide) and through Arts and Crafts Nationwide (an association that sponsors craft shows, offers insurance, and publishes a quarterly listing of shows around the country).

The Crafts Report   *$15 to $35 (1-year subscription)*
Arts and Crafts Nationwide   *$15 to $35 (annual dues)*

⚑ Catalogs

For the biggest selection of just about any art or craft item you could
want, look through one of the major art-supply catalogs. They have a
complete line of materials for ceramics, weaving, woodcarving and
woodburning, painting, drawing, copper enameling, jewelrymaking,
decorative tole, leathercraft, beadcraft, decoupage, stained glass, can-
dlemaking, metalwork, string art, needlepoint, embroidery, rug hooking, macrame, fabric decorating, and calligraphy, along with many
how-to books.

Dick Blick   *Free catalog*
NASCO   *Free catalog*

⚑ Quilting

Quilting preserves a very American tradition. It is a satisfying hobby
that results in beautiful objects to decorate the home or to wear. If
you weren't fortunate enough to have learned this craft from a family
member, it's not too late to learn it now. The **National Quilting Association** can provide lists of certified teachers in your area as well as
books and videotapes. They even have a consumer service to which
members can call and obtain assistance with their quilting problems.
The *Quilting Quarterly* magazine is published four times a year and
is included in the price of membership.

$5 to $15 a year

Another quilting association, the **American Quilter's Society,** provides the *American Quilter* quarterly magazine, books, and a Quilts
for Sale program that gives members a free listing (including full-color
photographs and descriptions) in AQS publications so that they can
show and sell their work.

$15 to $35 a year

❧ Sewing

People who enjoy sewing may want to join neighborhood and national groups for sewing enthusiasts. Bimonthly newsletters cover developments in fabrics, patterns, and new products and publications. Lectures, classes, demonstrations, seminars, and informal support systems are offered.

American Sewing Guild   *$15 to $35 a year*

❧ Needlework

Beginning or advanced stitchers who enjoy appliqué, counted-thread embroidery, crewel, drawn-thread embroidery, fine handsewing, lacework, painting and dying fabrics, patchwork, and smocking may want to develop their skills by joining a national needle arts association. The bimonthly *Needle Arts* magazine is provided, as well as a lending library, slide library, videos, workshops and seminars, correspondence courses, and advanced study/master craftsmen/teaching certification studies.

Embroiderers' Guild of America   *$15 to $35 a year*

Just about every type of needlework project anyone could want is available through the mail. Cross-stitch, needlepoint, latch hook, and tapestry kits and supplies can be ordered.

The American Needlewoman, Inc.   *Free catalog*

❧ Decoupage

Decoupage is the creative art of assembling and composing paper cutouts for decorating objects such as wall hangings, lamps, bowls, boxes, screens, and furniture. Fabric, glass, ceramic, and wood objects can be decorated with the cutouts, which are lacquered or varnished. Although this craft requires precision and a good eye for arranging, you don't have to be artistic in the traditional sense of being able to draw designs. Books on the craft as well as correspondence courses with experienced pen-pal teachers are available.

National Guild of Decoupeurs   *$15 to $35 a year*

❧ Working with wood

Older persons may not be able to do heavy-duty construction work, but they can still find projects that utilize their building skills. One unique possibility is building a playhouse for grandchildren, neighborhood children, or for a park or playground. Playhouses can range from simple to complex. The more sophisticated ones can be quite challenging. Plans and blueprints for three different styles (Tudor, contemporary, and gable-front) of unique miniature homes include such features as skylights, porches, and bay windows. The height is 7½ feet.

Munchkin Playhouses *$15 to $35 for each style*
(cost of materials estimated at $350 to $600)

Grandchildren can enjoy a variety of homemade gifts made from wood. Plans, parts, and kits are available for projects such as toys, clocks, banks, dollhouses, whirligigs, music boxes, and weather stations. All skill levels can be accommodated. These handmade items can also be produced as very special Christmas gifts for needy children.

Cherry Tree Toys *under $5*
If you carve or whittle wood (or would like to learn), join the **National Wood Carvers Association.** They can provide how-to books as well as lists of suppliers and teachers. The yearly membership includes the bimonthly magazine *Chip Chats*.

$5 to $15 a year

Marquetry is another variation of wood craft. Also known as wood mosaic, wood inlay, or intarsia, it involves cutting, gluing, and finishing pieces of different woods together to make decorative objects. It can easily be done at the kitchen table with a simple knife. The national association devoted to the craft provides a monthly newsletter as well as a pattern library service, books, videos, and a correspondence service in which members can have their questions answered and problems solved by experienced experts.

Marquetry Society of America *$15 to $18 a year*

EDUCATION

Any type of learning experience is a productive way to spend leisure time. A few possibilities are suggested, but there is an infinite number of resources for improving your knowledge. Take advantage of any opportunity (formal or informal) to learn something new.

❦ Home study

A variety of courses is available through universities and other educational institutions. You can study at home at your own pace. The **National Home Study Council** can provide a listing of all the opportunities. Ask for their free *Directory of Accredited Home Study Schools*.

Most of us don't have the money, time, or ability to attend Harvard or Yale. But a new product can enable any interested person to enjoy Ivy League courses at home. The Super Star Teachers College Lecture Course cassette series features condensed lectures from semester-long classes taught by top-rated professors from the leading colleges. Possibilities include Classic and Modern Political Theory, Ancient Greek Civilization, Introductory Psychology, Comparison of World Religions, and Poetry. Each course is packaged as a set of eight 45-minute lectures.

The Teaching Company   *$75 to $125, audio*
                                             $125 to $200, video

❦ College classes

Many colleges and universities allow older persons to audit regular classes on a noncredit basis. Some offer special programs specifically designed for mature learners. The Academy of Lifelong Learning at the University of Delaware is one noteworthy example. Participants form an intellectual cooperative and volunteer as instructors, planners, and committee members. Courses include sculpture, investing, current events, Oriental rugs, world religions, beginning Italian, Broadway music, and geography. The AARP has two publications that provide specific details about programs throughout the country: *Learning Opportunities for Older Persons* (D171) and *Directory of Centers for Older Learners* (D13973).

AARP Fulfillment   *Free*

❦ High school equivalency

A number of older persons regret never completing high school. They may have been forced by circumstances beyond their control (such as economic need) to quit high school or they may have chosen to marry instead of completing their education, but years later they wish they had received their diploma. Many older adults in their fifties, sixties, seventies, and even eighties and nineties decide to attain their high school equivalency by studying for and passing the GED (general educational development) test. Contact your local school board's Department of Adult Basic Education for more information. There are a number of study guides, motivational books, and practice tests available for adults who haven't been to school, taken a test, or studied anything in years. Contact the **General Education Development Institute** for a listing of its materials. Costs vary according to the publication, but are fairly low because the organization is nonprofit.

ENTERTAINMENT

Everyone likes to be entertained. The following suggestions offer some fun ways for older persons to enjoy some relaxing leisure time.

ᨆ Nostalgia television

No one would suggest that an older person be glued to the television set, but TV in moderation can be entertaining. While much of current programming is aimed at young people, there is a special 24-hour cable channel geared for the over-45 population. In addition to reruns of old network shows such as *Dragnet* and *Ben Casey*, the following programs are featured:

Jukebox Gym: aerobic workouts for mature exercisers.

Narrative Television Network: classic films adapted for persons with limited eyesight. Voiceovers describe the action, setting, and actors' expressions between the dialogue.

Dr. Ruth's Never Too Late: sexuality in later life.

Washington Report: Politicians and activists debate issues relevant to the older population (such as mandatory retirement and Social Security).

More than 700 affiliates carry the Nostalgia channel. Check to see if your cable company offers this station and request that it be added if it's currently not offered.

ᨆ Audiocassettes

A whole world of learning and entertainment is available on audiocassettes. Choices need not to be limited to the rock or rap music that most music stores at the mall seem to specialize in. Mail-order companies have a variety of music and nostalgic programs. Old-time radio shows from 1928 to 1959 can be heard again. Representative offerings in 1-hour tapes include such comedy and dramatic classics as *Fibber McGee and Molly*, *The Baby Snooks Show*, *The Bickersons*, *The Amos 'N Andy Show*, *The Abbott & Costello Show*, *The Third Man*, *The Green Hornet*, and *Sherlock Holmes*.

Adventures in Cassettes   *$5 to $15*

❧ *Old-Time Radio Programs* networking

Traders and collectors of old-time radio shows will enjoy this bi-monthly newsletter. It discusses problems and techniques in tape dubbing, tape quality, news and requests from collectors, and logs related to old-time radio shows.

Hello Again   *$5 to $15 a year*

❧ Videos

Even if going to the local video store to rent and return videos is inconvenient or impossible due to a lack of transportation, it's still possible to enjoy movies at home. A video store in Philadelphia sends tapes through the mail. Orders can be placed through their toll-free line and sent through UPS to addresses in the eastern half of the country and via the Postal Service's priority mail to the western half. Tapes may be enjoyed for 3 nights after receipt and then returned in the same shipping box. (Labels, postage, and tape are provided.) The package can be deposited in any mailbox. In addition to convenience, the service has another advantage over most video stores: the selection. More than 13,000 titles are available! Instead of concentrating on the newest mainstream releases like most retail outlets, the Video Library concentrates on classic mystery, adventure, musical, drama, and comedy, as well as foreign films, vintage movies, documentaries, fine arts, and instructional titles. They'll provide a 76-page list and regular updates; a catalog with brief reviews is also available.

Video Library   *$5 to $15 per title plus round-trip shipping (under $5 per title)*

⚥ Magazines

New Choices for the Best Years (formerly called *Fifty Plus*) is a lively magazine that covers health, fitness, travel, relationships, money management, and other topics for people over 50.

New Choices for the Best Years   *$15 to $35 a year*

GAMES

Whether you've been playing bridge for over 40 years or have always wanted to learn chess, one of the following games should provide you many enjoyable hours. They offer mental stimulation, social opportunities, and the possibility of winning recognition and prizes for your efforts.

⚥ Bridge

Bridge can be a great game for older people, but you may have stopped playing if you don't have anyone to play with. If it's difficult to get a foursome together, you can still learn and play bridge. Solo Bridge functions as your teacher, partner, both opponents, dealer, and scorekeeper. The small hand-held computer is programmed to eight skill levels. It bids the other three hands in response to your bids, then leads and plays the correct cards for the other three "players." You can view the "hidden hands" with the touch of a button, deal a new hand when desired, or rebid and replay the same hand as a learning exercise. Four AAA batteries are needed.

Herrington (C818)   *$75 to $125*

A less expensive version is Solobridge. Instead of a computer, the game comes with a playing board, instructions, and 50 hands (of real cards). Every bid and trick can be checked against the expert commentary for insights about how the hand could have been better played. All hands as dealt are completely unknown to the player, as in real bridge. Every aspect of bridge skills (bidding, play, and defense) can be improved as the game proceeds as if it were being played with a foursome.

Cardinal Company   *$15 to $35*

The **American Contract Bridge League** can put you in touch with one of their 4,200 local clubs and offers many publications about bridge. They also sponsor local, regional, and national tournaments.

✹ Checkers

You may not have looked at a checker board since you were a kid, but hundreds of older persons are rediscovering the challenges of this ancient game of strategy. It's easy to learn the basics, but higher levels of play require a good deal of time and energy before skills are refined. Tournaments are held throughout the country, with many held through the mail (players make a move and then contact the opponent for him or her to make the next move). The national organization devoted to the game has a large number of books and other instructional media available.

American Checker Federation   *$15 to $35 a year*

✹ Mah Jongg

This traditional Oriental game, played with tiles engraved with jokers, flowers, and Chinese symbols such as a dragon, is played by four persons. Although it is definitely a game of strategy, it is not as difficult to learn as bridge and is much more social than chess. To learn to play the game, send for *Mah Jongg Made Easy*.

National Mah Jongg League   *under $5*

✹ Poker

Poker has had a back-room image over the years. The stereotypical poker player was believed to be a middle-aged, hard-drinking, chain-smoking male. But thousands of individuals who don't fall within this category have discovered that the game is fun and stimulating. Famous poker players have included Lillian Carter, Jesse Helms, Groucho Marx, and Harry Truman. You don't have to travel to Las Vegas to play. Tournaments and private groups exist all over the country. Contact the organization for home poker players to learn more. Beginners and advanced players are welcome.

IH3PA   *$5 to $15 a year*

✹ Postal chess

Some would-be chess players aren't able to play this intellectually stimulating game because they don't have a partner. Postal chess can solve this problem by allowing all games to be played by correspondence. Players exchange cards containing the date the opponent's card was received, the date the reply was sent back, section number, acknowledgment of the opponent's last move, the current move, and a signature and return address. Players are assigned to a game by the tournament director. A variety of ongoing matches throughout the year and special tournaments are available for players at every level of chess proficiency (beginner to advanced). Membership includes bimonthly newsletters about chess, results, ratings, tournament news, and other announcements.

$5 to $15

American Postal Chess Tournaments
Knights of the Square Table
The Chess Correspondent

✺ Scrabble

As one of the best-loved word games of all time, Scrabble is played all over the world. If you're looking for people to play with or would like to play on a competitive basis, join the **National Scrabble Association.** They'll put you in touch with one of the more than 200 local licensed clubs, alert you to upcoming tournaments, and send you the *Scrabble News* eight times a year.

$15 to $35 a year

GARDENING

Growing plants, vegetables, and flowers indoors or outside is a leisure activity that has almost universal appeal. Just about everyone finds it satisfying to work with growing things and nurture them. You don't have to have an acre of land or be extremely physically fit to enjoy growing and taking care of plants. There are many possibilities for the mature gardener.

✺ African violets

African violets are considered to be the world's most popular houseplant because they can bloom year round. Although beautiful and somewhat delicate looking, they are not difficult to grow. They do need adequate light (bright but filtered, such as the morning sun coming through an east window or double-tube fluorescent lights for 12 to 14 hours a day) and moderate temperatures and humidity. Membership in the plant's national society includes a subscription to the bimonthly *African Violet Magazine* and affiliation with one of the more than 450 local clubs.

African Violet Society of America   *$15 to $35 a year*

⚘ Bonsai

Bonsai is the art of creating living trees in miniature. Although it originated in China and Japan, it is now practiced by people all over the world. Because the trees are so small, they can easily be handled by older persons. They do require a great deal of tender loving care, including bud pinching, root pruning, trimming, fertilizing, and watering, but the results are worth it. Becoming a member of the leading bonsai organization entitles you to a yearly subscription to *Bonsai Magazine*, as well as access to their lending library, discounts on books, and a directory of plant, tool, and pot suppliers. A number of communities have local clubs as well.

Bonsai Clubs International   *$15 to $35 a year*

⚘ Gardening catalogs

Catalogs contain a greater variety of plants than are carried by local nurseries. There are many items that are appealing to the mature gardener. Hanging strawberry baskets (F28792, $5 to $15 per basket) are easy to grow and can yield edible fruit year round. Bush cherry plants (N28125, three for $5 to $15) allow thousands of cherries to be picked without climbing a tree. Instant vegetable gardens of radishes, lettuce, carrots, and tomatoes (A31940, $5 to $15) and butterfly flower gardens of marigolds, zinnias, poppies, cornflowers, and cosmos (A31930, under $5) are easy to plant. Simply roll out the preplanted strips (10 running feet and 8 inches wide) onto bare soil, cover lightly, and water.

Gardener's Choice   *Free (catalog)*

⚘ Greenhouse gardening

Greenhouses are a perfect supplement or substitute for outdoor gardening activities. They offer a less physically demanding venue for gardening and more controlled environmental conditions. The *Directory of Manufacturers—Hobby Greenhouses, Solariums, Sunrooms, and*

Window Greenhouses is an annotated list of more than 40 manufacturers and is accompanied by an article on selecting a hobby greenhouse.

Hobby Greenhouse Association   *under $5*

❧ Indoor Gardening Society of America
Because this organization's focus is on growing indoor plants, it's ideal for older gardeners who want or need to pursue their hobby inside their homes. The organization publishes *House Plant Magazine* as well as other publications, such as *Learn to Grow Under Fluorescent Lights*. Round-robin letters enable members without an active local chapter to communicate and share information through the mail.

$15 to $35 a year

❧ Orchids
Orchids were once considered to be a rich person's hobby, but they're now within the reach of anyone, regardless of income. They also have the reputation of being difficult to grow, but this really isn't the case. They do require the right growing conditions of water, fertilizer, light, and air, just like any other plant. If you can grow house plants, you can grow orchids. These beautiful blooms of infinite variety and intense fragrance don't necessarily require a greenhouse; many can be grown successfully under normal household conditions. Find out more by joining the national orchid association with more than 26,000 members in 500 local groups. Membership includes a monthly magazine (the *AOS Bulletin*) with tips and articles on orchid culture and an advertising directory of sources for plants and supplies, as well as a handbook for beginners and discounts on other publications. Joining a local chapter will put you in direct contact with people who share your interest and who are willing to provide assistance as needed.

American Orchid Society   *$15 to $35 a year*

❧ Roses
Growing roses is a demanding but satisfying pastime. More than 20,000 persons belong to over 385 local societies that provide information, education, and social opportunities for rose lovers. About 70 percent of the members are over 50. Benefits include a subscription to

the monthly magazine *The American Rose*, access to other publications, discounts on products, and membership in local societies.

American Rose Society   *$15 to $35 a year*

⚘ Succulents

Succulent plants, including cacti, come in a variety of shapes, colors, and textures. Some species are flowering. Many are ideal for growing indoors. By joining one of the 80 local succulent clubs throughout the United States, you'll meet fellow hobbyists and learn more about growing succulents through lectures and slide programs. Lending libraries, plants on exhibit, and plants for sale are also offered. Membership in the national society includes a subscription to the bimonthly *Cactus and Succulent Journal,* which features articles for beginners, advanced collectors, and scientific botanists. Its advertising section offers plants, seeds, books, and accessories for sale.

Cactus and Succulent Society of America   *$15 to $35 a year*

MODEL AERONAUTICS

You're never too old to build model airplanes (or boats, cars, and train sets). Model aeronautics (the building and flying of miniature aircraft) is actually quite a complex activity. Beginners can learn to build and fly radio-controlled planes with the help of instructors available through one of the more than 2,500 chartered hobby clubs. Flying fields are also provided to members. Although the hobby was once viewed as being for children, the current membership of the club for model aeronautics is predominantly mature adults.

Academy of Model Aeronautics   *$15 to $35 a year annual dues*
A large selection of kits for beginning to advanced hobbyists is available through mail-order catalogs.

America's Hobby Center   *Free catalog*

MUSIC

There's no question that making music is as satisfying for older adults as it is for younger persons. Some of us were fortunate enough to have taken music lessons as children and continued playing throughout our lives, but most either didn't have these lessons or didn't keep up our skills as we grew older. Many adults wish that they had learned to play when they were younger but are convinced that they couldn't begin at this point in their lives.

Piano lesson booklets

Two booklets, *So You've Always Wanted to Play the Piano* and *The Possible Dream,* show that it's never too late to start. Helpful suggestions can benefit anyone of any age.

National Piano Foundation *Free (with a self-addressed stamped envelope)*

Music instructors (all instruments)

A nationwide listing of certified music instructors is yours for the asking.

National Association of Music Teachers

Photography

There's always something new to learn about photography. Improve your skills by joining a national photography organization. In addition to receiving the monthly *PSA Journal* (the oldest consumer photographic magazine published in the United States), your membership will also put you in touch with local and national workshops, competitions, and a technical information service. Special-interest divisions include color slides, pictorial prints, nature, video and motion picture, stereo or three-dimensional photography, photojournalism, and photo travel.

Photographic Society of America *$35 to $75 a year*

Radio

A number of leisure radio activities go beyond listening to commercial broadcasts. These include monitor radio listening, shortwave radio, and ham radio.

Monitor radio listening

"Eavesdropping" on two-way radio conversations from public safety departments (highway patrol, state/city/county police, fire, and emergency services), aircraft (commercial, military, private planes, and airports), government (local, county, state, and federal), railroads, and news media (TV and radio remotes) can be fascinating. Listening on a scanner is legal but does need to be done in an ethical and responsible manner. A national radio club can provide advice about equipment and facilitate sharing between members on searching the spectrum and locating local frequencies.

Radio Communications Monitoring Association   *$15 to $35 a year*

✺ Shortwave radio

Listening to broadcasts from China, eastern Europe, or the Middle East can be a fascinating pastime. Hundreds of stations around the world broadcast in English. Programs can range from nature to stamp collecting to sports to popular culture. They may even provide some foreign language lessons as well. A portable shortwave unit is around $200, while larger, more sophisticated units can cost a few thousand. Unlike amateur radio operators (hams) who must obtain a license issued by the FCC, shortwave listeners need only have a shortwave receiver to participate. Either the **North American Shortwave Association** or the **American Shortwave Listeners Club** can provide more information. Program guides to stations around the world are available from **Grove Enterprises** (*The Monitoring Times*) and **International Broadcasting Services** (*Passport to World Band Radio*).

$15 to $35

✺ Ham radio

Listening to broadcasts on shortwave receivers is an enjoyable passive activity. For more active involvement, owners of shortwave receivers can tune into the frequencies used by ham radio operators. Interesting QSOs (ham talk for conversations) make this a very enjoyable pastime. Communicating through voice, digital (computer), and Morse code, amateur radio operators can make hundreds of friends around town and around the world. They can also handle messages for police and relief organizations during such emergencies as hurricanes, tornadoes, floods, earthquakes, motor vehicle accidents, fires, chemical spills, and search and rescues. To learn the Morse code, novices can listen to code practice sessions on W1AW (the station operated by the American Radio Relay League). Codes at 5 to 15 words per minute are aired at 7 P.M. on Monday, Wednesday, and Friday; 10 P.M. on Tuesday, Thursday, Saturday, and Sunday. Megahertz frequencies are 1.8180, 3.5815, 7.0475, 14.0475, 18.0975, 21.0675, 28.0675, 147.5555. The multiple-choice test for an entry-level novice license isn't much more difficult than the written portion of a driver's license exam. Successful examinees also need to be able to copy Morse code sent at 5 words per minute. For those persons who are convinced that they couldn't learn Morse code, the technician class of ham license allows hams to talk using frequencies above traditional ham radio bands. Only a written exam is required. Study guides for the exams (such as *Technician Class FCC License Preparation* by Gordon West, under $5) are available at bookstores or Radio Shacks. As the national organization of amateur radio operators, the American Radio Relay League provides educational support for new hams, including *Your Introduction to Morse Code* (set of Morse code–learning audiotapes, $5 to $15) and *Now You're Talking!: Discover the World of Ham Radio* (an introduction to the hobby as well as information for passing the novice or technician license written exams, $15 to $35 for the book). A used transceiver (combination transmitter and receiver) costs about $350 to $600. An antenna can cost from $75 to $125 more.

American Radio Relay League, Inc.   *$15 to $35 annual dues*
Persons with physical disabilities can get assistance with specialized equipment for amateur radio operation and can network with each other through the **International Handicappers' Net.** Membership is free.

SOFTBALL

Physical activities such as walking and swimming are profiled in the Exercise section of Chapter 2. But softball, played just for fun, is a terrific way to spend some leisure time. Men and women over 50 who enjoy softball can see if there's a senior team that plays in their community. There's even a senior softball world series held every year.
Seniors Softball USA

TRAVEL

Older persons who have the time, money, and energy to travel find this to be one of the most rewarding activities of their later years. The possibilities for travel are endless. While seniors can participate in virtually any travel experience they wish, the following options and resources are especially geared toward their interests and needs.

(See also the Travel section earlier in this chapter.)

✖ Companion services

If you would like to travel but don't have anyone to travel with, you can obtain a traveling companion through special services that match up mature travel companions. Newsletters provide brief descriptions of members (such as gender, age, destination preferences, likes, and dislikes), but don't actually publish members' addresses and phone numbers. Club members contact each other through a mail-exchange service, club get-togethers, and group trips. Sample newsletters can sometimes be obtained for a nominal fee before purchasing an annual membership.

Traveling Companions   *$15 to $35 annual membership*

✖ *Travel Tips for Older Americans*

The State Department has put together a booklet suggesting ways in which mature travelers can enjoy safe and satisfying vacations abroad.

Consumer Information Center (157X)   *under $5*

✖ *Going Abroad: 101 Tips for Mature Travelers*

This highly informative booklet provides a wealth of information on trip preparation (packing, home security, currency, getting travel documents in order), the trip itself (plane travel, driving abroad, communicating, shopping, size conversions, phones, tipping, sightseeing, photography, and health care), returning home (clearing customs, cashing in used traveler's checks), and cruise tips, all with a focus on the mature traveler.

Grand Circle Travel   *Free*

✖ *The Mature Traveler*

This newsletter provides information about travel offers, discounts, and special packages, all aimed at older travelers.

$15 to $35 a year

✖ Travel agencies specializing in mature travel

Most older persons aren't interested in the types of vacations that appeal to people in their twenties. They look for bus and train tours, cruises, and packaged deals that suit their temperament, interest, and physical abilities. If local agents seem to cater to younger people, consider the services of travel firms that have interest and experience in serving the older traveler.

Grand Circle Travel, Inc.
Senior Escorted Tours

⚲ Travel/study: Elderhostel
Elderhostel offers noncredit adult education courses in the liberal arts and sciences. Any individual 60 or older is welcome to participate, regardless of educational background. Most programs are a week in length and consist of three courses that each meet for about an hour a day. There are no exams, grades, or homework. Programs are held at colleges, universities, retreat centers, and national parks. Participants stay in college dorms and eat in college cafeterias. Provisions are made for touring the local area and for cultural and recreational activities. The cost is extremely low and all-inclusive (registration costs, 6 nights' accommodations, all meals, five days of classes, and extra-curricular activities) except for airfare or other transportation costs. A limited number of "hostelships" (scholarships) are available for people who can't afford the fees. A sampling of recent offerings includes Making Maple Syrup (North Park College, Wisconsin), Advanced Genealogy Workshop (Brigham Young University, Utah), Shaker basketry (Calumet Conference Center, New Hampshire), George Washington: The Myth and the Man (Salisbury State University, Maryland), and Decoding TV in the 1990s (Mercer University, Georgia). International courses are offered as well, in countries ranging from France to Kenya to Costa Rica to Norway. Elderhostel programs provide high-quality intellectual and social stimulation to older persons in a safe, comfortable environment.

Elderhostel   *Cost varies; typical program is $200 to $350*

⚲ Travel/study: college noncredit programs
Many colleges and universities offer noncredit 2- and 4-week courses specifically for older students. Typically held in the summer, these courses may range from Conversational Chinese to Exploring Values to Music American Style to The Assassination of President Kennedy to Understanding Wall Street. Central Washington University's Senior Ventures offers a regionally and nationally organized program

that incorporates weekday classes taught by professors and weekend social functions and field trips. Extra side trips are also available so that participants can tour through more of the Pacific Northwest. Participants choose their housing, ranging from single furnished residence hall suites to double-occupancy student apartments. The only requirement for enrollment is the ability to climb stairs (since housing accommodations and classrooms are not always on the first floor) and to walk between classroom buildings (which may be as far as six blocks apart).

Senior Ventures   *approximately $350 to $600 per week (includes housing, meals, classes, and field trips but not transportation)*

⚴ Travel/study: Haystack Mountain School of Crafts

Instead of bringing back a store-bought souvenir from your next vacation, consider a vacation from which you can bring back both handmade souvenirs *and* a new hobby to continue pursuing. A very special summer program teaches crafts and arts to both beginning and advanced students. Course offerings include clay, drawing, blacksmithing, wood, baskets-fiber, glass, papermaking, printmaking, and metals. Sessions last 1 to 3 weeks. The school is located in a rustic lakeside setting 60 miles from Bangor, Maine. Scholarships are available for needy students.

Haystack Mountain School of Crafts   *$200 to $350 for 1-week tuition; $125 to $350 per week room and board (depending on accommodations)*

⚴ Travel/study: Augusta Heritage Center

Educational programs in the folk arts are available in week-long sessions held mainly during the summer at the Augusta Heritage Center of Davis & Elkins College in West Virginia. Possibilities for novices through advanced students include the following:

· music (harmony singing, hammered dulcimer, old-time banjo, harmonica, Scottish fiddle, flat-pick guitar)

· dance (clogging, Cajun dance, Irish folk dance, swing, dance calling)

· crafts (basketry, broommaking, bookbinding, paper marbling, calligraphy, wood carving, blacksmithing, stained glass, quiltmaking, weaving)

· folklore (herbs, Appalachian literature, Cajun cooking, Gaelic language and song, storytelling)

Participants may stay in the college dormitories or nearby economy hotels.

Augusta Heritage Center   *$200 to $350 a week*

❧ Travel/study: TraveLearn

The TraveLearn company specializes in setting up university-sponsored study trips. Under the auspices of TraveLearn, more than 170 universities and colleges provide international tours as part of their commitment to lifelong learning and global understanding. Tours are led by professors and include on site lectures, seminars, and field experiences conducted by local specialists. Specifically designed for adult learners (not undergraduates), these tours provide luxury accommodations for the mature traveler while offering opportunities to visit sites often not available to the average tourist on conventional tours. Participants tend to be over 50, educated, and representing a variety of backgrounds and interests. TraveLearn tours typically range from $2,500 to $5,000 and feature such destinations as the Dominican Republic, Ireland, Russia, Brazil, Galapagos Islands, and China.

TraveLearn

❧ Travel/study: writer's conferences, seminars, and workshops

A number of people of all ages feel that they have a novel in them but never get around to writing it. Older persons have the time and a lifetime of experiences to put pen to paper (or fingers to computer keyboard) and write that book. Some people have no problem just sitting down and writing, but others need some instruction. Colleges and adult community schools usually offer semester-long classes. A more intensive alternative is to attend a writing conference or seminar. *Writer's Digest*, a monthly magazine available in libraries and at bookstores, lists national conferences, seminars, and workshops in its May issue every year. They're typically held at colleges and universities. Recent offerings have included New England Writer's Workshop at Simmons College in Boston (4 days of general writing assistance, including individual consultations and manuscript evaluations from prominent agents and editors), University of Alaska's 6-day travel writing course (combining actual travel through Alaska with classroom instruction), and Summer Writing Workshops at Idyllwild School of Music and the Arts in California (featuring week-long creative writing and writer's journal courses). Other possibilities include romance novels, mystery writing, photojournalism, poetry, and screenwriting. Expenses vary according to the school/sponsor, accommodations, and travel, but they may be tax-deductible if you sell some of your writing!

⚶ Travel/outdoor activities

Persons 50 years young or older can join "The Gang" on its skiing, biking, rafting, sailing, hiking, and other outdoor trips. Many trips are offered throughout the year both in and out of the United States.

Over the Hill Gang   *Costs vary*

⚶ Travel/study: Close Up

The Close Up Foundation, a nonprofit, nonpartisan educational organization, offers a special learning adventure in the spring and fall for persons 50 and older. The Close Up week in Washington allows citizens to take a behind-the-scenes look at the federal government in action. Seminars, tours, and meetings enable participants to leave with a better understanding of the democratic process. This new appreciation, gained from meetings with senators, representatives, policy analysts, media representatives, diplomats, lobbyists, and program instructors, will make reading the newspaper and watching television news a much richer and involving process in the future. At all-inclusive price (everything but transportation to and from Washington is included), the week in Washington is a unique experience that can't be duplicated by typical tours to the nation's capital.

Close Up Foundation   *$600 to $1,000*

⚶ Travel/sports

Sporting vacations (primarily in golf, but also tennis, bowling, and skiing) are geared for those 50 and older. Tournaments are mostly recreational in nature, but there can be an element of competition for those who want it (with accompanying prizes and recognition). Participants range in skill levels but share common perspectives and experiences gained from the vantage of maturity. Instead of having to contend with partners or other players whose youth gives them an unfair advantage, participants in the National Seniors Sports Association (NSSA) sporting holidays can enjoy being with their peers. New friendships also develop between singles and couples who play together. Vacations are arranged in Florida, California. Hawaii, or the Caribbean during the winter and in Michigan, Oregon, or Canada during the summer. Fees vary depending on the resort, season of the year, and length (usually 4 nights). Prospective participants must join the NSSA; membership entitles them to a monthly newsletter that features articles describing upcoming outings and articles of interest.

National Senior Sports Association   *$15 to $35 a year*

❧ Travel/employment

Mature persons with special skills and talents can enjoy virtually free cruises if they're willing to share their expertise with the other passengers. A special booking bureau places speakers (who give five different 45-minute presentations on such topics as health, self-development, humor, genealogy, image, beauty/fashion, science, communication, and regional history/geography/culture) and instructors (who lead a number of 45-minute classes in fitness, dancing, golf, tennis, foreign language, computers, needlework, drawing, ceramics, calligraphy, and photography) on luxury cruise ships. In exchange for the presentation services, presenters receive their cruise, cabins, and meals for free. To be considered, applicants must provide a biography, a list of proposed titles and brief descriptions of the presentations, and a videotape. Men who are 45 and older, witty conversationalists, and excellent dancers can also be considered for the gentleman Host Program. These men act as ambassadors for the cruise ship, mingling with all the other passengers while concentrating on playing host to mature single females who are traveling alone. They must interact with all women and not show any favoritism toward any one female. The hosts participate in all activities, including dancing, dining, and other social events. Cruise lines provide free accommodations, meals, and round-trip airfare. Applicants must provide a photo, résumé, and letters of recommendation. Because they must be good dancers, a dance review is required. Dance reviewers in various cities spend half an hour to review the level of dance proficiency and provide helpful hints; the applicant is charged $15 to $35 for the review. A personal interview must be scheduled, either at the company's headquarters in San Jose, California or at various principal cities throughout the country; the applicant travels at his own expense to the interview. The booking agency charges $125 to $200 placement fee per week for every week that a host or presenter is aboard the ship.

The Working Vacation

⚘ Evergreen/Travel Club

This is ideal for those who dislike the impersonal feeling and expense of hotels. Members stay at other members' homes for a small fee. They make their own arrangements from a nationwide listing of prospective hosts. The typical stay is one or two nights. At their convenience, Evergreen members open up their homes to other members. If a guest wants to visit at an inconvenient time, would-be hosts can decline. Persons interested in traveling but who lack guest quarters can join the Travel Club. Both Evergreen members and Travel Club members find new friendships as they share their lives for a night or two. Annual dues are the same for Evergreen and Travel Club members, but accommodation prices differ. Evergreen members pay $5 to $15 nightly and couples pay $15 to $35; Travel Club members pay $15 to $35 as a single or as a couple.

Evergreen/Travel Club   *$35 to $75 annual dues*

⚘ Hosteling

Some travelers don't want or can't afford high-priced hotels. A hostel is the perfect alternative. It enables travelers to stay in Paris or New York City for $15 to $35 a night. Accommodations are usually dorm style, with separate quarters for males and females, fully equipped self-service kitchens, dining areas, and common rooms for socializing. Accommodations may range from a castle in Germany to a lighthouse on the California coast. There are more than 6,000 hostels in 70 countries (with 200 in the United States). Most have special programs and activities, such as historic neighborhood walking tours, photography workshops, or sailing and cycling trips. Although originally developed as a means for young travelers to afford to explore the world, persons of all ages are welcome. The informal atmosphere encourages guests to mingle as they cook and live together. Guests must bring their own linens (sheets, pillowcases, and towels; bed, blankets, and pillows are provided) and clean up after themselves. Because the philosophy of hosteling is to get out and see the world, guests must vacate the premises immediately after breakfast and can't return until evening.

Hosteling International/American Youth Hostels   *$15 to $35 a year membership fee*

⚐ RVing

An estimated 9 million Americans 50 and older use recreational vehicles for their vacations. Motor homes are an extremely popular way to travel around the U.S.A. Complimentary packets of information about RVing, including listings of RV rental sources, camping clubs, and campground and RV resort sites can be obtained through the national recreational vehicle association.

Recreational Vehicle Industry Association   *Free*

Many older persons do not have a spouse to travel with and may be interested in hooking up with other singles. Loners of America enables compatible individuals to connect. This organization allows travelers to maintain their privacy and independence while enjoying some companionship through organized recreational activities, campouts, rallies, and caravans. Although membership is limited to single persons, it is not a matchmaking service. Its 1,450 members are mostly retirees in their forties to nineties who vary in their RV use (as infrequently as a few days a year to living in it full time). Dues include a monthly newsletter and annual membership directory.

Loners of America   *$15 to $35 a year*

Women can find support and camaraderie in RVing Women. This organization enables them to meet and socialize with other women traveling independently. Over 40 rallies and caravans are planned each year. More than 3,000 women from the U.S., Canada, Mexico, and abroad belong. Some are married women whose husbands don't want to travel in RVs, and others are single. In addition to the social aspects, the group also educates members about issues such as security and RV maintenance. Members can hook up with other women who don't own a RV and want to travel with someone who does, as well as with other RV owners who are seeking a caravan companion.

RVing Women   *$35 to $75 a year*

WORK

Many people can't wait to retire, but once they leave the 9-to-5 grind discover that they feel bored and unfulfilled. A yearning to feel productive again (as well as pressing financial needs) may lead an older person to want to re-enter the work force.

❧ Finding work

Job hunting is never easy at any age. It's even more challenging the older a person gets. An older job seeker should take advantage of all available assistance. AARP WORKS sponsors nationwide seminars that help workers evaluate their skills and talents, enhance their self-esteem, and learn how to successfully look for employment.

American Association of Retired Persons   *$35 to $75*
for four 2-hour sessions

❧ *Second Careers: New Ways to Work After 50*

This book, written by Caroline Bird and published by Little, Brown, and Company, focuses on innovative career changes. It profiles mature workers who made dramatic switches from one career to a completely different one (such as an attorney who became a commercial salmon fisherman). The majority of the second careers discussed in the book allow workers to help others, become their own bosses, or simply feel more challenged and satisfied. At local bookstores
$15 to $35

❧ Green Thumb

As a national nonprofit organization dedicated to improving the quality of life for older Americans and to providing essential services to local communities, Green Thumb offers training and employment opportunities for older Americans in 44 states and Puerto Rico. Although it originally focused on rural participants who helped with beautification of the nation's parks and highways, current participants perform a wide range of community services: child care, elder care, tutoring, library assisting, computer operation, and skilled trades and crafts. Participants must be 55 years of age or older and have a limited income. They receive the minimum wage for approximately 20 hours of community service work at a public or nonprofit agency while receiving training, work experience, and supportive services to prepare them for eventual employment outside the auspices of the program. Contact the **Green Thumb** organization for further information.

⚘ Becoming an entrepreneur

Anyone with a good idea and some time and energy may want to think about launching his or her own business. Possibilities can be as modest as selling a few homemade crafts or providing child care services or as ambitious as running a restaurant or store, working as a consultant, or developing a new company. Some possibilities require significant capital, while others can be started without any money at all. Bookstores and libraries offer many books and magazines about entrepreneurship. One excellent resource specifically geared toward older persons is *Start Your Own Business After 50—or 60—or 70!* by Lauraine Snelling, published by Bristol Publishing.

$5 to $15; special order through any bookstore

RESOURCES

AAA Foundation for Traffic Safety
1730 M Street NW, Suite 40
Washington, DC 20036
(202) 775-1456

AARP Fulfillment
1909 K Street NW
Washington, DC 20045

AARP Home Equity Information
  Center
601 E Street NW
Washington, DC 20049

AARP—Membership Division
P.O. Box 199
Long Beach, CA 90801

AARP National Headquarters
601 E Street NW
Washington, DC 20049
(202) 434-2277

AARP Pharmacy Service
(800) 456-2277

AARP Volunteer Talent Bank
601 E Street NW
Washington, DC 20049

AARP Widowed Persons Services
1909 K Street NW
Washington, DC 20045

Academy of Model Aeronautics
1810 Samuel Morse Drive
Reston, VA 22090
(703) 435-0750

Access Real Estate
SEA Realty
22 Sunset Avenue
Westhampton, NY 11978
(516) 288-6244

Access to Recreation
2509 East Thousand Oaks Boulevard,
  Suite 430
Thousand Oaks, CA 91362
(800) 634-4351 or (805) 498-8186

ACTION—Volunteers in Service to
    America
1100 Vermont Avenue NW
Washington, DC 20525
(800) 424-8867 or (202) 606-4855

adaptAbility
P.O. Box 515
Colchester, CT 06415
(800) 243-9232

Adaptations
1758 Empire Central
Dallas, TX 75235
(800) 688-1758 or (214) 630-1537

Adaptive Equipment Center
Newington Children's Hospital
181 East Cedar Street
Newington, CT 06111
(800) 344-5405 or (203) 667-5405 in
    Connecticut (860)

Adventures in Cassettes
Metacom, Inc.
1401-B West River Road North
Minneapolis, MN 55411
(800) 328-0108

Advil
Forum on Health Education
1500 Broadway, 25th floor
New York, NY 10036

African Violet Society of America Inc.
P.O. Box 3609
Beaumont, TX 77704
(404) 839-4725

Agency for Health Care Policy and
    Research (AHCPR)
Publications Clearinghouse
P.O. Box 8547
Silver Spring, MD 20907

Aging Network Services
4400 East–West Highway, Suite 907
Bethesda, MD 20814
(301) 657-4329

Aids for Arthritis
3 Little Knoll Court
Medford, NJ 08055
(609) 654-6918

Alcoholics Anonymous
P.O. Box 459, Grand Central Station
New York, NY 10163

Alda Industries
292 Charles Street
Providence, RI 02904
(800) 544-9769 or (401) 751-6775

Allergy Information Center and
    Hotline
(800) 727-5400

Alsto Company (The)
P.O. Box 1267
Galesburg, IL 61401
(800) 447-0048 or (309) 343-6181

Alzheimer's Association
919 North Michigan Avenue, Suite
    1000
Chicago, IL 60611
(800) 272-3900, (800) 621-0379, or
    (312) 335-8700

Alzheimer's Disease Education and
    Referral Center
P.O. Box 8250
Silver Spring, MD 20907
(800) 438-4380

AMC Cancer Information and
    Counseling Line
(800) 525-3777 or (303) 233-6501

American Academy of Ophthalmology
P.O. Box 7424
San Francisco, CA 94120

American Association for International
  Aging
1836 Lomos Boulevard NE
Albuquerque, NM 87131
(505) 277-0911

American Association for Marriage and
  Family Therapy
1100 17th Street NW, 10th floor
Washington, DC 20036
(202) 452-0109

American Association of Individual
  Investors
625 North Michigan Avenue
Chicago, IL 60611
(312) 280-0170

American Association of Kidney
  Patients
111 South Parker Street, Suite 405
Tampa, FL 33606
(800) 749-2257

American Association of Oral and
  Maxillofacial Surgeons
9700 West Bryn Mawr Avenue
Rosemont, IL 60018
(800) 822-6637 or (708) 678-6200

American Association of Retired
  Persons—Membership Division
P.O. Box 199
Long Beach, CA 90801

American Association of Retired
  Persons—National
Headquarters
601 E Street NW
Washington, DC 20049
(202) 434-2277

American Automobile Association
Traffic Safety and Engineering
  Department
Driver Safety Services
1000 AAA Drive
Heathrow, FL 32746
(407) 444-7961

American Board of Medical Specialties
  Certification Hotline
(800) 776-2378

American Cancer Society
1599 Clifton Road NE
Atlanta, GA 30329
(800) 227-2345 or (404) 320-3333

American Checker Federation
P.O. Box 365
Petal, MS 39465
(601) 582-7090

American College of Obstetricians and
  Gynecologists
409 12th Street SW
Washington, DC 20024
(202) 863-2518

American College of SurgeonsPublic
  Information Office
55 East Erie Street
Chicago, IL 60611
(312) 664-4050

American Contract Bridge League
2990 Airways Boulevard
Memphis, TN 38116
(901) 332-5586

American Diabetes Association
1970 Chain Bridge Road
McLean, VA 22109
(800) 232-3472

American Dietetic Association
216 West Jackson Boulevard, Suite 800
Chicago, IL 60606
(800) 366-1655 or (312) 899-0040

American Field Service (AFS)
313 East 43rd Street
New York, NY 10164
(800) 876-2377

American Foundation for the Blind
Product Center
100 Enterprise Place
P.O. Box 7044
Dover, DE 19903
(800) 829-0500

American Foundation for the Blind
   Information Line
15 West 16th Street
New York, NY 10011
(800) 232-5463 or (212) 620-2000

American Heart Association
7272 Greenville Avenue
Dallas, TX 75231
(214) 373-6300

American Hotel and Motel Association
Safety Tips
1201 New York Avenue, NW
Washington, DC 20005

American Lung Association
1740 Broadway
New York, NY 10019
(212) 315-8700

American Medical Association
515 North State Street
Chicago, IL 60610
(312) 464-5000

American Needlewoman, Inc. (The)
P.O. Box 6472
Fort Worth, TX 76115

American Numismatic Association
818 North Cascade Avenue
Colorado Springs, CO 80903
(800) 367-9723

American Optometric Association
243 North Lindbergh Boulevard
St. Louis, MO 63141

American Orchid Society
6000 South Olive Avenue
West Palm Beach, FL 33405
(407) 585-8666

American Parkinson Disease
   Association
60 Bay Street
Suite 401
Staten Island, NY 10301
(800) 223-2732 or (718) 981-8001

American Philatelic Society
P.O. Box 8000
State College, PA 16803
(814) 237-3803

American Podiatric Medical
   Association
9312 Old Georgetown Road
Bethesda, MD 20814
(800) 366-8227 or (301) 571-9200

American Postal Chess Tournaments
P.O. Box 305
Western Springs, IL 60558
(708) 246-6665

American Quilter's Society
P.O. Box 3290
Paducah, KY 42002

American Radio Relay League
225 Main Street
Newington, CT 06111
(800) 326-3942 or (203) 666-1541

American Rose Society
P.O. Box 30000
Shreveport, LA 71130
(318) 938-5402

American Sewing Guild
P.O. Box 8476
Medford, OR 97504

American Shortwave Listeners Club
16182 Ballad Lane
Huntington Beach, CA 92649
(714) 846-1685

American Society for Geriatric
  Dentistry
1121 West Michigan Street
Indianapolis, IN 46202

American Society for Geriatric
  Psychiatry
P.O. Box 376-A
Greenbelt, MD 20768
(301) 220-0952

American Society for the Prevention of
  Cruelty to Animals
441 East 92nd Street
New York, NY 10128
(800) 395-2772 or (212) 876-7700

American Society of Plastic and
  Reconstructive Surgeons
444 East Algonquin Road
Arlington Heights, IL 60005
(800) 635-0635 or (708) 635-0635

American Speech-Language
  Association
10801 Rockville Pike
Rockville, MD 20852
(800) 638-8255 or (301) 897-8682 in
  Maryland

American Telemarketing Association
444 North Larchmont Boulevard, Suite
  200
Los Angeles, CA 90004

American Tinnitus Association
P.O. Box 5
Portland, OR 97207
(503) 248-9985

American Volkssport Association
1001 Pat Booker Road, Suite 101
Universal City, TX 78148

American Wild Bird Company
617 Hugerford Drive
Rockville, MD 20850
(800) 942-4737

America Remembers
P.O. Box 261804
San Diego, CA 92196
(619) 695-0031

America's Hobby Center
146 West 22nd Street
New York, NY 10011
(800) 989-3989 or (212) 765-8922

America the Beautiful Fund (ABF)
219 Shoreham Building
Washington, DC 20005
(202) 638-1649

Amnesty International USA
322 Eighth Avenue
New York, NY 10001
(212) 627-1451

Ann Morris Enterprises
890 Fams Court
East Meadow, NY 11554
(516) 292-9232

Aquatic Exercise Association
P.O. Box 497
Port Washington, WI 53074

Architectural and Transportation
  Barriers Compliance Board
1111 18th Street NW
Washington, DC 20036
(800) 872-2253 or (202) 653-7834

Arthritis Foundation
1314 Spring Street NW
Atlanta, GA 30309
(800) 283-7800 or (404) 872-7100

Arts and Crafts Nationwide
P.O. Box 2246
Paducah, KY 42002
(800) 755-0226

Ask A Nurse
(800) 535-1111

Ask the Pharmacist
(900) 420-0275

Assistance Dogs International
c/o Robin Dickson
10175 Wheeler Road
Central Point, OR 97502
(503) 826-9220

Association for Macular Diseases, Inc.
210 East 64th Street
New York, NY 10021

Association of Professional Sleep
  Societies
604 2nd Street SW
Rochester, MN 55902

Association of Radio Reading Services
University of South Florida
WSUF Radio Reading Service
Tampa, FL 33620
(813) 974-4193

Association of Retired Americans
P.O. Box 610286
Dallas, TX 75261
(800) 622-8040

AT&T National Special Needs Center
2001 Route 46, Suite 310
Parsippany, NJ 07054
(800) 233-1222

Audio Optics, Inc.
24 Hutton Avenue, #26
West Orange, NJ 07052
(201) 736-5490

Augusta Heritage Center
Davis & Elkins College
100 Sycamore Street
Elkins, WV 26241
(304) 636-1903, ext. 209

Bauer Financial Reports
P.O. Box 145510
Coral Gables, FL 33114
(800) 388-6686

Better Hearing Helpline
(800) 327-9355

Better Hearing Institute
P.O. Box 1840
Washington, DC 20013
(800) 327-9355 or (703) 642-0580

Better Vision Institute
1800 North Kent Street, Suite 904
Rosslyn, VA 22209
(703) 243-1528

Betterway Publications
P.O. Box 219
Crozet, VA 22931
(804) 823-5661

Bible Alliance, Inc.
P.O. Box 621
Bradenton, FL 34206
(813) 748-3031

Bits and Pieces
1 Puzzle Place
Stevens Point, WI 54481
(800) 544-7297

Bonsai Clubs International
Virginia Ellermann, Business Manager
2636 West Mission Road, #277
Tallahassee, FL 32304

Books on Tape, Inc.
P.O. Box 7900
Newport Beach, CA 92658
(800) 626-3333

Brookstone
5 Vose Farm Road
Peterborough, NH 03458
(603) 924-9541

Bruce Medical Supply
411 Waverly Oaks Road, P.O. Box 9166
Waltham, MA 02254
(800) 225-8446

Bruno Independent Living Aids
1780 Executive Drive, P.O. Box 84
Oconomowoc, WI 53066
(800) 882-8183 or (414) 567-4990

B. Young
P.O. Box 56
Stanfordville, NY 12581

Cactus and Succulent Society of
    America, Inc.
c/o Seymour Linden
1535 Reeves Street
Los Angeles, CA 90035
(310) 556-1923

Calcium Information Center
The New York Hospital/Cornell
    Medical Center
515 East 71st Street, S-904
New York, NY 10021
(800) 321-2681

Cancer Information Service
National Cancer Institute
Office of Cancer Communications
Building 31, Room 10A16
9000 Rockville Pike
Bethesda, MD 20892
(800) 422-6237 or (301) 496-5583

Canine Companions for Independence
4350 Occidental Road
P.O. Box 446
Santa Rosa, CA 95402
(707) 528-0830

Cardinal Company
P.O. Box 9
Moorestown, NJ 08057

Center for Accessible Housing
North Carolina State University,
    School of Design
P.O. Box 8613
Raleigh, NC 27695
(919) 515-3082

Center for Clothing/Physical
    Disabilities
Buffalo Street College
Caudell Hall
1300 Elmwood Avenue
Buffalo, NY 14222
(716) 878-5704

Center for Science in the Public
    Interest
1875 Connecticut Avenue NW, Suite
    300
Washington, DC 20009
(202) 667-7483

Center for Therapeutic Applications of
  Technology
University of Buffalo
3435 Main Street, 515 Kimball Tower
Buffalo, NY 14214
(800) 628-2281

Century 21 Real Estate Corporation
P.O. Box 19564
Irvine, CA 92713
(714) 553-2100

Chair Dancing order service
(800) 551-4386

Cheapskate Monthly
P.O. Box 2135
Paramount, CA 90723
(310) 630-8845

Cherry Tree Toys
P.O. Box 369-140
Belmont, Ohio 43718
(614) 484-4363

Chess Correspondent (The)
P.O. Box 3481
Barrington, IL 60011

Children of Aging Parents
1609 Woodbourne Road, Suite 302-A
Levittown, PA 19057
(215) 945-6900

Choice in Dying
200 Varick Street
New York, NY 10014
(212) 366-5540

Chrysler Corporation
Physically-Challenged Resource
  Center
1220 Rankin Street
Troy, MI 48083
(800) 255-9877

Civitan International
P.O. Box 130744
Birmingham, AL 35213
(800) 248-4826 or (205) 591-6307 in
  Alabama

Cleo, Inc.
3957 Mayfield Road
Cleveland, OH 44121
(800) 321-0595 or (216) 382-9700

Clinical Nutrition Research Unit
Division of Nephrology, Hypertension,
  and Clinical Pharmacology
Oregon Health Sciences University
3314 SW Veterans Hospital Road
  PP262
Portland, OR 97201
(800) 321-2681

Close Up Foundation
44 Canal Center Plaza
Alexandria, VA 22314
(800) 232-2000

Clowns of America, International
P.O. Box 570
Lake Jackson, TX 77566
(409) 297-6699

Colonial Garden Kitchens
P.O. Box 66
Hanover, PA 17333
(800) 752-5552 or (717) 633-3330

Comfortably Yours
2515 East 43rd Street, P.O. Box
  182216
Chattanooga, TN 37422
(800) 521-0097 or (615) 867-9955

Commission on Voluntary Service and
  Action
P.O. Box 117
New York, NY 10009
(212) 581-5082

CompuServe Information Service
Department L, P.O. Box 18161
Columbus, OH 43272
(800) 848-8199

Conservation Corporation of America
56 Radcliffe Road
Weston, MA 02193
(800) 344-7283

Consumer Education Research Center
350 Scotland Road
Orange, NJ 07050

Consumer Information Center
P.O. Box 100
Pueblo, CO 81002

Consumer Product Safety Commission
Office of Information and Public
  Affairs
5401 Westbard Avenue
Bethesda, MD 20207
(301) 504-0580

Contest Center (The)
59 DeGarmo Hills Road
Wappingers Falls, NY 12590

Cornell University
Media Services Resource Center
7 Cornell Business and Technology
  Park
Ithaca, NY 14850

Council of Better Business Bureaus
4200 Wilson Boulevard, Suite 800
Arlington, VA 22203
(703) 276-0100

Council on Family Health
225 Park Avenue South, Suite 1700
New York, NY 10003

Courage Stroke Network
Courage Center
3915 Golden Valley Road
Golden Valley, MN 55422
(800) 533-6321 or (612) 588-0811

Crafts Report (The)
P.O. Box 1992
Wilmington, DE 19899
(800) 777-7098

Critics' Choice Video
P.O. Box 749
Itasca, IL 60143
(800) 367-7765

Cruises Unlimited
9200 West Cross Drive, Suite 201
Littleton, CO 80123
(800) 875-6533

Dancin' Grannies
10 Bay Street, Suite 3
Westport, CT 06880
(800) 331-6839

Dearborn Trade
520 North Dearborn Street
Chicago, IL 60610
(312) 836-4400

Delo Books
3800 NW 126th Avenue, P.O. Box
  8447
Coral Springs, FL 33075

Dentsply
P.O. Box 872
York, PA 17405

Descriptive Video Service/WGBH-TV
125 Western Avenue
Boston, MA 02134
(617) 492-2777, ext. 3490

Diabetic Traveler (The)
Box 8223 RW
Stamford, CT 06905
(203) 327-5832

Dick Blick
P.O. Box 1267
Galesburg, IL 61401
(800) 723-2787

Direct Marketing Association
P.O. Box 3861
New York, NY 10163

Dr. Leonard's Health Care Catalog
74 20th Street
Brooklyn, NY 11232
(718) 768-0010

Doctors By Phone
(900) 773-6286

Earthwatch
680 Mount Auburn Street, P.O. Box
   403N
Watertown, MA 02272
(800) 776-0188 or (617) 926-8200

Easy Access Hotline
(800) 875-4663

Easy-Up
2917 Union Road, Suite D
Paso Robles, CA 93446
(800) 848-8706

Echo Corporation
(800) 832-4624

Effective Learning Systems, Inc.
5221 Edina Industrial Boulevard
Edina, MN 55439
(800) 966-5683 or (612) 893-1680

Eldercare Locator
(800) 677-1116

Elder Craftsmen, Inc.
135 East 65th Street
New York, NY 10021
(212) 861-5260

Elder-Health Program
University of Maryland
School of Pharmacy
The Parke-Davis Center for the
   Education of the Elderly
20 North Pine Street
Baltimore, MD 21201

Elderhostel
75 Federal Street
Boston, MA 02110
(617) 426-7788

Embroiderers' Guild of America, Inc.
335 West Broadway, Suite 100
Louisville, KY 40202
(502) 589-6956

Energizer Batteries
9711 Fuesser Road
Mascoutah, IL 62288

Enrichments
145 Tower Drive, P.O. Box 579
Hinsdale, IL 60521
(800) 323-5547

Evergreen/Travel Club
P.O. Box 441
Dixon, IL 61021

Evergreen Travel Service
(800) 435-2288 or (206) 776-1184 in
   Washington State

Eye Care Project
P.O. Box 7424
San Francisco, CA 94120
(800) 222-3937

Fashion Ease
1541 60th Street
Brooklyn, NY 11219
(800) 221-8929 or (718) 853-6376

FDIC
(800) 934-3342

55 Alive/Mature Driving
AARP
601 E Street NW
Washington, DC 20049

Food and Nutrition Information
   Center
U.S. Department of Agriculture
National Agricultural Library Building,
   Room 304
Beltsville, MD 20705
(301) 504-5719

For Convenience Sake
4092B Howard Avenue
Kensington, MD 20895
(800) 242-9763 or (301) 493-5810

Ford Mobility Motoring Program
P.O. Box 529
Bloomfield Hills, MI 48303
(800) 952-2248

Foster Grandparents Program
1100 Vermont Avenue NW
Washington, DC 20525
(202) 606-4849

Foundation for Glaucoma Research
490 Post Street, Suite 830
San Francisco, CA 94102
(415) 986-3162

Friendship Force
Suite 575, South Tower
One CNN Center
Atlanta, GA 30303
(404) 522-9490

Friends of the Earth
218 D Street SE
Washington, DC 20003
(202) 544-2600

Frontgate
9180 Le Saint Drive
Fairfield, OH 45014
(800) 626-6488

Games
P.O. Box 605
Mount Morris, IL 61054
(800) 827-1256

Gardener's Choice
County Road 687, P.O. Box 8000
Hartford, MI 49057
(616) 621-2481

Genealogists Bookshelf
343 East 85th Street
New York, NY 10028
(212) 879-1699

General Education Development
   Institute
16211 6th Avenue NE
Seattle, WA 98155
(206) 362-2055

Global Volunteers
375 East Little Canada Road
St. Paul, MN 55117
(800) 487-1074

GM Mobility Program for the
   Physically Challenged
P.O. Box 9011
Detroit, MI 48202
(800) 323-9935

Golden Companions
P.O. Box 754
Pullman, WA 99163
(509) 334-9351

"Golden Years" (*The*)
P.O. Box 391236
Mount View, CA 94039

Good Housekeeping order service
(800) 847-8700

Gourmets and Friends
P.O. Box 11652
Houston, TX 77293
(713) 442-7200

Grand Circle Travel
347 Congress Street
Boston, MA 02210
(800) 221-2610 or (607) 350-7500 in
    Massachusetts

Grandparents' Little Dividends
P.O. Box 11143
Shawnee Mission, KS 66207

GRANDTRAVEL
The Ticket Counter
6900 Wisconsin Avenue, Suite 706
Chevy Chase, MD 20815
(800) 247-7651 or (301) 986-0790 in
    Maryland

Gray Panthers
2025 Pennsylvania Avenue NW, Suite
    821
Washington, DC 20006
(202) 466-3132

Green Thumb Inc.
2000 North 14th Street, Suite 800
Arlington, VA 22201
(703) 522-7272

Grove Enterprises
P.O. Box 98
Brasstown, NC 28902
(704) 837-9200

Guideposts Associates, Inc.
39 Seminary Hill Road
Carmel, NY 10512

Habitat for Humanity
121 Habitat Street
Americus, GA 31709
(912) 924-6935

Hartford Insurance Group
Hartford Plaza
Hartford, CT 06115

Harvard Medical School Health Letter
P.O. Box 380
Boston, MA 02117

Haystack Mountain School of Crafts
P.O. Box 518
Deer Isle, ME 04627
(207) 348-2306

Health Care Financing Administration
U.S. Department of Health and
    Human Services
6325 Security Boulevard
Baltimore, MD 21207
(800) 638-6833 or (202) 245-6113

HealthDesk Corporation
1801 Fifth Street
Berkeley, CA 94710
(800) 578-5767 or (510) 843-8110

Health Insurance Association of
    America
1025 Connecticut Avenue NW, Suite
    1200
Washington, DC 20036
(800) 942-4242 or (202) 223-7780

Healthy Dialogue
Department HD-1
1147 West Jackson Boulevard
Chicago, IL 60607

Hear You Are, Inc.
4 Musconetcong Avenue
Stanhope, NJ 07874
(201) 347-7662

Hello Again
P.O. Box 4321
Hamden, CT 06514
(203) 248-2887

Help for Incontinent People
P.O. Box 544
Union, SC 29379
(800) 252-3337 or (803) 579-7900

Herrington
3 Symmes Drive
Londonderry, NH 03053
(800) 622-5221 or (603) 437-4638

HITECH Group International, Inc.
8205 Cass Avenue, Suite 109
Darien, IL 60559
(800) 288-8303 or (708) 963-5588 in
    Chicago

Hobby Greenhouse Association
8 Glen Terrace
Bedford, MA 01730
(617) 275-0377

Home Automation Laboratories
5500 Highlands Parkway, Suite 450
Smyrna, GA 30082
(800) 466-3522 or (404) 319-6000

Homecare Products, Inc.
15824 SE 296th Street
Kent, WA 98042
(800) 451-1903 or (206) 631-4633

Home Trends
779 Mount Read Boulevard
Rochester, NY 14606
(716) 254-6520

Hosteling International/American
    Youth Hostels
733 15th Street NW, Suite 840
Washington, DC 20005
(202) 783-6161

House of Fabrics
P.O. Box 9110
Van Nuys, CA 91409

ID Marketing
6914 Canby Avenue, Suite 111
Reseda, CA 91355
(800) 859-1150

IH3PA (International Home and
    Private Poker Players Association)
Route 2, Box 2845
Mantistique, MI 49854
(906) 341-5468

Independence Builders, Inc.
1718 Rugby Avenue
Charlottesville, VA 22901
(800) 562-0669 or (804) 977-5516

Independence Dogs
146 State Line Road
Chadds Ford, PA 19317
(215) 358-2723

Independent Living
P.O. Box 202
Centerport, NY 11721

Independent Living Aids, Inc.
27 East Mall
Plainview, NY 11803
(800) 537-2118

Indiana University Medical Center's
    Sleep Center
(800) 726-3626

Indoor Gardening Society of America
c/o Horticultural Society of New York
120 West 58th Street
New York, NY 10019

Institute of Certified Financial
    Planners (ICFP)
3443 South Galens, Suite 190
Denver, CO 80231
(303) 751-7600

Institute of Public Law
1117 Stanford NE
Albuquerque, NM 87131

International Association for Widowed
    People
P.O. Box 3564
Springfield, IL 62708
(217) 787-0886

International Association of Financial
    Planners (IAFP)
2 Concourse Parkway, Suite 800
Atlanta, GA 30328
(800) 241-2148 or (404) 395-1605

International Broadcasting Services,
    Limited
P.O. Box 300
Penn's Park, PA 18943

International Executive Service Corps
P.O. Box 10005
Stamford, CT 06904

International Handicappers' Net
P.O. Box 1185
Ashland, OR 97520

International Healthcare Products, Inc.
4222 South Pulaski Road
Chicago, IL 60632
(800) 423-7886 or (312) 247-7422

International Hearing Society
20361 Middlebelt Road
Livonia, MI 48152
(800) 521-5247 or (313) 478-2610

International Implant Registry
2323 Colorado Avenue
Turlock, CA 95380
(800) 344-3226 or (209) 668-1111

International Mailbag Club
c/o Mrs. James T. Shepard
130 Center Street
Findlay, OH 45840
(419) 422-2362

International Pen Friends
P.O. Box 290065
Brooklyn, NY 11229

International Senior Citizens
    Association
537 South Commonwealth Avenue,
    Suite 4
Los Angeles, CA 90020
(213) 380-0135

International Tremor Foundation
360 West Superior Street
Chicago, IL 60610

In Touch Networks, Inc.
15 West 65th Street
New York, NY 10023
(212) 769-6270

IRS
(800) 829-1040

Ishi Press
76-H Bonaventure Drive
San Jose, CA 95134
(800) 859-2086 or (408) 944-9110

JC Penney Catalog
(800) 222-6161

J.L. Pachner Limited
13 Via Di Nola
Laguna Nuguel, CA 92677
(714) 363-9831

Joan Cook Housewares
3200 SE 14th Avenue
Fort Lauderdale, FL 33350
(800) 327-3799

*Johns Hopkins Medical Letter—Health
   After 50*
Subscription Dept., P.O. Box 420176
Palm Coast, FL 32142

Kiwanis International
3636 Woodview Trace
Indianapolis, IN 46268
(317) 875-8755

Knights of the Square Table
111 Amber Street
Buffalo, NY 14220

Kohler Company
Kohler, WI 53044

LensCard Systems
P.O. Box 025491
Miami, FL 33102
(800) 322-3025

Letter Exchange (*The*)
P.O. Box 6218
Albany, CA 94706

Lever-Aide Products Inc.
1357 Park Road
Chanhassen, MN 55317
(612) 470-1264

Library of Congress
Division of the Blind and Physically
   Handicapped
1291 Taylor Street NW
Washington, DC 20542

Lifeline Systems, Inc.
One Arsenal Marketplace
Watertown, MA 02172
(800) 642-0045 or (617) 923-1384

Lifescan Tele-Library/Johnson and
   Johnson
(800) 722-6037 or (800) 227-8862

Lifescope Videos
1327 Milvia Street #8
Berkeley, CA 94705
(510) 528-1177

Lifestyle Resource
4814 Taylor Road, Department
   BBKA03
Batavia, OH 45103
(800) 872-5200

Lighthouse Low Vision Products
36-02 Northern Boulevard
Long Island City, NY 11101
(800) 453-4923 or (718) 937-6959

Lighthouse National Center for Vision
   and Aging (The)
800 Second Avenue
New York, NY 10017
(212) 808-0077

Lions Clubs International
300 22nd Street
Oak Brook, IL 60521
(708) 571-5466

Literacy Volunteers of America
5795 South Widewaters Parkway
Syracuse, NY 13214
(315) 445-8000

Little Brothers—Friends of the Elderly
1121 South Clinton
Chicago, IL 60607
(312) 786-0501

Living At Home/Block Nurse Program,
    Inc.
Suite 225—Ivy League Place
475 Cleveland Avenue North
St. Paul, MN 55104
(612) 649-0315

Living Bank (The)
P.O. Box 6725
Houston, TX 77265
(800) 528-2971 or (713) 528-2971

Loners of America
Route 2, Box 85E
Ellsinore, MO 63937
(314) 322-5548

Long Distance Love
P.O. Box 2301
Ventnor, NJ 08406

Look Good—Feel Better
(800) 395-5665

LS&S Group
P.O. Box 673
Northbrook, IL 60065
(800) 468-4789 or (708) 498-9777 in
    Illinois

Lung Line Information Service
National Jewish Center for
    Immunology and Respiratory
    Medicine
1400 Jackson Street
Denver, CO 80206
(800) 222-5864

Make-A-Wish Foundation of America
100 West Clarendon, Suite 2200
Phoenix, AZ 85013
(800) 722-9474 or (602) 279-9474

Make Today Count
101½ South Union Street
Alexandria, VA 22314

MARK56 Records
P.O. Box 1
Anaheim, CA 92815
(800) 227-7388

Marquetry Society of America
P.O. Box 224
Lindenhurst, NY 11757

MasterMinds
c/o Jerre Bellerue
52 South Washington
Denver, CO 80209
(303) 722-9291

Mature Investor
QXO Publishing
P.O. Box 2741
Glen Ellyn, IL 60135

Mature Outlook
6001 North Clark Street
Chicago, IL 60660

Mature Traveler (The)
P.O. Box 50820
Reno, NV 89513
(702) 786-7419

Mature Wisdom
P.O. Box 28
Hanover, PA 17333
(800) 638-6366

Maxi Aids
P.O. Box 3209
Farmingdale, NY 11735
(800) 522-6294 or (516) 752-0521 in
   New York

Maze Magazine
17 North Avenue
Manchester, MA 01944

MCI
(800) 444-3333

MedEscort International
P.O. Box 8766
Allentown, PA 18105
(800) 255-7182 or (215) 791-3111

Medical Assistance Passport Plan
   (MAPP)
(800) 933-4627

MedicAlert
2323 Colorado Avenue, P.O. Box 1009
Turlock, CA 95380
(800) 432-5378 and (800) 423-6333

Medic-Light, Inc.
34 Yacht Club Drive
Lake Hopatcong, NJ 07849
(201) 663-1214

Med/West
702 South Third Avenue, P.O. Box 130
Marshalltown, IA 50158
(800) 843-8978 or (515) 752-5446

Merck
(800) 635-4452

Metropolitan Life Insurance Company
Health and Safety Education, Area
   16-UV
1 Madison Avenue
New York, NY 10010

Mike Moldeven
P.O. Box 71
DelMar, CA 92014
(619) 259-0762

Miles Kimball Company
41 West Eighth Avenue
Oshkosh, WI 54906

Mosby-Year Book, Inc.
11830 Westline Industrial Drive
St. Louis, MO 63146
(800) 453-4351

Munchkin Playhouses
P.O. Box 622
Lynbrook, NY 11563
(800) 247-6553

Narrative Television Network
5840 South Memorial Drive, Suite 312
Tulsa, OK 74145
(918) 627-1000

NASCO
901 Janesville Avenue, P.O. Box 901
Fort Atkinson, WI 53538
(800) 558-9595

National Academy of Elder Law
   Attorneys
655 North Alvernon, Suite 108
Tucson, AZ 85711

National Action Forum for Midlife and
   Older Women
P.O. Box 816
Stony Brook, NY 11790

National Apartment Association
111 14th Street NW, 9th floor
Washington, DC 20005
(800) 421-1221

National Association for Retired Credit
Union People (NARCUP)
P.O. Box 391
Madison, WI 57701
(608) 238-4286

National Association of Investors
Corporation
1515 East Eleven Mile Road
Royal Oak, MI 48067

National Association of Letter Carriers
100 Indiana Avenue NW
Washington, DC 20001

National Association of Music Teachers
617 Vine Street
Suite 1432
Cincinnati, OH 45202

National Association of Partners in
Education
601 Wythe Street, Suite 200
Alexandria, VA 22314
(800) 992-6787

National Association of Private
Geriatric Care Managers
655 North Alvernon #108
Tucson, AZ 85711

National Association of State Units on
Aging
2033 K Street NW, Suite 304
Washington, DC 20006
(202) 785-0707

National Audubon Society
950 Third Avenue
New York, NY 10022
(212) 832-3200

National Bird-Feeding Society
P.O. Box 23
Northbrook, IL 60065
(708) 272-0135

National Captioning Institute
5203 Leesburg Pike
Falls Church, VA 22041
(800) 533-9673 or (703) 998-2400

National Center for Home Equity
Conversion (NCHEC)
1210 East College, Suite 300
Marshall, MN 56258
(800) 247-6553 or (507) 532-3230

National Center for Nutrition and
Dietetics
216 West Jackson Boulevard
Chicago, IL 60606
(800) 366-1655

National Chronic Pain Outreach
Association, Inc.
7979 Old Georgetown Road, Suite 100
Bethesda, MD 20814
(301) 652-4948

National Coalition for the Homeless
1621 Connecticut Avenue NW, Suite
400
Washington, DC 20009
(202) 265-2371

National Consumer League
815 15th Street, Suite 928-N
Washington, DC 20005
(800) 876-7060

National Council of Senior Citizens
Nursing Home Information Service
925 15th Street NW
Washington, DC 20005
(202) 347-8800

National Council on Alcoholism and
Drug Dependence Hopeline
12 West 21st Street
New York, NY 10010
(800) 622-2255

National Digestive Diseases
   Information Clearinghouse
BOX NDDIC, 9000 Rockville Pike
Bethesda, MD 20892
(301) 468-6344

National Easter Seal Society
70 East Lake Street
Chicago, IL 60601
(312) 726-6200

National Eye Care Project
P.O. Box 6988
San Francisco, CA 94101
(800) 222-3937 or (415) 561-8500

National Guild of Decoupeurs
807 Rivard Boulevard
Grosse Pointe, MI 48230
(313) 882-0682

National Headache Foundation
5252 North Western Avenue
Chicago, IL 60625
(800) 843-2256

National Health Information Center
Department of Health and Human
   Services
P.O. Box 1133
Washington, DC 20013
(800) 336-4797 or (202) 429-9091
   locally

National Heart, Lung, and Blood
   Institute
Information Office
Building 31, Room 4A21
9000 Rockville Pike
Bethesda, MD 20892
(301) 496-4236

National Home Study Council
1601 18th Street, NW, Suite 2
Washington, DC 20009
(202) 234-5100

National Hospice Organization
1901 North Moore Street, Suite 901
Arlington, VA 22209
(800) 658-8898 or (703) 243-5900

National Institute of Dental
   Research/NIH
Public Inquiries Office
Building 31, Room 6A32
9000 Rockville Pike
Bethesda, MD 20892
(301) 496-5248

National Institute of Mental Health
Office of Inquiries
Room 15C-05
5600 Fishers Lane
Rockville, MD 20857
(301) 443-4513

National Institute of Neurological and
   Communicative Disorders and
   Stroke/NIH
Public Inquiries Office
Building 31, Room 8A06
9000 Rockville Pike
Bethesda, MD 20892
(301) 496-5751

National Institute on Aging
Public Information Office
Building 31, Room 5C27
9000 Rockville Pike
Bethesda, MD 20892
(800) 222-2225 or (302) 496-1752

National Institutes of Health
Building 31, Room 2B23
9000 Rockville Pike
Bethesda, MD 20892

National Jewish Center for
   Immunology and Respiratory
   Medicine
1400 Jackson Street
Denver, CO 80206
(303) 388-4461

National Kidney and Urologic Diseases
  Information Clearinghouse
P.O. Box NKUDIC
9000 Rockville Pike
Bethesda, MD 20892
(301) 468-6345

National Kidney Foundation
30 East 33rd Street, Suite 1100
New York, NY 10016
(212) 889-2210

National Kitchen and Bath Association
c/o Donna Luzzo, Public Relations
687 Willow Grove Street
Hackettstown, NJ 07840
(800) 843-6522

National League For Nursing
350 Hudson Street
New York, NY 10014
(800) 699-1656, ext. 242, or
  (212) 989-9393 in New York City

National Library Service for the Blind
  and Physically Handicapped
Library of Congress
Washington, DC 20542
(800) 424-9100

National Mah Jongg League, Inc.
250 West 57th Street
New York, NY 10107

National Mental Health Association
1021 Prince Street
Alexandria, VA 22314
(800) 969-6642

National Odd Shoe Exchange
P.O. Box 56845
Phoenix, AZ 85079-6845

National Organization of Mall Walkers
P.O. Box 191
Hermann, MO 65041
(314) 486-3945

National Osteoporosis Foundation
2100 M Street NW, Suite 602
Washington, DC 20037
(800) 223-9994

National Piano Foundation
4020 McEwen Street, Suite 105
Dallas, TX 75244
(214) 233-9107

National Psoriasis Foundation
6443 Southwest Beaverton Highway,
  Suite 210
Portland, OR 97221
(503) 297-1545

National Quilting Association, Inc.
  (The)
P.O. Box 393
Ellicott City, MD 21041
(410) 461-5733

National Safety Council
444 North Michigan Avenue
Chicago, IL 60611

National Scrabble Association
P.O. Box 700
Greenport, NY 11944

National Senior Sports Association
10560 Main Street, Suite 205
Fairfax, VA 22030
(800) 282-6772 or (703) 385-7540

National Sleep Foundation
122 South Robertson Boulevard, 3rd
  Floor
Los Angeles, CA 90048
(310) 288-0466

National Stroke Association
300 East Hampden
Englewood, CO 80110
(800) 787-6537

National Underwriter Company
420 East Fourth Street
Cincinnati, OH 45202

National Wildlife Federation
1400 16th Street NW
Washington, DC 20036

National Wood Carvers Association
P.O. Box 43218
Cincinnati, OH 45243

New Choices for the Best Years
850 Third Avenue
New York, NY 10022

New York Times Large-Type Weekly
P.O. Box 9564
Uniondale, NY 11555
(800) 631-2580 or (212) 556-7078

Nolo Press
950 Parker Street
Berkeley, CA 94710
(415) 549-1976

NordicTrack
104 Peavey Road
Chaska, MN 55318
(800) 858-2453

North American Shortwave Association
45 Wildflower Road
Levittown, PA 19057

Older Women's League (OWL)
666 11th Street NW, Suite 700
Washington, DC 20001
(202) 783-6686

Olsten HealthCare
(800) 462-9556

One Shoe Crew (The)
86 Clavela Avenue
Sacramento, CA 95828
(916) 364-7463

OTT Light Systems Inc.
28 Parker Way
Santa Barbara, CA 93101
(800) 234-3724 or (805) 564-3467

Over the Hill Gang
3310 Cedar Heights Drive
Colorado Springs, CO 80904
(719) 685-4656

Pace Link
89 Haddon Avenue, P.O. Box 117
Haddonfield, NJ 08033
(800) 242-7137

Palmer Industries Inc.
P.O. Box 707
Endicott, NY 13760
(800) 847-1304 or (607) 754-1954

Paralyzed Veterans of America
Information Specialist
801 18th Street NW
Washington, DC 20006
(202) 416-7710

Pedigree Selectadog Service
P.O. Box 58853
Vernon, CA 90058

Philanthropic Advisory Service
1515 Wilson Boulevard
Arlington, VA 22209

Photographic Society of America
3000 United Founders Boulevard,
    Suite 103
Oklahama City, OK 73112
(405) 843-1437

Pixel Perfect
(800) 788-2099

Positive Parenting Inc.
612 West Stratford Drive
Chandler, AZ 85224
(800) 334-3143

Prison Pen Pals
P.O. Box 1217
Cincinnati, OH 45202

Probus Press
(800) 395-3733

Project LINK/Center for Therapeutic
   Applications of Technology
515 Kimball Tower
Buffalo, NY 14214
(800) 628-2281 or (716) 829-3141

Promises Kept, Inc.
2525 Xenium Lane
P.O. Box 47638
Plymouth, MN 55447
(800) 989-3545 or (612) 553-1787

Purina Pets for People Program
Checkerboard Square 6T
St. Louis, MO 63164

Radio Communications Monitoring
   Association
P.O. Box 542
Silverado, CA 92676

Rational Recovery
P.O. Box 800
Lotus, CA 95651
(916) 621-4374

Reader's Digest Large-Type
P.O. Box 241
Mount Morris, IL 61054

Readmaster Corporation
Olney, IL 62450
(800) 251-0025

Recorded Books, Inc.
270 Skipjack Road
Prince Frederick, MD 20678
(800) 638-1304

Recording for the Blind
20 Roszel Road
Princeton, NJ 08540
(609) 452-0606

Recreation Vehicle Industry
   Association
P.O. Box 2999
Reston, VA 22090

Refundle Bundle
P.O. Box 9605
Clinton, IA 52736

Relax Video
419 West 119th Street, Suite 81
New York, NY 10027
(212) 496-4400

RE/MAX ACTION Specially
   Challenged Network
(800) 276-6291

RESULTS
236 Massachusetts Avenue NE, Suite
   300
Washington, DC 20002
(202) 543-9340

Retired Senior Volunteer Program
1100 Vermont Avenue NW, Room
   6100
Washington, DC 20525
(202) 634-9353

Retirement Living Publishing
28 West 23rd Street
New York, NY 10010

Right Start (The)
5334 Sterling Center Drive
Westlake Village, CA 91361
(800) 548-8531

Rockport Fitness Walking Guide
c/o Stella Croker
MetLife Managed Care Services
  Group
57 Greens Farms Road
Westport, CT 06880

Rodale Press
33 East Minor Street
Emmaus, PA 18098
(215) 967-5177

RVing Women
P.O. Box 8206
Kenmore, WA 98202
(800) 333-9992

Safety Zone (The)
215 East 43rd Street, P.O. Box 182247
Chattanooga, TN 37422
(800) 999-3030

Scudder
160 Federal Street
Boston, MA 02110
(800) 322-2282 or (800) 424-2430

Sears HealthCare
P.O. Box 19009
Provo, UT 84605
(800) 326-1750

Secular Organizations for Sobriety
P.O. Box 5
Buffalo, NY 14215

SelfCare Catalog
349 Healdsburg Avenue
Healdsburg, CA 95448
(800) 345-4021

Self Help for Hard of Hearing People,
  Inc. (SHHH)
7800 Wisconsin Avenue
Bethesda, MD 20814
(301) 657-2248

Senior Escorted Tours
P.O. Box 400
Cape May Courthouse, NJ 08210
(800) 222-1254

Senior Fitnessize
P.O. Box 2567
Morganton, NC 28655
(704) 438-9274

Senior Neighbors of Chattanooga
10th and Newby Streets
Chattanooga, TN 37402
(615) 622-7645

SeniorNet
399 Arguello Boulevard
San Francisco, CA 94118
(415) 750-5030

Seniors Abroad
12533 Pacato Circle North
San Diego, CA 92128
(619) 485-1696

Senior Software Systems
8804 Wildridge Drive
Austin, TX 78759
(800) 637-9949

Seniors Softball USA
9 Fleet Court
Sacramento, CA 95831
(916) 393-8566

Senior Ventures
Center for Lifetime Learning
Continuing Education
Central Washington University
Ellensburg, WA 98926
(800) 752-4380 or (509) 963-1526

Service Corps of Retired Executives
  (SCORE)
655 15th Street NW, Suite 901
Washington, DC 20005
(202) 653-6279

Shared Housing Resource Center, Inc.
6344 Greene Street
Philadelphia, PA 19144
(215) 848-1220

Shield Mail Order Medical Supply
P.O. Box 922
Santa Clarita, CA 91380
(800) 232-7443

Showersafe, Inc.
335 DeMott Avenue
Teaneck, NJ 07666
(800) 453-5662 or (201) 836-4433

Sierra Club
Department J-420, P.O. Box 7959
San Francisco, CA 94120
(415) 923-5576

Signals
WGBH Educational Foundation
P.O. Box 64428
St. Paul, MN 55164
(800) 669-9696

Simon Foundation for Continence
P.O. Box 815
Wilmette, IL 60091
(800) 237-4666 or (708) 864-3913

Singles for Charities
c/o Jan Krivosheiw
12 Split Rock Road
Syosset, NY 11791

Skinflint News
1460 Noell Boulevard
Palm Harbor, FL 34683
(813) 785-7759

Social Security Administration
Office of Public Inquiries
6401 Security Boulevard
Baltimore, MD 21235
(800) 772-1213 or (410) 965-1234

Solutions
P.O. Box 6878
Portland, OR 97228
(800) 342-9988

Special Olympics International
1350 New York Avenue NW, Suite 500
Washington, DC 20005
(202) 628-3630

Sporty's Preferred Living Catalog
Cleremont County Airport
Batavia, OH 45103
(800) 543-8633

Sprint
(800) 867-2000

St. Croix Railing
2525 Nevada Avenue North, Suite 302
Golden Valley, MN 55427
(612) 542-3118

Support Dogs for the Handicapped,
  Inc.
301 Sovereign Court, Suite 113
St. Louis, MO 63011
(314) 394-6163

Support Plus
99 West Street, P.O. Box 500
Medfield, MA 02052
(800) 229-2910

Susan G. Komen Breast Cancer
    Foundation
(800) 462-9273

Syntex Labs
3401 Hillview Avenue
Palo Alto, CA 94303

Taylor Gifts
355 East Conestoga Road, P.O. Box
    206
Wayne, PA 19087
(215) 789-7007

Teaching Company (The)
P.O. Box 96870
Washington, DC 20090
(800) 832-2421

Telephone Preference Service
P.O. Box 3861
New York, NY 10163

Temasek Telephone Inc.
260 East Grand Avenue #19
South San Francisco, CA 94080
(800) 647-8887 or (415) 875-6666

THEOS Foundation
1301 Clark Building, 717 Liberty
    Avenue
Pittsburgh, PA 15222
(412) 471-7779

Tightwad Gazette (The)
RR 1, Box 3570
Leeds, ME 04263

Time Dollar Network
c/o Essential Information
P.O. Box 19405
Washington, DC 20036

Travel Companion Exchange
P.O. Box 833
Amityville, NY 11701

TraveLearn
P.O. Box 315
Lakeville, PA 18438
(800) 235-9114

Travel Information Service
Moss Rehabilitation Hospital
1200 West Tabor Road
Philadelphia, PA 19141
(215) 456-9600

Traveling Companions
P.O. Box 3139
Binghamton, NY 13902
(607) 724-1364

Travelin' Talk
P.O. Box 3534
Clarksville, TN 37043
(615) 552-6670

TTY of Carolina
308-D Sherwee Drive
Raleigh, NC 27603
(919) 779-0481

TTY/TDD Store
1250 Womack Avenue
East Point, GA 30344
(404) 755-0256

20/20 Vision National Project
30 Cottage Street
Amherst, MA 01002
(800) 669-1782 or (413) 549-4555

Twin Peaks Press
P.O. Box 129
Vancouver, WA 98666
(800) 637-2256 or (206) 694-2462

United Seniors Health Cooperative
1331 H Street NW, Suite 500
Washington, DC 20005
(202) 393-6222

United States Peace Corps
1990 K Street NW
Washington, DC 20526
(800) 424-8580 or (202) 606-3010

United States Servas, Inc.
11 John Street, Suite 407
New York, NY 10038
(212) 267-0252

United States Water Fitness
   Association
P.O. Box 3279
Boynton Beach, FL 33424

Veribanc
P.O. Box 461
Wakefield, MA 01880
(800) 442-2657

Vermont Country Store (The)
P.O. Box 3000
Manchester Center, VT 95255
(802) 362-2400

VibraSonics
7811 Froebel Road
Laverock, PA 19118

Video Library
7157 Germantown Avenue
Philadelphia, PA 19119
(800) 669-7157

Voicespondence Club (The)
1711 Bellevue Avenue, D-1214
Richmond, VA 23227

Walt Nicke Company
36 McLeod Lane, P.O. Box 433
Topsfield, MA 01983
(800) 822-4114 or (508) 887-3388

Waupuca Elevator Company, Inc.
P.O. Box 246
Waupaca, WI 54981
(800) 238-8739

Weiss Research
(800) 289-9222

Well Spouse Foundation
P.O. Box 28876
San Diego, CA 92198
(619) 673-9043 or (914) 357-8513

Wheaton Medical Technologies, Inc.
P.O. Box 205
Pennsville, NJ 08070
(800) 654-5455

Wheelers Accessible Van Rentals
(800) 232-7443

Whirlpool Corporation
LaPorte Division/Literature
   Department
1900 Whirlpool Drive
LaPorte, IN 46350
(616) 926-5000

Williams-Sonoma
P.O. Box 7456
San Francisco, CA 94120
(800) 541-2233

Working Vacation (The)
4277 Lake Santa Clara Drive
Santa Clara, CA 95054
(408) 727-9655

World At Large (The)
P.O. Box 190330
Brooklyn, NY 11219
(800) 285-2743

Yarns of Yesteryear Project
University of Wisconsin—Madison
Continuing Education in the Arts
    Department
610 Langdon Street, Room 722
Madison, WI 53706
(608) 263-3494

Young Grandparents Club
P.O. Box 11143
Shawnee Mission, KS 66207

Zelco Industries Inc.
630 South Columbus Avenue
Mount Vernon, NY 10550
(800) 431-2486 or (914) 699-6230

Index